THE
GREAT
TEXAS
MURDER
TRIALS

ALSO BY DAVID ATLEE PHILLIPS

The Night Watch: 25 Years of Peculiar Service

The Carlos Contract

THE GREAT TEXAS MURDER TRIALS

A COMPELLING ACCOUNT OF THE SENSATIONAL T. CULLEN DAVIS CASE

• • •

DAVID ATLEE PHILLIPS

MACMILLAN PUBLISHING CO., INC.   NEW YORK

Macmillan Publishing Co., Inc.
866 Third Avenue, New York, N.Y. 10022
Collier Macmillan Canada, Ltd.

Library of Congress Catalog Card Number: 79-12413

First Printing 1979

Printed in the United States of America

Fort Worth multimillionaire T. Cullen Davis has been brought to trial twice on criminal charges involving murder. He has steadfastly maintained that he is innocent of all accusations made against him, and the state of Texas has failed twice to convince a jury of his guilt. The first trial, for the murder of his stepdaughter, Andrea Wilborn, lasted five months and ended in a verdict of acquittal. His second trial was for soliciting the murder of the judge who had presided at his divorce trial. After twelve weeks of testimony from almost one hundred witnesses, the jurors stalemated and the judge declared a mistrial. The prosecutors say they will try Mr. Davis again, but no immediate plans have been announced.

In relating the bizarre history of the two trials, I have found it helpful to use a character whom I have named "Judge Matthew Willard." Though in a sense a fictional character, he is based on a real person, who, though knowledgeable of the law, is not a judge.

CONTENTS

ACKNOWLEDGMENTS

The T. Cullen Davis case has been the biggest story covered by the *Fort Worth Star-Telegram* in its seventy-three-year history. I relied on the newspaper's files from mid-1976 to early 1979 in documenting portions of this book. Frequently, the *Star-Telegram* material and the reporters who prepared it are recognized in the text, but not always, especially in quotations from the reporting on the Amarillo and Houston trials written by Evan Moore, Jim Jones, and Glen Guzzo.

The most frequently quoted newsman is Glen Guzzo, who was assigned to the Davis beat for more than thirty months and performed in a manner which merits national recognition. I am also indebted to *Star-Telegram* reporter John Makeig and to the able staff of the newspaper's reference library. Carl Freund of the Fort Worth bureau of the *Dallas Morning News* and Bill Hix of KXAS-TV, Fort Worth, also provided valuable assistance.

Reference sources on Texas crime and Southwest lore included *In Old Fort Worth* by Mack Williams, the Tomlinson *Lone Star Book of Texas Records*, and the excellent *How Fort Worth Became the Texasmost City* by Leonard Sanders.

And I am grateful to many individuals who agreed to be interviewed in Texas, nearly all of whom requested anonymity.

THE
GREAT
TEXAS
MURDER
TRIALS

PROLOGUE

The precise sequence of events and the circumstances of that bloody Sunday night/Monday morning were subsequently the subject of spirited and sometimes acrimonious debate but one conclusion was indisputable: A man dressed in black wearing a woman's wig shot and killed two people and wounded two others. The first to die was a young girl and the second victim, a thirty-year-old man who stood eighty-one inches. The murder weapon was a .38 revolver partially concealed in a plastic garbage bag.

It was before midnight in August of 1976 when the mayhem commenced in Fort Worth; thirty minutes later the gory chores were done. The murderer must have perspired profusely. The temperature had topped the 100-degree mark during the day and there had been no cooling breezes in the evening off the scrub-and-brush plains around the Texas city. The last of the revelers at the adjoining Colonial Country Club had gone home; it was quiet except for an occasional forlorn clank from the nearby T & P Railroad freight yards. A slice of moon was not bright enough to cast shadows. The aroma of mimosa drifted from the cluster of trees surrounding the mansion.

The killer may have driven up the hill to the palatial residence by either of two roads or he could have approached on foot. From any direction he would have had to drive or trudge up a steep incline. The mansion grounds were 140 in-town acres of garden, lawn, and open field below the hilltop manor. The architect had characterized this edifice as "a rambling-type home of contemporary design with a Southwest regional flavor...." Most agreed that it was an impressive building, but others believed it looked more like a fortress than a home. One described the architecture as "art deco mausoleum." Texans admire the immense, but the ostentatious homestead wasn't the sort of place where people *lived*. Before the killings it was referred to by friends of the occupants as "the Davis place." Afterwards it was called "the murder mansion."

It was assumed the luxurious house was a gift of love. T. Cullen Davis, one of the wealthiest men in America, proffered it to his new bride Priscilla when they wed in 1968, her third and his second marriage. Cullen promised Priscilla she would have a dream house—"just as she wanted it built," he said at the time. Priscilla's dream came true in 1972 after two years of construction. The cost of the land and building was six million dollars. In Fort Worth society the dowagers clucked and remarked that the rich abode was...well...tacky. And the mansion's furnishings were described by many, including those who had never seen them, as flashy. Others disagreed, finding the mansion striking and its interior sumptuous, if perhaps a touch gaudy.

Priscilla *was* gaudy. She was blonde and curvaceous, provocative and audacious. She shocked and titillated Fort Worth by appearing in scanty attire at the nearby Colonial Country Club and the exclusive Petroleum Club downtown. Her blouses and hot-pants were creaseless-tight on her full, lush body. Her décolletage plunged so deeply at times that, as one awed spectator put it, "On a clear day you could see her knockers from Dallas."

Priscilla relished the notoriety. She gave the back of her hand to Fort Worth society whenever she could. Her favorite pendant was two words spelled out in diamonds on gold: "Rich Bitch."

But, within a matter of a few years, the marriage between Cullen Davis and his princess from across the tracks soured and went terribly awry. They separated in 1974. A bitter divorce

4

proceeding ensued. She lived in the mansion with one of her three children by previous marriages. She rejected Cullen's settlement offers as parsimonious after her lawyers told her that the profits from Cullen's worldwide business enterprises were $52 million in 1975. The judge presiding over the squabble, Joe Eidson, enjoined Cullen from visiting the mansion or approaching Priscilla. Soon there was a new resident, a six-foot nine-inch ex-basketball player named Stan Farr; he was referred to, delicately, as Priscilla's "live-in companion." There were allusions to the size of the stud-athlete's main attraction. The mansion became an arena for memorable parties.

The mansion was an ideal place to entertain. The indoor pool. The collection of expensive art. The tall cabinets filled with jade, a fabulous chess set, an antique snuff box from the Manheim Galleries, the popcorn wagon from Hammacher Schlemmer, the crystal butterfly from Steuben. All sorts of conversation pieces. Everybody in Fort Worth talked about the $400,000 Renoir hanging on the wall of a bathroom. The parties spawned persistent rumors of wild evenings spiced with dope and orgies.

Perhaps Priscilla needed parties. Being alone with her eighteen-year-old daughter Dee in a mansion with 19,000 square feet of floor space was hardly titillating; Priscilla worried about intruders. Her jewelry alone was tempting loot: The platinum and diamond bracelet; the yellow gold, diamond, and emerald necklace; the diamond and platinum pendant; and all the other baubles and trinkets were of immense value. Booze and music and merriment made the mansion livable; being alone there was scary. Before the murders Priscilla talked with a man who was expanding the electronic alarm system which protected the mansion. "When I'm alone in this place at night," she confided, "it's so big that it gets creepy and spooky."

There was a particular reason for a celebration in early August 1976. Judge Eidson had ruled that Cullen must increase his temporary alimony payments to Priscilla from $3500 monthly to $5000 and give Priscilla over $42,000 for attorney's fees and other expenses related to the divorce. Cullen was advised of the injunction on August 2, eight hours before the murders.

Priscilla was absent when the man dressed in black entered the mansion, but her younger daughter Andrea was there. Usually she lived with her father and brother, but she was a visitor on this night. Andrea was alone. Her body was found later, sprawled on the concrete floor of a basement storeroom. Had Andrea lived to her next birthday she would have become a teenager.

Shortly after midnight Priscilla and Stan Farr returned to the mansion. The killer was still inside the house when they entered. Perhaps he was standing near the large composite portrait of Cullen and Priscilla painted in happier times, Cullen in a sombre pose, Priscilla smiling and showing an expanse of bare thigh. The man in black shot Priscilla. The bullet entered her chest between her extravagant breasts, then perforated her liver before emerging.

As Priscilla staggered in shock, the gunman turned on Stan Farr. He felled the giant with four bullets.

Priscilla escaped the mansion, perhaps because the murderer had to reload his hot revolver. Clutching her abdomen, she ran down the hill a thousand yards to the home of a neighbor.

The killer coolly lurked at the scene. Young Gus Gavrel, Jr., escorted his eighteen-year-old girlfriend, Beverly Bass, to the mansion where she was to spend the night with Priscilla's elder daughter Dee. It was 12:30 A.M. Dee had not yet arrived, but the murderer waited. And he shot Gus from a distance of three feet. The steel-jacketed bullet nicked the lower part of Gus's spinal cord. Beverly screamed and ran out of the mansion, pursued by the man in black. She eluded him in the darkness.

The police, summoned by Priscilla's neighbors, were by then on the way. They found the wounded Gus in a pool of blood...and Andrea and the basketball player. After verifying that the latter two were dead, they sought the perpetrator.

The murderer had fled.

·1·

THE OLD JUDGE

Judge Matthew Willard had already shaved, fed the dog, and read a passage from the Bible before he turned on the early morning news at six o'clock and heard about the shooting spree at Cullen Davis's place on Mockingbird Lane. When the news account was completed he snapped off the radio and spoke to his dog.

"Did you hear *that*, Oliver?" The black Labrador had been dozing at the Judge's feet and looked up at the sound of his name. "That Priscilla woman is Cullen Davis's fancy wife who's been in the newspaper so much. You remember Cullen...that slender, baby-faced boy who lived down the street until just a few years ago. His brother William lives there now."

The Judge shook his head in disbelief. "*Son* of a bitch! What kind of person is it that can kill a twelve-year-old girl?"

He pushed himself from his black leather chair and strode from the room and through the hall to fetch the *Fort Worth Star-Telegram*. Normally, the newspaper waited until after breakfast, but now the Judge was eager to read the details of the astonishing development at the Davis mansion. He opened the paper anxiously.

"Goddamn *it!*" The blasphemy was directed to the newspaper. There was nothing on the front page about the murders. The banner headline, Monday morning, August 3, 1976, read: COLORADO FLASH FLOOD KILLS 60. The only photograph on the page was a silly one of a man smiling inanely while hugging a huge block of ice to cool himself in Sunday's hundred-plus heat.

The Judge delivered his opinion of the man. "*Horse's* ass."

He flipped through the pages of the first section of the paper, then through the local news. Nothing about the shootings. He paused at the sports section because of the eye-catching photograph of a nude young man dancing in a field among dozens of women. He read the caption: "Montreal (AP) *A young man ran into the center of the Olympic Stadium at the closing ceremony Sunday night, stripped off his clothes, and cavorted naked with 500 garbed women who were part of the ceremony.*" The Judge chuckled.

The Judge looked west. Through the trees he could see the old Davis place, now occupied by William. The sprawling English manor house was opposite the fifteenth tee of the Rivercrest Country Club; the Judge had passed it almost every morning for the past twenty years during his regular morning hike around the course. Before they moved into that monstrous house on Mockingbird Lane, Cullen Davis and Priscilla had lived there. They had inherited the place from Cullen's father, Ken Davis, Sr.

The Judge looked at the *Star-Telegram* again, then slammed it against his thigh. "Goddamn *it*!" he repeated. What kind of newspaper is it that doesn't have an important story like the murders at the Davis mansion? If Amon Carter were still alive and heading that paper there would have been some ass *kicking*. Amon would have....The Judge reflected. Of course. All that carnage had occurred too late last night, or too early this morning, to get in the paper before it went to press. He would have to wait for the afternoon edition.

The Judge returned to the house, went into the kitchen, and turned on the burners under the kettle, for his tea, and the small pot, for his soft-boiled eggs.

The Judge stepped from the kitchen to the adjacent studio-office-library where he had slept and worked since the death of his wife eighteen years ago. For all practical purposes, the rest of the house might as well have been sealed off; the Judge seldom ventured into the other downstairs rooms or the bedrooms upstairs. The commodious room he now preferred had been an addition to the original fifty-year-old brick house. When the Judge had been elected to the state Supreme Court he had need-ed a place to keep his books and to work whenever he was able to return to Fort Worth from Austin. Then, after his wife died, he brought down the four-poster bed and confined his activities to that area.

In addition to the bed there was the Judge's leather chair where he liked to sit in the evening with his single drink of the day, a small sofa for visitors, a rolltop desk which had been in his father's office in the family dry-goods store on Main Street, a second, stand-up desk where he read the ponderous law books, and a podium on which rested a massive King James version of the Bible.

There were two paintings, both valuable, side by side on one wall. The first was a Remington—a cowboy plunging from his crophorse onto a steer—which the Judge had won in a poker game in Lubbock when the rancher who owned it placed undue faith in four kings while the Judge held a bobtailed flush. The other painting was a formal portrait of the Judge's triple-great grandfather done by a student of Charles Wilson Peale. The jux-taposition of the aristocratic Eastern gentleman and the Western scene was not incongruous. Fort Worth has always been called "the city where the West begins," and if this is true it is also where the East ends.

There was a large picture window. It framed a view which the Judge thoroughly enjoyed, especially when he watched the sun sink in the clear air following a summer storm, his single drink of the day in hand.

The other walls were solid books: history, biography, Southwest lore, and the law. The Judge didn't read fiction; he figured he owned two thousand books but only one novel, and that by Owen Wister and printed in 1889. The Judge liked to read books, but sometimes he was content simply to hold them. When he acquired a new volume—the purchase always an agonizing decision because it meant the displacement of one already on the shelves—he opened the pages a few at a time, first in front, then in the back, and ran his thumbnail down the page near the spine. His father had taught him that, to lengthen the life of the binding. The truth of the matter was that the Judge loved his books, particularly Blackstone's *Commentaries* and those of the British barrister's American counterpart Kent, more than anything or anyone. Certainly the Judge had been devoted to his wife and was lonely for a while after her death. But, my, she had been a *talker*. And the Judge was genuinely fond of his companion Oliver, and liked to talk to him. Oliver's formal name should have been Oliver IV, because he was the fourth Labrador retriever the Judge had named in memory of the greatest justice of them all.

But the books and what he discovered in them concerned the most important thing in the Judge's life. The Judge was deeply in love with the law.

All in all, the Judge believed himself a fortunate man. He knew he was honest. Charitable. He was devout; he had given up church-going years ago, but read the Bible each day. And he was convinced he had been a damned *good* lawyer and a damned *great* trial judge.

But the Judge did recognize in himself two weaknesses and one eccentricity. The latter was that he carried on one-sided conversations with Oliver, but that didn't bother him too much. He long ago ceased worrying about what people thought of that.

But the two weaknesses did worry him: foul language and bourbon.

Since the Judge considered himself a man of rectitude he had a guilty conscience about using expletives, but he enjoyed them so he couldn't break the habit, though he never used the ugly four-letter words that referred to sexual activity. The Judge had reached a compromise with his conscience in the way he employed curse words—he always put the emphasis on another word. Sometimes the stress would be on the adjective—as in "a *randy* bastard" or "*horse* shit." Sometimes the emphasis would be on a noun or pronoun—as in "Goddamn *him*." One of his favorite expressions was "in a *pig's* ass."

The other sin was the bourbon. That single drink of the day. When he had been practicing and while on the bench, the Judge had often remarked that he had only one drink a day and that was true. It was still true. That hadn't changed. But the glass had. In the beginning it was a tumbler. The Judge switched to a regular highball glass. Then he found a taller one. Then he changed to one of the same height but of greater circumference. Finally he settled on just the right one—an excessively large iced-tea mug he found in a novelty shop. It held, over ice, almost a pint.

So, each day, enjoying the bourbon even while at odds with his conscience, the old Judge sat in his chair and looked out his window and sipped his single drink.

After his breakfast of tea, two soft-boiled eggs, and milk on bran (the menu never varied), the Judge took Oliver's leash from the closet. The Labrador pranced with anticipation at the signal that the daily excursion around the perimeter of the golf course was to begin.

In previous years the Judge usually had the sidewalks and fairways to himself except for a few early golfers or insomniacs. No more. The area was crowded with joggers. What a pack of idiots they were. The Judge simply didn't understand what they were up to—there's nothing better than a brisk walk, but why run your ass *off*? It couldn't be more obvious that the joggers weren't enjoying themselves. When they ran past, their faces were invariably contorted with fatigue and anguish. What ass*holes*!

Despite their twisted countenances the Rivercrest joggers always managed a smile of recognition when they ran near the Judge. Even those who had never met him were aware of his reputation as a legal giant in the Southwest. And, at the age of eighty-two, he was a remarkably virile and handsome figure. He stood almost six feet and his body was trim. He kept his back erect. He always wore a white shirt and a dark tie, even on hot days like this one, and a town-size Stetson hat. His white hair was long enough to flow below the hat, and his hirsute eyebrows and hawklike nose gave him a fierce, Old West look.

The Judge and his dog walked along near the stately houses. They paused frequently while Oliver sniffed for insects in the grass or pawed at a gopher's burrow. The Judge was patient; he enjoyed gazing at the estates of his neighbors, pondering each inhabitant's foibles and virtues. There was one common denominator among them: great wealth. First, of course, the oil people. Then the landowners; some of them had oil also. Bankers, lawyers, professional people, a few doctors. Then there was a large group of inheritors. Some of them had never worked a day in their lives. They just inherited.

Of course, some of them, like the Davis boys, were inheritors who worked and expanded already sizeable fortunes. (When the Judge used the word "boy" he often referred to men in their forties and fifties.) Whether they worked or not, some of the inheritors found it difficult to handle the problems they inherited along with the money.

"Oliver, come here." The dog heeled. The Judge pointed to a large, rambling home. "See that place, Oliver? The man who built that house had more money than you have fleas. He was a barber in Kilgore. Everybody was digging wells. He had a little-bitty yard behind his barbershop. Just big enough for one derrick. That's all he needed, Oliver."

At the tee on the sixth hole the Judge paused to drink from the water cooler. He filled his cupped hands so the dog could lap water.

"Now look at that place, Oliver." The Judge gestured toward an opulent home just across Rivercrest Drive. "Moncrief. I wouldn't be surprised at all if Monty wasn't one of the ten richest men in Texas. Once he summoned his two sons just before Christmas to give them a special little gift. A million dollars. Each. But Monty was not just family-generous. He must have paid for half that new All Saints' Hospital out of his own pocket.''

The Judge crossed the street. The house next to the Moncrief place had been the home of Gaylord Chizum. Lawyer. Then the Judge and the dog continued at a leisurely pace, enjoying the trees and birds.

They had come to the Batts place. The Judge squinted at the spacious dwelling. ''There was violence in this house, Oliver.'' The Judge was sombre. ''Bob Batts shot and killed his wife there. Bob was a lawyer. They didn't get along. He wanted a divorce, but she was R.C. and wouldn't go along. She was a strange woman; some folks thought she should have been in an asylum. They owned a ranch a couple of hours from town and one night she telephoned Bob from the ranch because she was suspicious he was entertaining a woman at their house in town. She wouldn't believe him when he told her he was playing poker with friends. They had a hell of a fight on the phone until Bob hung up on her. He was boiling mad. Didn't win a hand after that. Nobody should play poker when they're not thinking straight.''

The Judge leaned down and unsnapped Oliver's leash. He picked up a stick and threw it; he waited until the retriever had returned with the stick before continuing.

''Bob and his friends were just starting to play the last round when Bob's teenage boy came in. He was scared. He had seen someone hiding in the shrubbery in the backyard. There had been several cases of breaking and entering around the neighborhood, so Bob thought there was a prowler on his premises.

''Bob took a deer rifle off the rack in his den and loaded it. Then he went to the back of the house, flipped on the floodlight that illuminated his yard, opened the door, and raised his rifle.

13

His guests saw him shoot. One time. Then Bob turned toward his friends with a stunned look on his face.''

The Judge exhaled slowly.

''It was his wife. They found her dead in the bushes, barefoot. Later, a witness said he saw her take off her shoes and go around behind the house. She had driven down from the ranch to check on Bob, to be sure he wasn't entertaining a woman. Took off the shoes so she could tiptoe around without being heard. Bob said he didn't recognize his wife, just saw a dark figure in the bushes holding what he thought were two guns. So he shot first. In self-defense, he said.

''Now you listen to me, Oliver.'' The Judge shook the stick at the dog. ''Don't you *ever* forget that story. Because it demonstrates the *complexity* of the law. Bob Batts was a clever lawyer with a thorough awareness of the rules of evidence. He had wanted to shed his wife for years. Suddenly he found himself with *someone* in the sights of his rifle. Was it an accident? Or was it murder? I reiterate, Oliver, the law is *complex*! Is murder premeditated if the premeditation lasts only a split second? Usually not. But what if that instant decision is taken in the wake of one arrived at long before to murder should the opportunity safely arise? And murder has to be proved by that golden maxim—*beyond a reasonable doubt*. And, how often can others know, or, to be more accurate, guess *beyond a reasonable doubt* what was going on in another person's mind?''

The Judge pulled at pursed lips, reflecting, and then resumed his walk. After passing one house he stopped again at the next, a square, white-brick abode of Moorish design: 805 Rivercrest Drive.

That place belonged to Ed Phillips. Fine young lawyer. Died when he was in his late thirties. Played golf in the rain and caught pneumonia. Didn't have penicillin then, in 1928. Young as he was, Ed had his own law firm, with a batch of partners. Chizum, from that house we passed back aways, and David Trammel, who lived not far from him. Ed left a wife and four sons. The Depression came and they were the poorest rich people in Fort Worth. But she went to work and was able to educate them. Two became lawyers; they practice in Fort Worth now. A third boy wrote a book about Rivercrest and he shook the skeletons in every closet around this golf course. *Holy* shit, it did cause a scandal! He left town and he's been writing ever since.

The fourth Phillips son was named for David Trammel. The Judge knew him better than the other boys because as a lad the boy made extra spending money cutting the grass and clipping the hedges in his yard. He ran around the neighborhood with Ken Davis, Jr., Cullen's older brother. He left Fort Worth about '39, but through the years sometimes dropped by to chat with the Judge during visits to Fort Worth. Never had much to say about what he was doing, though. Apparently he had become some sort of spy.*

The excursion continued until the Judge resumed his conversation with Oliver at another of the sumptuous homes.

"Do you know what kind of violence occurred here, Oliver?" The Judge paused. "*Patricide!* The Parker family. J. Lloyd Parker shot and killed his father in the kitchen of that house. For a long time J. Lloyd had been living on a grand scale on money that his mother gave him—I'm not sure he ever worked a day in his life. Then his mother and father were in an automobile accident. The father was driving; he survived but the mother died. Now they say that J. Lloyd blamed his father for his mother's death. In any event, J. Lloyd wasn't able to get as much money from the old man as he had before. The resentment festered. They had an argument and J. Lloyd shot his father. Right in that kitchen, Oliver. J. Lloyd had plenty of money then, and spent a lot of it on lawyers. He spent some time in the Rusk Psychiatric Hospital, but tried every way his lawyers could think of to stay out of jail. It was ten years before he exhausted his appeals, and spent a few years in prison. He's free now. He

---

*Judge Willard refers to the author, who retired from the CIA in 1975.

15

doesn't do anything, I understand. He just likes to drive around town in his Cadillac. He buys one each year when the new models come out, and just drives around town.''

A few moments after the Judge and his dog had resumed their walk a pretty jogger, a young girl in a T-shirt and running shorts, approached them. She smiled at the Judge, and he touched the brim of his Stetson.

The dog and his master turned the corner at the Polk place. Young George had gone off to be a journalist. Did well, until he got killed. They found him floating in a bay in Greece, his hands tied behind his back and his body full of holes. Still see his name in the newspapers once a year because of some journalism award named for him.

The smell of honeysuckle hung in the hot morning air as the Judge turned into a cul-de-sac and gestured toward a large home. ''Amon Carter. He was born out in Wise County in—and this is absolutely *true*, Oliver—a log cabin. Moved into Bowie and discovered that the train which stopped in town didn't have a dining car. So Amon sold box lunches, mostly chicken sandwiches, and when there was no chicken the passengers didn't know the difference when they got rabbit instead.

''Amon Carter founded the *Fort Worth Star-Telegram*. A powerful influence in the Southwest, read by every cattleman and dirt farmer for five hundred miles around. Then Amon went into the oil business and made a bundle from that. He was generous with his money. Left Fort Worth that Amon Carter Museum, which has the finest collections of Remingtons and Russells in the world.'' The Judge's Remington, according to his will, would hang there some day.

When the Judge turned the corner returning to the golf course he lingered, as he always did, at the estate where the Waggoner girl lived. Her husband liked animals and kept a thoroughbred horse behind the high wall. Used to keep a longhorn steer, noble animal, as well, but the Judge hadn't seen any recently. The

16

Waggoner girl was Dan's great granddaughter. Dan Waggoner owned oil and land. His ranch was *five hundred thousand acres*! When he died there was a squabble about his estate. Twenty-six lawyers fighting it out. Young Bucky Waggoner got most of it. Forty-five million dollars. There was a picture of Bucky in the newspaper. It showed Bucky sitting with his legs crossed. There was a hole in his shoe. Undoubtedly, with that forty-five million, Bucky was able to get his shoe fixed.

How much money was there around this golf course? A billion? Two?

The Judge crossed the street and walked down the broad fourteenth fairway. He was becoming tired. He and Oliver had almost completed the cirle around the golf course; the Judge had once clocked the distance at close to four miles.

He rested, sitting on the cool concrete bench in the tee house on the fifteenth hole, a short par three. It was almost eight o'clock, and the temperature must have climbed to eighty degrees.

Only a few feet from where the Judge sat there was a bronze plaque on a stone base in the grass. It was two feet by one and featured a sculpted bas-relief portrait of a man. There was an inscription: "In Memory of John B. Collier III." When the Judge had first seen that plaque he considered it curious. Had Collier dropped dead at that spot? Then he read the inscription further. Yes, Collier had died, but elsewhere. Finally: "He Scored a Hole-in-one Here on #15 June 14, 1969. "

The Judge still thought it curious.

Oliver barked, then streaked to a high fence not far from where the Judge sat. The Judge turned to see what had attracted the dog's attention. It was the camel on the Lowe place. What a *big* ass house that is, the Judge mused, gazing beyond the camel to the manor. Ralph Lowe made a lot of money in his time, but had some bad luck, too. He owned a horse that ran in the Kentucky Derby. In the home stretch the horse was ahead of the field, looking like a sure winner. But then Willie Shoemaker made some sort of mistake. Thought the race was over and pulled on the reins. So Ralph Lowe lost the Kentucky Derby.

Now, how did the camel come to be there? Ah, yes, the Judge remembered—a pair of camels was the his-and-her Christmas gift at Neiman-Marcus a few years back.

The Judge turned and looked across the narrow street at the Davis place.

Ken Davis came to Texas eighty-three years ago from Pennsylvania. He bought into a little oil-supply equipment outfit, took over, and expanded it into a worldwide industrial empire. He was a short, pugnacious bantam. Everyone called him Stinky. He lived in that house across from the fifteenth tee with his wife and three sons, Ken, Jr., William, and Cullen. When he died he left them a family business valued at three hundred million dollars.

The Judge remembered that Stinky doted on the three boys. But that didn't deter Stinky from being hard-nosed when it came to educating them about money. Frequently he would interrupt when Cullen was playing with his friends. He would walk up to Cullen and demand: ''How much money do you have in your pocket, Cullen?''

Cullen would respond. Maybe thirty-six cents.

Then Stinky would insist that Cullen clean out his pockets and they would count the coins. If Cullen had been accurate in assaying his wealth, Stinky would allow him to return the money to his pocket, perhaps with a bonus.

But if Cullen had not remembered the precise amount, Stinky took the money away from Cullen.

''Don't ever forget this,'' Stinky would admonish Cullen when he confiscated the boy's pocket change. ''A man who doesn't know how much he's worth doesn't deserve to keep the money he has.''

The Judge stood and stretched. He gazed again at the Davis place. When Stinky died in 1968, Cullen and Priscilla moved into the house, and when they went to the bigger place on Mockingbird Lane, William moved in.

"Do you know how Cullen came to inherit this mansion, Oliver?" The dog was attentive. "The story is that Stinky's will specified that his house was to go to the son who married first. I haven't seen any *evidence* to support that story. But one thing I *do* know. The day Stinky died Cullen and that flamboyant blonde Priscilla were married in that house. That same day."

The Judge pulled at his pursed lips. He shook his head, slowly, from side to side.

"Come on, Oliver. Time to go home."

When the old Judge arrived at his house the telephone was ringing. It was some time before the Judge understood who was calling from the state of Maryland; it was that youngest Phillips boy, the one who used to take care of the Judge's yard after school and usually visited the Judge when he was in Fort Worth. He had heard on the radio about the murders and that Cullen was being sought by the police. He wanted to know if the Judge had more details. The Judge told him what he could and said certainly, he would be glad to have him visit again when next he was in Fort Worth.

After he hung the phone in its cradle the Judge turned on his radio. The announcer reported that the big house on Mockingbird Lane had a new name: Murder Mansion.

·2·

CULLEN IN
THE CROSS-BAR HOTEL

By the time the first reporters and photographers arrived at the mansion Priscilla Davis had been rushed to the Peter Smith Hospital. On the way she told the ambulance attendant that her estranged husband Cullen had "put on a black wig and started shooting all my kids." A police officer at the hospital told a reporter that he understood Farr had been shot by Cullen. Beverly Bass was asked if she was certain the man dressed in black was Cullen; she was sure, Beverly said, because "I've known him for years."

The police began to look for Cullen Davis and took steps to protect those who might be in jeopardy. Tarrant County District Judge Joe H. Eidson* was awakened at 2 A.M. and advised that police guards had been dispatched to his home. Judge Eidson had presided for almost two years over the turbulent divorce proceeding involving Cullen and Priscilla. Her attorneys, Ronald Aultman and Jerry Loftin, also soon had police protection at their homes.

It was a very open secret in Fort Worth that Cullen was living with an attractive, blonde divorcée, Karen Master, in her home in the Edgecliff Village section of town. He had moved in with her shortly after his separation from Priscilla two years before.

The police surrounded the Master residence. Patrolman H. L. Ford went next door and dialed Karen Master's number. He

---

* Pronounced "Edson."

spoke with Cullen. He instructed Cullen to come out. Cullen asked if it would be all right if he took the time to dress and Ford said yes, but to be sure that his hands were visible at all times when he did come out.

At 4:30 A.M. Cullen Davis walked quietly out of Karen Master's home. Ford advised Cullen of his rights and escorted him to the back seat of a patrol car.

The multimillionaire industrialist was on his way to the city jail, sometimes referred to in Fort Worth as the Cross-Bar Hotel.

Shortly after Cullen's arrival at the Fort Worth jail Detective Claude R. Davis (no relationship) talked with Karen Master in the homicide office, and later with Cullen. In a notarized statement the police officer recounted that Karen had told him she had taken a sleeping pill about 10 P.M. the previous evening. She said she did not see Cullen again until about 4 A.M. when the telephone rang with police on the line asking Cullen to surrender.

In the same statement Detective Davis claimed that he had talked with Cullen for about forty-five minutes. The detective reminded Cullen that an oral statement could not be used against him in court. But the police officer did want Cullen to tell him why two people had to die and why two others were shot. "I asked Cullen Davis point blank, 'Why?' and Cullen replied, 'There are some things that a person does not need a reason for.'"

Detective Davis's statement was not admissible in criminal proceedings because the conversation occurred before Cullen posted bond. The statement was not mentioned during Cullen's subsequent criminal trials, nor would it become public for more than two and a half years.

While the events at the Davis mansion at 4200 Mockingbird Lane had developed too late to be in the morning edition of the *Star-Telegram*, the news spread rapidly through the telephone

21

gossip mill. A morning exchange of society intelligence is a ritual among the wives and widows in the affluent sections of Fort Worth. The right side of the tracks is the western area of town, the most prestigious enclaves located in the vicinity of the River-crest Country Club and the exclusive Westover Hills and in the newer but only slightly less desirable neighborhoods of Ridgelea and Colonial Country Club. The telephone is an essential in these golden ghettos. In some cases the listings in the three-inch telephone book (the most recent cover depicts surf on a beach although Fort Worth is 300 miles from the nearest wave in the Gulf of Mexico) include numbers for an office, the residence, the guest house, and the servants' quarters. Most homes have two or more numbers and several extensions throughout the house. Almost everyone in society uses a recent innovation offered by the telephone company. It is a beeper attachment which allows one talking to know if another call is coming in; that person can be instructed to hold while the original conversation is com-pleted. Many of the telephone numbers are unlisted. But they are almost always available in another register in which few among Fort Worth's elite wish to remain anonymous: *The Social Directory.*

The plastic buttons on the telephones generally begin to light up around 9 A.M. when Fort Worth wives are alone after their husbands depart for downtown offices. The sun had scarcely ap-peared over the horizon on the morning of August 3 when the telephone wires became conduits of hot, delicious gossip: *Have you heard?*

The life-styles of Cullen Davis and his colorful wife Priscilla had generated a variety of mouth-watering anecdotes since Cullen had married Priscilla on the day his father Stinky died. Some were true, most exaggerated, others patently false, and a few downright ugly and mean.

Priscilla, you know, had her breasts injected with silicone. Her monthly beautician's bill ran over $3000. She never went to the shop, a beautician came to the mansion every morning just to comb her hair. Everyone knows she lived with that Rufner man after she split up with Cullen

22

and before that basketball player moved in with her. Some of the stories about those parties at the mansion you simply wouldn't believe.

The earliest version of Priscilla's flight from the mansion after the shooting was that she was nude or at best scarcely clothed. That was disputed:

What saved her life was that her jeans were so tight that they kept her from bleeding to death.

The men listened to the latest radio reports while they drove. Soon their business lines were buzzing in offices in the Fort Worth National and Continental Bank buildings.

Cullen did have a fiery temper, you know. I was there that night he came out of that debutante bash and went to the parking lot for his Mark IV. He got tired of waiting for the attendant to bring the car, so he grabbed his own keys from the board, then threw the board with everybody else's car keys down into the mud.

She certainly is a piece, I can promise you that (meaningful pause, the intimation of firsthand knowledge of Priscilla's charms).

They say that Cullen inherited a big collection of pornography from Stinky along with the Rivercrest house.

And, do you believe the story that Cullen really got his rocks off by taking strangers to the mansion and watching while they screwed Priscilla?

The revelations in radio reports had been shocking and sensational, but skimpy. The headlines in the afternoon edition of the *Star-Telegram*—DAVIS JAILED AFTER SLAYING—was more satisfying.

There were two photographs on the front page. In the featured one, a grim but composed Cullen, his cheek against a closed fist, sat in the back seat of the patrol car which was to whisk him to the county jail. The second was a snapshot of Priscilla and Stan Farr which had been taken at a Colonial Country Club golf tournament in 1975. She seemed diminutive alongside the basketball player who towered over her; her head only reached his chest. Priscilla was wearing brief shorts and a bikini top. She wore three ornamental necklaces; the first circled her neck, the second dropped to the beginning of her cleavage, and the third plunged into the chasm between her almost bare breasts.

On the second page there was an aerial scene of the murder mansion and a portrait of Angela Dee Davis, Priscilla's daughter from her marriage to Jasper Baker. Dee was the adopted daughter not only of Cullen but of Jack Wilborn, Jr., Priscilla's second husband and father of her son John and her daughter Andrea.

The sixth page, too, offered two photographs: the first of policemen searching the garage area for the murder weapon, the second of a policeman turning his back on a white marble neoclassical statue of a woman which was located 100 yards from the mansion.

The seventh page was devoted entirely to photography. The broken glass in the dining-room window. The kitchen area of the manse, where a "trail of blood" had been found. Stan Farr's body being loaded into an ambulance, his normally large feet grotesquely enlarged because of the camera angle. Policemen crouching behind a car, guns drawn, outside Karen Master's house, as they waited for Cullen to emerge. A remarkably attractive Karen with a white scarf around her hair. Karen's garage with Cullen's car in it, as police searched for weapons. Then, back at the mansion, Beverly Bass in the sanctuary of the automobile of a private security guard she had flagged down after escaping from the wigged killer; her face still showing panic in the flashbulb's glare. Finally, a view of the rear of the mansion as investigators combed the area.

Priscilla was not aware that Andrea was dead until she had undergone surgery and was taken off the critical list.

The readers of the *Star-Telegram* waited anxiously for the next day's morning edition. When it arrived there was a large photograph of Priscilla, attractive, smiling, almost demure in a party frock, as she stood before a huge painting of Cullen, dressed in a conservative business suit, and of herself. The second picture was of twelve-year-old Andrea's father, Jack Wilborn, Jr., after he arrived at the Dallas-Fort Worth airport from an interrupted Colorado vacation. Wilborn was a grittily handsome man, with long hair and the face a casting director would seek for the role of a cowboy-actor-poet. Wilborn had been approached by a reporter when he stepped off the plane; he had broken into tears when asked the first question.

The lead story carried Glen Guzzo's by-line, the first of almost daily accounts he was to write on the sensational case over the next two and a half years; the second story was by Dan Frazier. There were others by *Star-Telegram* reporters John Makeig, Jim Street, and Jon McConal. The entire first page of the second section of the paper was devoted to feature stories involving the principals. Stan Farr had once been the manager of the Rhinestone Cowboy Saloon, and a mourner there, between drinks of bourbon and Coke in a pint fruit jar, lamented the loss of his friend, saying Stan had been a "good ole boy." A friend who had dined at the Swiss House with Priscilla and Stan the night before said that Priscilla had been "in a real good mood" before she left the restaurant for the Rangoon Racquet Club and had had one for the road before returning to the mansion. Andrea's presence at the mansion was explained: She was alone in the mansion when the murders occurred, having just returned from Houston where she had been visiting her grandmother.

A friend recalled the narrow swath Cullen had cut in Fort Worth social circles and mentioned that Cullen had escorted Suzy Knickerbocker, the glamorous syndicated columnist, to a local charity ball in 1975. For all his wealth and social prominence, Cullen was a quiet man in public, dressed conservatively, and worked diligently in a series of executive posts in the family enterprises. "Really," one friend of Cullen's put it, "an ordinary guy."

The police had completed a search of Cullen's white and blue Cadillac parked in Karen Master's garage. They found two snub-nosed revolvers in a Styrofoam chest in the trunk of the car, a small automatic pistol in a cardboard box also in the trunk, and another handgun in a cardboard box under the driver's seat. In a closet in Karen's house they found a fifth weapon.

Cullen was charged with murder on August 4. Judge Byron Matthews set the bond at $80,000. There was an outcry. What was to keep Cullen from jumping in his private Lear jet and flying away? The judge defended the bond as adequate, opining, "He'll probably never hurt anybody again. He was just drunk....The police told me he was quite drunk and they say when he gets drunk, he gets mad." Matthews's assertion was immediately challenged by Patrolman Ford and the squad which had apprehended Cullen at Karen Master's house. *They had said no such thing, and Cullen had been sober when arrested.* The judge backed down, saying that "someone" had told him that. The bond remained unchanged.

Cullen paid the $80,000 and checked out of the Cross-Bar Hotel. He hired a Dallas attorney, Phil Burleson. The same day Gus Gavrel, listed in critical condition after surgery and facing permanent, partial paralysis from the injury to his spinal cord, sued Cullen in the Seventeenth District Court for three million dollars in damages.

On August 5 the *Star-Telegram* revealed a chink in the family empire which had been presided over by the Davis sons since Stinky's demise in 1968. The youngest brother, William, claimed that he had been forced out of the family business by his older brothers, Ken, Jr., and Cullen. The suit had been filed two years earlier but was still in its early stages and had been held secret up to this point. Cullen was the primary target in William's legal feud: "T. Cullen Davis feels compelled to engage in a continuous series of [multimillion-dollar] expenditures based on his emotional needs rather than any exercise of business judgement." Cited as an example of impulse spending were "a number of business ventures [made] without any adequate examination into their affairs and the construction of a multimillion-dollar home.'' The suit further maintained that Cullen had accumulated $16 million in personal debts by late 1974 and more than $150 million in business debts through mismanagement.

On August 5, Andrea was buried. In the eulogy it was said that she fell victim to ''an adult world of confused and distorted values.''

On August 7 an attorney representing the surviving family of Priscilla's lover Stan Farr filed suit against Cullen. The same day District Attorney Tim Curry carried his murder charge to the grand jury.

For two weeks gossip proliferated while readers of the *Star-Telegram* waited to hear a golden slipper drop: Priscilla's version of what had occurred at the murder mansion.

In the August 24 issue of the *Star-Telegram* the Cullen Davis affair was still front-page news, but second-best to a slaying which had occurred that day: MAN KILLED WOMAN TELLER THEN HIMSELF told the story of a ''crime of passion'' which unfolded in the Continental National Bank. A man with a gun entered the lobby not to rob but to confront an ex-girlfriend. He disposed of the young woman teller with three shots and with a fourth, himself.

Fort Worth heard for the first time Priscilla's version of what had happened in the murder mansion three weeks previously when she testified before a grand jury from her wheelchair.

She said that she and Stan Farr had returned to the mansion at 12:30 A.M. on Monday morning after dining out with friends. Stan went directly upstairs to the bedroom. Priscilla noticed that the door to the cellar was open. She approached and saw a bloody handprint on the door, then more blood on the wall....

''I screamed, 'Stan come here! Stan come here!' Only much louder. Then Cullen stepped out from the direction of the washroom....

"He was dressed all in black and he had a black wig...like a woman's wig that was curly on the ends. He had both his hands together and there was a black or dark-colored plastic bag around them.

"He stepped out and said, 'Hi!' Then he shot me....I grabbed where I had been shot. I screamed. I said I had been shot. I said, 'Cullen shot me. Stan, go back!' I could hear Stan coming."

Priscilla then told the grand jury that Cullen had run past her to the door and tried to tug it open but couldn't. Farr must have been holding it.

"Then Cullen fired the gun [through the door] and I heard Stan cry out. It was like 'Uhhh.' Cullen stood there and he opened the door and Stan came out and grabbed him. They were wrestling around when Stan turned his back to me. I heard a shot, then Stan jerked back. He turned around and fell down and was just kind of looking at me and breathing in a very raspy voice. And Cullen stood at his feet and shot him twice more. Then Stan just kind of laid his head down and died."

Then Priscilla described a scene in which Cullen grasped Farr's ankles and dragged his body into the kitchen. When her husband was out of view she staggered to her feet and escaped through a patio door to the lawn.

"I knew the door made noise when I opened it. I knew Cullen was after me. I ran down the walkway and turned and saw him. I said, 'Cullen, I love you. I've never loved anyone else!' He grabbed me by the arm and started dragging me back the way I had exited. All he kept saying was, 'Come on, come on!'"

She pleaded with Cullen to release her, that he was hurting her. Then Cullen abruptly dropped her and returned to the kitchen; she was on the ground just outside the patio door.

"I reached down and jerked off my shoes and jumped up. I wrapped my skirt around me real tight and ran."

Priscilla hid from her husband in garden shrubbery. Peering through the bushes she observed Cullen leave the house and walk down the path, searching for her. He was no longer wearing the wig, Priscilla said. He went past her into the darkness. Then: "I heard a female voice saying, 'Who is it?' It sounded like Dee. I heard her saying, 'Who is it? Who are you?' I could tell the voices were going away around toward the garage, the back door."

At that point, Priscilla testified, she crawled out from the shrubbery and began to run. She had only just started when she heard a shot, a woman screaming, and then more shots.

Priscilla ran as fast as she could, holding her hands to her body, over the lawn and down the hill to the vast field which surrounds the mansion. Finally she reached the edge of the property and sought refuge at one of a row of homes adjacent to the mansion grounds. She pounded on the door, Priscilla said, but the occupants of the house refused to let her inside. But they did call an ambulance.

The next day Gus Gavrel, Jr., twenty-one, known as "Bubba," testified at the separate but related bond hearing, which was being conducted simultaneously with the grand jury session. As Priscilla had been, he was in a wheelchair. He said that he had been with his girlfriend, Beverly Bass, at the Rangoon Racquet Club. Beverly was a friend of Dee, Priscilla's daughter, and Gus had driven her to the mansion, where she planned to spend the night with Dee. Gus said he heard a woman screaming when he stopped the car. That, and his subsequent testimony, coincided with and corroborated Priscilla's declarations.

"I heard screaming and yelling...a woman's voice. She was yelling 'I love you!' Then a man's voice: 'Come on. Come on.' I saw a man dragging a woman back toward the house. I started walking toward the garage, and, as soon as I did, he came around by the gate. I asked him what he was doing, what he wanted. He just said, 'Come on, let's go inside.'"

He and Beverly followed the man, Gus said.

"And as soon as he got down by the lights Beverly told me it was Cullen. And, as soon as she said that, he shot me."

Gus continued. Once Cullen had shot him, Cullen ran past

him searching for Beverly. Gus attempted to stand and walk. He could not. He managed to crawl to the grass lawn near a door to the house before he realized that he was partially paralyzed. He could hear footsteps; Cullen was returning to the mansion. Cullen approached a window near the locked door and shot three times through the window glass, then broke out the remaining shards so that he could squirm through the opening. Then, Gus said, Cullen came out of the door after a few minutes and walked down the pathway and away into the night.

"After he left, I crawled up and crawled through the window [into] and [through] the breakfast room. I tried to use the phone but it didn't work."

Gus Gavrel then blacked out.

Priscilla Davis was the sole witness for the prosecution in the grand jury inquiry and one of several during the bond hearings. Called back for a second day of testimony for the latter, Priscilla characterized Cullen as a man with a quick temper, capable of violent acts. She recalled two episodes from her life with Cullen before their legal separation in 1974.

In the spring of 1972, Priscilla said, she and Cullen had spent an evening in a hotel in Palm Springs, California. In the lounge Cullen had danced in what Priscilla called a provocative manner with another woman.

"He had his hand on her backside, her rear end." Later in their room, "I jumped him about it...and he hit me with his fists."

Priscilla also claimed that a year before the Palm Springs incident Cullen had beaten her daughter Dee in the Rivercrest house, before they moved to the mansion on Mockingbird Lane. One night when preparing for bed she heard sounds from downstairs. When she descended to investigate, "Cullen and Dee were at the back door. Her nose was bleeding. I came down and I had a little yellow kitten in my arms. He came at me and grabbed the cat, then threw it down on the floor, and picked it up and threw it down again. It just lay there."

Phil Burleson objected when Priscilla told the story, but the judge overruled the objection.

During reexamination Priscilla claimed that Cullen had broken her nose twice, her collarbone once, and Dee's nose once. She also testified that Dee had left home about four years previously because Cullen had beaten her up. She said that she and Cullen had been visited by a social worker who asked Cullen what changes he would make if Dee returned. Cullen replied, according to Priscilla, that he would beat Dee severely should that occur.

"Has he even so much as said 'I'm sorry'?" she was asked.

"No, sir," Priscilla responded.

Burleson asked Priscilla if she could remember the name of the social worker. No. And Dee did return home, crying, and Cullen did not beat her up.

Assistant District Attorney Joe Shannon had further questions for Priscilla after she testified that she had visited Cullen at the Ramada Inn suite where he had lived temporarily after the separation.

"Did you have something to eat there?"

"Yes," she said.

"Drinks?"

"Yes."

"Did ya'll have sex?"

"Yes," Priscilla replied. "I had hoped that he'd show some sign of wanting to change."

Burleson asked if they had slept together in the Ramada Inn before or after Cullen had agreed to purchase a new luxury automobile for her.

Priscilla couldn't remember.

But she did have an answer of sorts. "The last time I was there and talked to him, I looked under his bed and saw a lot of pornography—"

Burleson interrupted, protesting that Priscilla was not being responsive to his question.

Priscilla confirmed that her twelve-year-old daughter was

alone in the mansion the night of the murders. Dee had picked Andrea up that day when Andrea returned from attending a Bible school in Houston. Because her father, Jack Wilborn, was in Colorado, Andrea stayed with Priscilla. When Priscilla and Stan Farr left, she said, Andrea "came to the back door with us and I watched her activate the security door locks."

Other witnesses established that two bullets had been removed from Stan Farr's body, and that perhaps two more passed through the six-foot nine-inch frame of the former ICU basketball star. There was no bullet in Andrea's corpse, but a witness from the Fort Worth Police Department's crime scene search team said that he found a slug on the basement floor near Andrea. All the bullets were from the same revolver; none was from any of the guns found in Cullen's car. Burleson asked the policeman what other evidence he had discovered. Joe Shannon objected, complaining to the judge that Burleson was "trying to rummage through our entire file" of evidence. The judge agreed; he sustained the objection.

Cullen's brother Ken testified for the defense. He said that he had first learned of the events at the Mockingbird Lane mansion when he received an early morning telephone call from Jim Hale, then general manager of the *Star-Telegram*, on August 3. Ken, in turn, had telephoned Cullen about 4:00 A.M. at Karen Master's home, before the police had arrived there. Karen answered, passed the phone to Cullen.

Cullen: "I was in bed."

Ken: "Have you been there all night?"

Cullen: "Most of the night."

Ken asked Cullen if he had heard about the shootings.

Cullen: "No, who was shot?"

Ken: "A man by the name of Stan Farr and a little girl were killed, and Priscilla was shot."

Then Ken advised Cullen the police were looking for him. There was no response to this.

Cullen closed the conversation: "Well, I guess I'll go back to bed."

The *Star-Telegram* reported that it had learned from "sources" that Cullen, after being released on bond the day of his arrest, stayed for three nights in a clinic which specialized in psychiatric treatment.

On August 16, Priscilla's daughter Dee was driving in an automobile with her boyfriend in Azle, a small town near Fort Worth. There was a single-car accident. Rescue workers spent forty-five minutes removing the young man from the wreckage; he was dead on arrival at the hospital. Dee was thrown from the car, suffered a broken nose and lacerations.

On August 20, Cullen was arrested on two counts of capital murder—which can bring a death penalty—as he was about to climb in his private jet at Meacham Field. The pilot was aboard and the plane ready to take off. Later, several witnesses were to testify that he was not attempting to flee, but the question remained in doubt. A bond hearing was scheduled.

On August 26 the suit filed against Cullen by his brother William was settled out of court. Henceforth William would be excluded from any management responsibilities; in effect, Cullen and Ken, Jr., had taken over the vast conglomerate created by their father Stinky. For his pain William was to receive ample balm: $100 million.

At the end of the month District Judge Tom Cave ordered that Cullen remain in jail without bond until his trial, which was scheduled for October.

On September 22, 1976, Cullen celebrated his forty-third birthday. It was the first, but not the last birthday he would spend in the Cross-Bar Hotel.

It was not what Old Stinky had envisioned for his son.

·3·

THE OLD JUDGE AND
THE JOURNALIST

The journalist had arrived in Fort Worth the evening before and had telephoned Judge Willard. The Judge had said he would be happy to see the visitor and had suggested that the journalist come in the morning. They could take a walk on the golf course. "I'll expect you," the Judge had said, "at 6:15 A.M."

There had been a pause at the other end of the line.

"It won't be too cold this late in February," the Judge had said.

"Fine," the journalist finally replied. "I'll be there at 6:15."

After a cup of tea the next morning at the Judge's house—the journalist asked for coffee, but there was none—the Judge took Oliver's leash from the closet and the two men and the dog went out for their walk along the golf course. The Judge remembered and commented on the time, forty years before, when the journalist had taken care of the Judge's lawn.

"Now, what have you really been up to all these years, young man?"

The journalist, age fifty-four, explained that he had been a writer and newspaperman, and then had served in the CIA until early 1975. Now he was a writer again.

"What in the world," the Judge asked, "ever made you become a spy?"

The journalist explained that he had been a manager of spies, then turned the topic of conversation to the surprising events at

34

the mansion on Mockingbird Lane. He said he was trying to decide if a book might be written about the escapade. If it came to that, he hoped the Judge would give him his thoughts on the murders and on the trial which was scheduled soon in Fort Worth.

"Seems to me," the Judge said, "you should start by poking around in the history of crime and punishment in Texas."

"Judge Roy Bean and the law west of the Pecos?"

"Don't *believe* all those stories," the Judge said, "although some of 'em are pretty good tales. I like the one about the time Judge Bean was presiding over the case of a man accused of killing a Chinese laundryman. Bean moved from behind his bar and sat in his armchair. That meant court was in session. He thumbed through the book which constituted his entire law library—*The Revised Civil Statutes of Texas, 1879.* After a while Judge Bean announced, 'Ain't nothing in the statutes of the state of Texas sez it's against the law to kill a Chinaman. Case dismissed.' "

The Judge unleashed Oliver so the dog could run free.

"Now don't *believe* that story, young man. Most everything ever written on Judge Roy Bean was mythical to the extreme. Only story I really ever found credible was about him refusing a gift from Lillie Langtry. She was pleased when she learned that Bean had named his town and his saloon after her, and she offered to erect a drinking fountain in the town. Bean turned her down, because water was the one thing people *never* drank in those days."

The journalist smiled and rubbed his arms briskly. He found it to be quite cold.

"Now if you want some authentic legal history," the Judge said, "you can begin right here in Fort Worth. There was an outstanding attorney named Captain Joseph Christopher Terrell here in the early days. He had a law office at First and Main streets for fifty years until he died in 1907. Terrell carried a weapon on his person. In fact, a pocket pistol in early Fort

35

Worth was a part of almost every gentleman's attire and essential to the practice of law. Now, I remember one story...."

The Judge paused, grimaced as a jogger panted past, and then resumed.

"No, that *wasn't* Terrell. I'm thinking of District Judge 'Three-Legged' Williamson down in Houston. He was on the bench once when a lawyer stated a point of law and mentioned a case to back it up. 'Give the court the book and the page where the case might be found,' Three-Legged said. The lawyer had had enough of the judge. He pulled a bowie knife and said, 'This is the page,' and drew a pistol and said, pointing the gun at the judge, 'and this is the law.' 'Your law is no good,' the judge said. Then he pulled his own six-shooter and aimed it at the lawyer's nose. 'The proper authority is Colt on revolvers.' And that lawyer fled right out of the court."

The journalist guided the Judge's reminiscences back to the Fort Worth lawyer.

"While Captain Terrell was practicing law in Fort Worth," the Judge said, "ordinary human life was held very cheaply. Justice could not travel on leaden feet. There were two crimes which were serious above all others and never condoned: the theft of horses or cattle and the act of disturbing a religious service."

"More serious than murder?" the journalist questioned.

"Yup," the Judge replied. "One lawman explained it once by saying that in Texas there were more folks around that needed killin' than there were horses that needed stealin'."

Then the Judge recounted the story of one of Captain Terrell's exceptional cases where a man beat the rap of disturbing a church meeting. Terrell's client had gotten all tanked up with cheap whiskey and fired his guns through the top of a tent where a band of the faithful were praying. He got away but his conscience began to bother him. He went to Terrell, confessed the awful thing he had done, and asked what to do. Terrell told his client that from the legal point of view there was no hope, no one was ever acquitted for that crime. Your only chance, Terrell counseled, is to about-face with your sin and *join* that church. "You reckon?" the dismayed offender queried. When Terrell said he did so reckon, the contrite culprit took the vows in the very church group he had shot up. And the Fort Worth marshal took no cognizance of the offense, the grand jury failed to indict, and Terrell lost his fee. And that man, true to his vows, was devout from that time on.

The journalist took advantage of the remark about the early Fort Worth grand jury to steer the Judge's discussion back to the present. He asked the Judge about the capital murder and attempted murder indictments against Cullen.

The Judge stopped the walk, pointing to a mansion near the fifth green. "I guess you remember Monty and his boys. Monty Moncrief is a very rich and generous man. His boys are rich, too, I've been told."

Yes, the journalist said, he remembered Moncrief and his sons, and it was true that they were quite wealthy. One of Monty's grandsons, in fact, had the middle name of Oil—literally.

The Judge hadn't known that, although he did know that a daughter of one of the wealthy families across the links had the middle name of Zillion.

The Judge eventually explained that capital murder was defined as murder carried out during the commission of another felony and must be tried by a jury. Cullen, if convicted, could be executed for those offenses. The attempted murder charges were for the unsuccessful attempts to slay Priscilla and Gus Gavrel. Those two indictments and the capital murder charge for the death of Stan Farr were being held in abeyance. The second felony was Cullen's trespassing on the mansion grounds after the divorce judge had enjoined him against approaching the property. District Attorney Tim Curry had elected to pursue, at least for the time being, only the single indictment for the capital murder of Andrea, the twelve-year-old girl.

When the Judge and the journalist arrived at the old Batts

place, the Judge related the story of the death of Bob Batts's wife in that house. The Judge added that a journalist should remember the incident and consider the complexity of the law in a case such as Cullen's. And the responsibility a jury had in determining—beyond a reasonable doubt—what went on in any man's head, and precisely why, when, and how a man might or might not have perpetrated murder.

Just around the corner the two men stopped at 805 Rivercrest, the white house where the journalist had lived as a child and where his father had died. The Judge had not known, until the journalist recounted the circumstances, that Edwin Phillips had collapsed on the golf course directly in front of his own residence, on the third green. The journalist's mother had sold the house in the early '40s. A number of people had lived there since, including John Held, Jr., once famous for his cartoons of short-skirted flappers and their greased-hair beaus.

As they continued down the shady street the journalist remarked that T. Cullen Davis was a very wealthy man who could afford the most expensive lawyers and perhaps could muster more money for his defense than Tarrant County could for his prosecution. Given those circumstances, how likely was it that Cullen would be found guilty? And, if he was, what were the chances of his spending some years in the penitentiary in Huntsville or dying in the electric chair there?

"Not the electric chair," the Judge corrected the journalist. "That's changed since you lived here in Texas. Now lethal injection is the form of execution. I was reading something about it in the *Star-Telegram* not long ago."

The Judge pointed to a large house. "That's the old Fender place. You must have known young Howard."

Yes, the journalist had known Howard Fender. He had heard that Howard had become the district attorney in Fort Worth.

"*Was*," the Judge said, "before Tim Curry. Now he's a judge. But the item I read in the paper was about when Howard was the district attorney and had a case where he won a death-sentence conviction. The defendant's lawyer protested that under the new lethal injection law his client could be subjected to cruel and inhuman punishment. The law was broad on the point of who had the authority to decide *what* injection. What was to keep the prison director from injecting a man with antifreeze or battery acid? A valid point. Oklahoma has the same law, but up there they give the condemned man a euphoria-inducing sedative before the injection so that he expires in a state of joy. Anyway, nobody's been executed in Huntsville since that law came into effect.''

The Judge delivered a history lesson on the Huntsville penitentiary. Back in 1871 the Texas state legislature passed a law which permitted the prison to be leased out to an entrepreneur who paid the state $3 a month for each convict placed there; he made his profit by hiring out the inmates as workers. That didn't really work out, and the operation of Huntsville returned to the state. Since that time, when convicts have worked, it has been on a farm or in a chain gang. In the early days the longest sentences went to horse thieves and cattle rustlers. Back in the '80s one Texas court sentenced a man to five years for cattle theft and the following day another man to four months for murder. In 1887 a nine-year-old boy was sentenced to and served most of nine years for homicide, and a girl guilty of infanticide began her three-year term when she was only eleven. The most notorious inmate was John Wesley Hardin, son of a Methodist minister from Bonham—that's Sam Rayburn's hometown near Fort Worth; he killed twenty people, in prison and out. And there was an unfortunate military prisoner named Turner. That soldier was sentenced to three years after being found guilty of ''worthlessness.'' That's a pretty vague charge, the Judge admitted, and the escutcheon of Texas justice is not any brighter because of it, but Turner did serve his time. Finally the Judge mentioned the Huntsville siege, just back in 1974, when four people died in ten days—the longest prison siege in U.S. history.

39

The two men rested near the Parker place. The Judge told the story of the murder in the kitchen there. The journalist remembered the details, having known J. Lloyd Parker during their school days.

The Judge had more stories to tell of famous criminals who had frequented the Fort Worth area. Belle Starr, the outlaw queen, and Bonnie Parker and Clyde Barrow all operated in Tarrant County. And, ranging around the state, the Judge described the dreadful massacre in Austin, just ten years ago, when a student killed his wife and mother, then climbed the tower at the University of Texas and sniped away until there were sixteen more dead and thirty-one wounded. The sniper was gunned down, finally, by police. And, just three years ago, twenty-seven young men and boys were found in shallow graves around Houston, where they had been buried after a thirty-three-year-old electrician had homosexually abused them.

Then the Judge, his face grim, mentioned that most *tragic* crime in Texas history, in Dallas, in Dealey Plaza, thirteen years before.

After the Judge stopped to look, as he always did, at the fine range horse inside the fence at the Waggoner girl's place, he told the journalist that old W. T. Waggoner had once sold a part of his land on the golf course to A. P. Barrett because Barrett wanted to have a place large enough for a private landing strip. The journalist said that he could recall the planes flying in and out of that estate.*

The journalist remarked that the families who lived around Rivercrest had a great deal of money.

The Judge confirmed the observation. At first the money came from land and the crops and cattle on it. Then more money was made when that land was spoiled for grazing by oil

---

* The First State Bank of Rio Vista, Texas, is the only bank in the world with fly-in service, having a landing strip for wealthy fliers.

seeping up through the surface. "Take old W. T., for instance," the Judge said. "When that happened to old Pappy Waggoner he's supposed to have said, 'Damn it, cattle can't drink that stuff.' And that quagmire in his pasture turned out to be the Electra field—named for his daughter—which became one of the great deposits of oil ever found in this country."

At the end of their hike, the Judge and the journalist were standing at the fifteenth tee, facing the Davis residence. Oliver barked at the camel on the nearby Lowe lawn.

The journalist still had not received an answer to the question he had put to the Judge half an hour before: Would Cullen be convicted? And, if so, might he be executed or sentenced to a long prison term?

"I don't know," the Judge said. He pushed his Stetson back on his head and pulled at his lips. "I just don't *know* enough about what actually happened that night. The question of motive is vital, of course. It obviously wasn't robbery. Cullen certainly had as good a motive as anyone. Maybe jealousy of Priscilla's giant lover. Or, more likely, the fear that Priscilla was going to get away with his money and his property. But I don't really *know*, and no one can until they have more facts in hand."

The Judge stooped to snap Oliver's leash onto the dog's collar.

"It's a question of evidence, son. *Evidence.* Now a while back I was standing right at this spot mulling over the story that most people in this town believe—that Cullen married Priscilla the day his father died because Stinky's will deeded the house to the first son married after his death. That story has been told so much it's accepted as fact. But, when it gets right down to it, I've never seen any *evidence* that it's true."

The Judge regarded the journalist. "Son, what kind of book is it you plan to write about Cullen?"

"I'm not sure I'll be able to sell the idea to my publisher," the journalist said. "But I'm thinking of something that would separate facts from fiction so the reader could make up his own mind. Maybe I can put some distance between rumors and what really happened.''

"You have your work cut out for you!" the Judge exclaimed. "You have a shit *pot* full of work. There'll be rumors and speculation and all sorts of wild stories and the people who will tell them to you may honestly believe they have found the truth, but most of what you hear will be myth. Don't forget, son, the tendency in this great state to exaggerate, to blow everything up until it's the best and especially the *biggest*. Remember the story about the man who came to Fort Worth from the East and stayed overnight in a millionaire's mansion. The Texans showed him through the place; it was the *biggest* house, with the *biggest* yard, the *biggest* everything! That night the visitor walked in his sleep and plunged right into the swimming pool. He came up out of the water sputtering, 'Don't flush it! Don't flush it!' ''

The journalist chuckled.

"Keep that story in mind," the old Judge admonished, "or you'll find yourself drowning in the biggest goddamned *pool* of hyperbole you've ever sunk in!"

The journalist looked at the Davis mansion. He told the Judge he remembered being in the house many times with the Landreth girl when he was growing up and before Stinky bought the place in 1943. And, later, there was a hazy memory of Stinky, and he clearly recalled Ken, Jr., with whom he had attended classes at Arlington Heights High School. But Cullen had been much younger; only the vaguest recollection of him remained. The journalist asked the Judge what he knew about Cullen.

"Why, I scarcely know the boy," the Judge answered. "Just saw him running up and down the street when he was a youngster, and driving in and out of Rivercrest in his Cadillac when he and Priscilla lived in the house for four years.

"Not knowing much about him," the Judge said, "I really shouldn't comment on his character. But I *must* say there's one thing about Cullen that puts me off. That T. Cullen Davis business. What's wrong with Thomas? Somehow it's always seemed to me that a man who insists on a first initial in order to be known by an uncommon second name, or for any other reason, always generates a lot of suspicion with respect to basics of human...uh...*beingness*, if there is such a word. I suppose that kind of judgment is not...very scientific, but I *do* feel that way.'' The Judge looked at the journalist. ''Did you ever know anyone who called themselves by a first initial?''

The journalist thought for a moment. ''Only one,'' he said. ''A man I used to work with. E. Howard Hunt.''

The Judge's eyes twinkled. ''Well, then. Do I recollect correctly that he later worked at the White House? With a man called G. Gordon Liddy?''

The journalist smiled and nodded.

''Well, if you're going to write the story of Cullen Davis, you'd better start with Stinky. There, I *can* help you. Any father has an influence on his son's life. I would say that Stinky's influence on Cullen was *profound*. Come along to the house now, and we'll have some lunch. You can have a drink if you want, but I won't. I only have one drink a day, and I save that for the evening.''

The Judge and the journalist and the dog turned back and began the trek along the golf course toward the Judge's home. As they walked the Judge began to tell the journalist what he knew of Stinky Davis.

·4·

STINKY'S EMPIRE,

CULLEN AND PRISCILLA

In the beginning it was the Mid-Continent Supply Company, which wasn't really very much when Kenneth W. Davis took it over soon after the Great Depression. It was quite something, however, when the old man died in 1968. It was KenDavis Industries International, Inc.—Kiii, the logo read—one of the world's most profitable privately owned conglomerates. Except for some of the shares in one segment of the giant complex, it was a family business. Ken Davis, Sr., left his three sons an industrial estate which was valued at more than a quarter of a billion dollars. That was just what he had in mind all along.

Davis was born in 1895 near Johnstown, Pennsylvania. As a young man he played semiprofessional baseball in Pittsburgh. During World War I he was an officer and pilot in the U.S. Army Air Service, and taught others to fly as an instructor. After the war he worked in Pennsylvania as an aircraft salesman, in real estate, and, briefly, in a steel mill.

Davis went to Texas in the mid-twenties and married a Fort Worth girl, Alice Bound. The couple moved to Arkansas where he became a roustabout in the oil fields and a clerk in a supply store. He learned about digging for oil and hawking the equipment needed to process it. After several years the Davises returned to Fort Worth and, with a stake accumulated in backbreaking labor on the derricks, Davis bought into Mid-Continent Supply Company. The company was dedicated to providing whatever paraphernalia was required by anyone in the oil business. Davis soon owned the business lock, stock, and oil barrels. He heeded Andrew Carnegie's advice and put all his eggs in that one basket—and watched that basket carefully. He and Alice lived in a modest brick house in the western section of Fort Worth. They were only a dozen blocks but still many years from Rivercrest. Davis toiled long hours to expand his business and Ms. Davis quietly bore three sons: Ken, Jr., Cullen, and finally the baby William.

Early on Davis acquired a nickname: Stinky. The sobriquet suggested the need for Life Buoy soap, but actually referred instead to the hard-nosed manner in which Stinky conducted his business and to the mean streak which he sometimes revealed in the office and at home. There were rumors of skulduggery in the acquisition of Mid-Continent—did he force his partners out with illegal tactics and didn't someone jump out of a window?—but if that were true any evidence of it vanished as time went by. Once *his* venture prospered Stinky was not accused of dishonesty, but many believed his shortcuts skirted the borderline of executive morality. Few of his associates or customers thought highly of Stinky as a person, but most respected his business acumen and accepted his normal pugnacity and occasionally erratic behavior.

When the boys were young they were sometimes embarrassed by their father's brusque manner and belligerent confrontations with their friends. Stinky's feisty demeanor became even more intimidating when he had been drinking. In his middle age, that was frequently. Usually he held his liquor well, but sometimes he would break up a teenage party by coming home roaring drunk—"Out! Everybody go home!"—and once one of his sons was red-faced when he saw Stinky, gloriously tanked at the helm of a boat, ram into and demolish a dock at Eagle Mountain Lake.

When Ken, Jr., and Cullen were in elementary school, neighborhood friends purchased a Model-T truck. After it had been decorated crudely in flamboyant hues it became the joy of the kids on the block. Though fun, the truck was seldom functional and broke down one day in front of the Davises' red brick house. The boys, attempting to repair the dilapidated truck, were soon making a racket that brought Stinky rushing out of the house with demands for quiet. William was napping and mustn't be awakened! Then Stinky noticed the disreputable heap. "Get it out! Get that thing away from here!" The boys protested that the truck would not start, no matter how much they cranked. Stinky ran at the vehicle, literally attacking it. His assault against the upright windshield was so ferocious that the glass shattered. But Stinky succeeded in pushing the offending jalopy away from his property without injury.

The next morning Stinky was furious when he found all four tires on his own automobile deflated. He suspected—quite accurately—that the culprits were the owners of the Model-T he had abused the previous evening. He knocked on neighborhood doors and roared his suspicion. One father convinced Stinky his own son was not involved, and Stinky advised the man to keep his boy away from "those goddamned hoodlums" who were responsible. When he did encounter the father of one of the guilty parties, Stinky threatened to send a bill for the wrecker he had hired to put even more distance between his property and that mechanical derelict. Stinky never did send the bill, but neither did he pay for the broken windshield on the Model-T*

So the neighborhood gang learned to be cautious in dealing with the quick-tempered Stinky. He didn't exactly terrorize them, but it became obvious that it wasn't worth the effort to cross or displease him. On Halloween nights there were no soap marks on the windows at the Davis house, nor were eggs splattered on the door. Certainly none of the boys dared contemplate Stinky's front porch as the locale for one of the *neat* Halloween stunts—defecating in a paper sack, igniting the sack on the stoop, ringing the doorbell, and then from the bushes watching

---

* The vehicle was purchased, subsequently, by the author and several friends, for $15.

the occupant open his door, see the burning bag, and stomp on it vigorously to put out the flames.

As the oil industry expanded Stinky's enterprises boomed. Soon he owned a number of companies which tended to spawn new ones. Cummins Sales and Service, Great Western Drilling, and, by the time Cullen was of high school age, Stratoflex, all of which quickly established satellite organizations around the world. The Davis family moved out of the small house into another larger and more comfortable, along the road which would lead eventually to Rivercrest.

During this period, Stinky began to invest in real estate in and near Fort Worth. One tract Stinky acquired was a huge parcel of 181 acres in the city, 140 acres of which later was the site of the murder mansion. On one edge of the huge field a wooden fence separated it from an adjacent home. Riding along the fence on his horse one day, Stinky was enraged to see that the occupant of the home had dumped a pile of grass clippings over the fence on-to Stinky's land. Stinky promptly spurred his horse around the corner, dismounted, knocked on the door, and, when the door opened, told the offender to get his goddamned grass clippings off Davis property.

The piece of real estate which Stinky guarded so zealously became extremely valuable and others coveted it. The property was alongside the links of the Colonial Country Club. The posh golf establishment had been the initiative of Marvin Leonard, a wealthy Fort Worth merchant. Leonard approached Stinky with the proposal that he sell a parcel of the acreage to Colonial for an additional nine holes. Stinky said no. Leonard persisted in his effort. In the end the two men had a bitter personal confrontation—and Stinky bellowed that he would *not* sell. Furthermore, he threatened to have written into his will a stipulation that Leonard would *never* get his hands on the land, even after Stinky was dead.

Stinky also purchased a large plot of lakefront ground at Eagle Mountain Lake, twenty miles northwest of Fort Worth and rapidly developing into a recreational area for the city's wealthy. Once again Stinky was riding about inspecting his domain when he surprised a group of young men enjoying themselves at a picnic. He charged them on his white horse, much in the manner of a rancher in days of yore scattering a band of marauding Indians. "Get out! Get out! This is private property!" After the boys explained they were friends of Ken and Cullen, Stinky reconsidered and grudgingly toned down his demands to: "Well, just hurry then."

Some years later, one of the young men who had been at the picnic asked Stinky if he would sell him a small plot of the lakeshore property. Stinky glared at him and barked, "I never sell anything."

Stinky was at least impartial: he intimidated his sons as well as their friends. He was a strict disciplinarian and insisted his boys learn to respect money and know the value of it—although in later years he no longer confiscated their pocket change if they could not accurately remember how many coins they had.

Those who knew or were even briefly associated with Ms. Davis recall her as an exceptionally pleasant woman. Alice collected snuff boxes, enjoyed the theater, and served on the board of the local opera group. She supported the Fort Worth Children's Museum. She spent much of her time in good works, often performing menial tasks such as sweeping out the office of a local charity which assisted families in temporary straits after a fire or a family tragedy. Everyone thought Alice was an exceedingly charitable and charming woman and marveled that she managed to survive a marriage to such a domineering tyrant. She was stoic when Stinky embarrassed her. Once the two of them were with a group of Fort Worth art patrons. Stinky described his own extensive collection of paintings and Alice's interest in it. It was suggested that Alice be nominated as a board member of the local art association. Stinky was suspicious. Perhaps he saw the proposal as a gambit to get at his own collection. He discouraged the proposal by saying, in

Alice's presence, "the old bitch will never get her hands on any of my paintings."

There was one family art project that Alice felt so strongly about that she was prepared to defy her husband. In 1964, Stinky purchased a lot in Greenwood Memorial Park as the site for a family tomb. He bought the largest lot ever acquired in the cemetery, paying $40,000 for the ground. The mausoleum of Carnelian Minnesota granite cost $45,000. There was to be a stained-glass window. Stinky selected a design which featured, among other details, an oil well. Alice protested. She wanted something of a religious nature.

Dominating Alice's life as he did that of their sons, Stinky insisted on approving any item of clothing Alice purchased. In Fort Worth she usually shopped at Wally Williams, a women's specialty store. She would select a dress and have it fitted with pins in the tucks and hems. Then Alice would take the dress home, returning for the final alterations only after Stinky had approved her choice.

Stinky often told the story of a shopping expedition to the tony Neiman-Marcus store in Dallas. He escorted his wife into the emporium and directed her to select any frocks, shoes, or accessories she wanted. As she did, he inspected each item. Some he would toss back. If he approved of the selection, he would throw it on a growing pile of apparel on the counter. He shouted instructions at the salesclerk in such an imperious voice that a crowd gathered. Finally Stinky asked the clerk to estimate the cost of the entire pile. The clerk's reckoning came to about $4000. Too much, Stinky declared. "I'll tell you what," Stinky bellowed, "I'll give you $3000 for the whole pile—cold cash. Take it or leave it!" According to Stinky's version, this offer was discussed with the management and accepted. Neiman-Marcus regulars to whom Stinky boasted of the episode were skeptical. But then, with Stinky, you never could be sure....

Alice Davis, in addition to being pleasant, must have been extraordinarily patient. She endured Stinky's temper tantrums and moods, and survived countless embarrassing incidents when he was drinking. Stinky consumed prodigious amounts of bourbon. It was difficult to believe that such a small man could surround so much whiskey and, usually, hold it so well.

Stinky was five feet five inches tall. He compensated for his pint-sized physique by keeping his body in excellent condition and taking some form of exercise daily, maintaining his weight at 145 pounds. He was usually tanned from shirtless rides on his white horse. He was a feisty, pugnacious little man; no one called him Shorty. He often sought and achieved—if he and the town talk were to be believed—extramarital sexual fulfillment. ''He is a randy banty'' was one description to which he did not seem to object.* Neither was he displeased, at that time, when addressed as Stinky.

During his prime, Stinky's sexual prowess and maneuvers became legendary. Stinky gave and received at the office. At a time when most in-house business publications were dull, not the Mid-Continent employees' magazine—which Stinky insisted be spiced up with double entendres and Petty-girl drawings. Copies were passed hand to hand by Fort Worthians with no interest whatsoever in oil field equipment. When an attractive woman sought employment at Mid-Continent, it was understood she might expect an advance from the boss during her first days on her job. If a husband worked there, he had to be prepared to witness mutely Stinky patting his wife on the fanny from time to time.

Fort Worth chuckled when a man with an uncommonly attractive blonde wife began to do very well at Mid-Continent, despite the fact that he had little aptitude and less qualification for the work. For a period the fellow received regular promotions. Then Stinky and the blonde had a parting of the ways. The husband was fired forthwith.

Another story was told of one of Stinky's employees, the husband of a blonde wife with whom Stinky had a relationship known and tolerated by the husband. Once the man was trying

*Banty, in the Southwest, is a variation of bantam.

to sell his house and was asked many legal questions he couldn't answer. He finally hung his head and admitted that the house *really* belonged to Stinky.

Stinky was aggressive in his amorous pursuits, but not always successful. On one occasion, it was said, he suddenly grasped a shapely secretary in his office, lifted her from her feet, and, in an obviously lascivious gesture, pulled her body against his. She cooled Stinky's ardor, however, by reaching into her desk, grabbing a letter opener, and jabbing Stinky in the ass until he released her.

Another such story concerns a tall, attractive blonde woman with whom Stinky was in daily contact, but not the kind he wished. At six feet she towered over him but, nonetheless, Stinky decided he just had to climb that mountain of pulchritude and so began his assault. Each morning he brought a single red rose to the office and deposited it in a vase on the woman's desk. He continued the stratagem over a period of weeks, each morning delivering a dew-fresh rose. Finally the time came when he realized that this campaign was not going to succeed. On the final morning he arrived with a plastic rose, jammed it into the vase, and tacitly conceded defeat with, "That'll just have to do from now on."

The ultimate put-down came when Stinky, in his cups, made a demarche to a charming lady high in Fort Worth society. He asked this married woman to go on a date with him, and she refused. Stinky persisted.

"Don't you know I have a nickname? People call me Sexy Davis."

"Oh," came the retort, "I always thought they called you Stinky."

It was about this time that Stinky let it be known that he no longer wished to be identified by his nickname.

In 1943, Stinky purchased the Landreth place on Rivercrest Road. It had been a long trek from the oil fields of Arkansas and the early days as a store manager at Mid-Continent. Between drinking bouts and sex excursions he had managed to expand and consolidate his empire. Further, it was said that after his initial foray into the oil prospecting business Stinky's wells alone produced 12,000 barrels a day.

The English manor house on Rivercrest was evidence that Stinky had accumulated a fortune and achieved social status, in that order. There were constant demands for charitable contributions. Stinky was reluctant; he was saving the money for his boys. His neighbors, Amon Carter and a regional Coca-Cola distributor, were more successful than most in persuading Stinky to fork over for good causes. A floor at All Saints' Hospital was partially financed by Davis largesse. But Carter—known as "Mr. Fort Worth"—persisted in his efforts as a fund raiser, chastising Stinky for shirking his civic responsibilities. Stinky had the duty, Carter insisted, of taking care of Fort Worth.

"Amon, Fort Worth is yours," Stinky said. "I'll take care of the rest of the world."

Stinky had indeed conquered that portion of the world which was engaged in the extraction and distribution of petroleum. KenDavis Industries International, Inc., had become a giant conglomerate. Its promotional brochure listed more than eighty corporations, companies, and subsidiaries around the globe. In Canada, Britain, and the European countries. Turkey, Morocco, Malaysia, Venezuela, and Bolivia. There were exotic titles indicating the extent of Stinky's foreign endeavors: Artic Terex, Ltd., Midco Caribe Company, Nigeria Drilling Company, Ltd., and Loftland Brothers North Sea. Stinky and his sons had learned only limited Spanish, but their resident managers had to do business in two dozen languages.

Despite the exigencies of becoming rich and powerful, Stinky found time for occasional relaxation. At times he napped briefly in a hammock at the Eagle Mountain Lake home. Shirtless, to absorb maximum sun, he took his powerboat out on the lake. He was adept with a billiard cue. He played horseshoes and once won the tournament of a Fort Worth business executives' club. He explained his victory: He tossed the first horseshoe with his eyes closed and had the good fortune to score a ringer. "That," Stinky explained, "usually has the desired effect on your opponent." A man who knew Stinky well described the claim as horse manure. "Stinky never closed his eyes," he said, "except to sleep, and that was usually with one eye open for a good deal."

Most of his waking hours Stinky devoted to keeping both eyes open to watch the business and to prepare his boys to take it over. He did not appreciate interference, even from well-meaning business associates. One of his executives once gave young William the money he needed to pay for repairs after his car had been wrecked. Stinky found out about it and complained. "I don't like it. I'm raising those boys the way I want to, and I want them to respect money."

According to the Davis family physician, Stinky rarely saw his boys at home, but the office was another matter. "The three sons were three very busy young men," the doctor said, and Stinky "saw the three sons when he would go to the office." While Stinky groomed the boys for their future he insisted they observe firsthand how business was conducted. Often he completed a business transaction only after summoning the three sons into his office to witness the final negotiations. During these training sessions Cullen, Ken, Jr., and William learned of Stinky's pride. He once contemplated a business arrangement with a Texas steel tycoon who matched him in the pride department. The two men never got around to actually discussing the matter as neither of them was willing to wait for the other to come on the telephone line. "Please put Mr. Davis on," one secretary would say, but Stinky's secretary knew better than to do that. The game of one-upmanship continued indirectly through the two secretaries until the prospect of collaboration expired.

The boys learned that their father did not tolerate anything

53

less than an hermetically sealed contract. Once, during a conference scheduled to culminate a long period of negotiation on a service contract, Stinky flipped through several pages of fine type until he spotted an inconsistency. "What's this?" Stinky demanded. The businessman who had prepared the proposal studied the item and then admitted that it was an error. A mistake had been made. "I don't have time to fool around with mistakes," Stinky said, tossing the papers and the contract away.

Stinky's aggressive and unorthodox business habits frequently provoked those he dealt with to sue or threaten to sue. "Line up," Stinky would say, "with the other claimants."

Although Stinky liked to keep the business a family one, he did allow outside participation to a limited degree. A very limited degree. In one magnanimous gesture Stinky decreed that Mid-Continent employees could buy stock in the company—up to a total of 0.5 percent. In 1948, Stinky established Stratoflex, a venture which diversified his empire beyond oil-related equipment and production. Stratoflex was geared to and grew with the space age, and few aircraft or space vehicles could lift off the ground anywhere without at least a few fuel lines and tube fittings from Stratoflex companies. The business world was surprised when Stinky announced that a small part of the shares of the company would be sold to the public. One analyst was quoted as viewing the development as suspicious: "The old man wanted to take the stock public to see if he could sell it for more than it was worth." As late as 1978—ten years after Stinky's demise—the *Star-Telegram* said, "It is not even clear why Stratoflex was ever public." And *Texas Business* reported, "Nobody seems to know why Stratoflex went public to a small degree." The true explanation of why Stratoflex sold some stock is a valid commercial one: United States government contracts are more likely to be awarded to a company with some public ownership than to one which is privately owned.

Stinky suffered a stroke in 1966 at the age of seventy-one; he was to be a semi-invalid for two years. He had four heart attacks and his right leg became partially lame. His physician later described him as a tough little man with a "neck beaten about from oil field incidents and falls from horses....He had pains. He had a good deal of pain in his neck, and he had pains in both shoulders. But he never took an aspirin or anything." He was dismayed that his once-stylish handwriting had become shaky and illegible; he tried to regain his aptitude by writing out the alphabet over and over again in a notebook.* His pride was such that he would not enter his office. He was driven there to read his mail and go over business papers in his limousine while his secretary took notes.

In February 1967, Alice Davis died of an apparent heart attack at the age of sixty-six. In the extensive archives of the *Star-Telegram* her obituary is the only clipping which records for posterity that Alice existed. It reports that she was the wife of Kenneth W. Davis, Sr., was a native of Fort Worth, and supported the opera association and the Children's Museum. The remainder of the death notice is about Stinky.

Stinky must have approached the end of his own life with a certain satisfaction. The boys were ready to take over the business, having learned to be managers in a variety of executive positions. His private physician said Stinky "expected his sons to carry on his enterprise. He had determined, from the time those boys were quite small, how he was going to raise them."

Stinky, age seventy-three, died fifteen minutes after a heart attack at 3:55 P.M. on August 29, 1968. The funeral service, two days later, at the First Presbyterian Church was followed by burial in Greenwood Memorial Park. Stinky was interred in the burnt-orange granite mausoleum where Alice already rested. The tomb of Marvin Leonard was on the adjoining lot. (Leonard was the man with whom Stinky had such an

---

* His handwriting was never the same after the stroke. The signature on his will, signed in 1954, is virile and flowing. On a codicil, signed in 1967, it is childlike and palsied.

acrimonious dispute over the Mockingbird Lane property which Leonard had hoped to acquire to expand the Colonial Country Club golf course.) Also nearby, amid the tombstones and sarcophagi of less affluent citizens, was the mausoleum of the wealthy and prominent Tandy family. Just around the corner of the cemetery lane was Amon Carter's mausoleum.

The grandest mausoleum in Greenwood is easily identified: "The Family of Kenneth W. Davis." There are two inscriptions carved in the granite. The first reads: "Man's Greatest Happiness Comes From The Joy He Gives To Others." The second is: "That Which We Create From God's Bounty Will Be Our Living Legacy."

The epitaphs are a wonderment to those who knew the stingy Stinky, the patriarch-tyrant, the businessman with a legendary mean streak. Did Alice choose the two inscriptions?

Alice won at least one argument with her husband. There are no oil wells in the stained-glass window in Stinky's mausoleum. The window depicts the Good Samaritan.

After Cullen and Priscilla were married in a Methodist church the night of the afternoon Stinky died, the couple had a brief honeymoon. Then Cullen was ready to assume his role. He was anxious to go to work and see that the family enterprise prospered.

"He was intense about it," a Mid-Continent executive said of Cullen, "with a spring wound up inside. I figure his Dad wound it up."

In his passage from youth to social and business recognition as an inheritor of a vast fortune, Cullen left few discernible footsteps. He delivered the old *Fort Worth Herald* (which was later absorbed by the *Star-Telegram)* in the neighborhood when he was a boy. His high school years were uneventful; in the Arlington Heights High School yearbook for Cullen's senior year his class photograph appears, but otherwise he is not mentioned as participating in school activities. He was careful but not stingy in making small loans to school pals. When attending Texas A & M he extracted a fee from classmates he drove to and from the college. He graduated with an engineering degree and served a stint in the navy.

Cullen grew into a slender, small man with a sweet countenance that women remembered. Unlike many wealthy Texans, he had no interest in politics. He moved in and out of society circles quietly, and the leisure time he spent in pool halls and clapboard dives spawned few anecdotes. The upper-crust crowd in Rivercrest was hardly aware Cullen existed until he gained notoriety by escorting Priscilla to annual galas.

One acquaintance remembered Cullen as being as "interesting as a paperweight." In a city where informality is tolerated and even encouraged, Cullen often wore dark suits, and a shirt and tie. His suits were sometimes so dark it was difficult to say whether they were navy blue or black. In 1972 one man voted Cullen the best-dressed man of 1962.

Despite the fact that his houses on Rivercrest Road and later on Mockingbird Lane both bordered on golf courses, Cullen was not seen on the links. He played some tennis. He was, unquestionably, a proficient skier—according to semiprofessionals who went to Colorado with him—and, with all those pool tables at his disposal, became a good pool player. A plaque in the Petroleum Club commemorates Cullen's victories as the club's snooker champion in 1971 and 1973 (snooker is played on a table with small pockets and requires the finesse of billiards). He liked to play chess. But most of his energy and time was devoted to business. The financial record proved Cullen talented in that area.

People recalled Cullen's first marriage, which had ended several years earlier. He and Sandra Masters had lived in a home in Edgecliff. Sandra was small, well-proportioned, and somewhat like Priscilla, except that her hair was jet black. Occasionally her dress was interestingly see-through. She bore two sons. The Edgecliff house had a pool table in the basement. In the divorce settlement Sandra received the house, its furnishings, an automobile, and an undetermined financial settlement. The rumors around town were that she elected to leave Cullen because he had physically mistreated her when drinking and she couldn't take any more. One version of the breakup is that Sandra was so fed up that she secretly took karate lessons and, when next Cullen abused her, chopped him to the floor before walking out of the marriage.

Then, after they met on a tennis court, Cullen married Priscilla.

As Ms. Davis, Priscilla became a member of Fort Worth society. Not a *part* of it, since she was not welcomed in that hermetic society because of her dubious background and pyrotechnic life-style. But when she married Cullen she became a member of the clubs where the quality folks congregated, and nobody could bar her from entering the golden portals of the Rivercrest Club, up the winding street from the Davis residence, and the Colonial Country Club, site of a prestigious, nationally televised, annual golf tournament. The Shady Oaks Country Club was out on the edge of town, while the Ridgelea Country Club had been developed on a vast tract of land alongside the Lake Como area, a black residential quarter where Fort Worth's wealthy families obtained maids and waiters. She also frequented the Petroleum Club, where businessmen and their wives lunched, and the Boat Club on Eagle Mountain Lake. And, as Cullen's wife, she attended the yearly party of the Steeplechase Club, which presented a bevy of debutantes each year.

Some say this was when Priscilla made her own debut into her Harlow era. She emulated the screen vamp by going into a white-on-white period. There was a white Lincoln Continental Mark IV and a white motorcycle which Priscilla gunned up and down Rivercrest, wearing a white jumper and white boots, her white-blonde hair blown back in the wind. And she wore a white mink coat and white boots. One society woman—an exception in that she liked Priscilla—commented that it was "really sort of pitiful."

Cullen and Priscilla, as dues-paying members, attended the pretentious extravaganzas sponsored by the various clubs, and they were always ready to buy expensive tickets to charity balls. There was a hush at Priscilla's entrances when she wore one of her shockingly brief outfits, often one which provoked soft whistles of admiration from the men and purse-lipped indignation from the women. Priscilla didn't wear clothes, she wore costumes, usually scanty. "I wouldn't be surprised to see her next time," one observer commented, "in the guise of a sugar cookie, wearing nothing but a raisin in her navel." Another woman said, "Fort Worth has its own Carol Doda now," comparing Priscilla with a San Francisco entertainer renowned at the time for the immensity of her siliconed breasts.

The busty, bouncy Priscilla and her husband Cullen were seldom invited into the homes of the rich or socially prestigious* for private parties or intimate dinners. More often they were seen in public places, perhaps after dinner at the convivial Carriage House or the Merrimac Restaurant down by the Trinity River, and later, at less desirable establishments. Sometimes they frequented dives where the walls were flyspecked and the urinals stank. In these proletarian bistros they would cavort with Priscilla's friends from her less affluent days before she married Cullen. Some were friends of Cullen—shiftless men who drifted from one job to another when they worked, which was seldom, or spent their days shooting pool and drinking Lone Star beer or Coke and bourbon when they were unemployed, which was often.

One of the drifters they met by chance was Charles David McCrory, whom Cullen challenged to a pool game one evening at a scabrous dive on Camp Bowie Boulevard called the Pink

---

* The two categories, despite considerable overlap, are not necessarily synonymous in Fort Worth.

Elephant. McCrory, age thirty-eight, had come to Fort Worth from Cisco, Texas, after dropping out of the tenth grade. A sometime carpenter and construction worker, he had failed consistently at each job or business endeavor he ever attempted. The one he had enjoyed the most was operating a karate studio under a franchise granted him by the owner of several such establishments, Pat Burleson (a distant relative of Phil Burleson, the Dallas attorney who worked for Cullen). After a while that endeavor failed too, and McCrory was unemployed when he met Cullen. Cullen liked McCrory. He was a good storyteller, even if it was said that most of his yarns were fabrications. Priscilla and McCrory's wife Judy became friends and the two women would sip beer or wine at the bar and feed coins into the jukebox while Cullen and Charles David shot a few games of rotation or eight ball.

While the Pink Elephant stayed open as late as almost any place in Fort Worth, it did eventually close and was not open at all on Sundays. Cullen was irritated one evening when he was told there was time for only one more rack. So McCrory purchased the Pink Elephant—with Cullen's money, it was said—so that they could shoot pool whenever they pleased.

Although Cullen and Priscilla spent much of their time in social seclusion sedately watching television or going to the movies, there were two public incidents that generated some waves and attendant notoriety. The first gave Fort Worthians valid reason to comment that Cullen had inherited Stinky's volatile temper.

In 1973 there was a downpour during the Steeplechase Club debutante ball at the Shady Oaks Country Club. When the orchestra played its final refrain Cullen and Priscilla joined a group crowding the front entrance of the club. Priscilla, outfitted in an audacious garment that framed more than it cloaked, chatted amiably with the men in formal dress and the women in long dresses. She had enjoyed a gala evening.

But Cullen's mood was not good. He had been waiting impatiently for the parking lot attendant who would fetch Priscilla's white Continental Mark IV. The parking lot crew had to slosh through water to find automobiles, and, when they located them, drive to where the owners waited. Cullen decided he would wait no longer. He persuaded an acquaintance who had already retrieved his own car to drive him to the Continental. Once there, Cullen realized he had no keys: they were still hanging on the club's wooden rack where they had been placed earlier. Cullen slushed back to the club. He could not find his keys on the board. Exasperated, Cullen wrenched the board from where it was fixed and threw it down into the quagmire. Cullen's customary sweet countenance was distorted with fury as he hissed to those who had observed him: "If I can't find *my* keys, nobody else will find theirs either!"

Priscilla began to assist others searching in the mud for their own keys. Cullen cursed and instructed his wife coldly to "get in this car this minute," and they drove off in the automobile of another couple, leaving the Continental in the parking lot for the night. Others, whose keys had been trampled in the muck, resorted to the same expedient or called a taxi.

The other much-commented-upon episode occurred two years later at a Ridgelea Country Club golf tournament. There were free movies in the parking lot. Cullen parked a large van among the automobiles there and invited acquaintances inside to view some pornographic films. A dozen men and women who had abandoned the links could squeeze into the improvised theater. There was a program of steamy selections, but the favorite was *Deep Throat*, which had not been screened in Fort Worth's X-rated movie houses yet. This incident revived stories about Stinky Davis's sexual promiscuity and his porn collection, and invited comparison between Stinky and Cullen in that department.

During the six years of their high-flying marriage, Cullen and Priscilla were often in the air. They flew to Aspen or Acapulco with Charles David and Judy McCrory in their Lear jet. Or, to New York where Priscilla would raid the exclusive stores for new outfits and expensive gimcracks for the mansion on Mockingbird Lane. "I had numerous charge accounts," Priscilla said, "all over the world."

On one occasion in 1972, Cullen and Priscilla winged to New York on an art expedition to buy paintings for the walls of their massive new mansion, which was in the final stages of completion. They hired an art expert from Fort Worth to go with them. During the flight in Cullen's Lear jet one passenger said that she had heard that Washington, D.C., was a lovely city, but that she had never seen it. Let's see it now, Cullen suggested, and he instructed the pilot to change course in order to fly over the national capital. Once there Cullen told the pilot to dive low so they could have a good look. They flew directly over the White House in violation of stringent FAA regulations and then resumed their journey to New York. At LaGuardia's terminal for private aircraft, spectators in the lobby were astonished at the spectacle of Priscilla striding through the gate to a waiting limousine. In honor of TCU, she was wearing the school colors: white boots, purple hot-pants, a white ermine shoulder wrap—and purple sunglasses.

Priscilla changed to an only slightly more conservative oufit before she and Cullen entered an art gallery on Fifth Avenue in Manhattan. Cullen selected the pieces to decorate the mansion back on Mockingbird Lane. In that particular gallery Cullen purchased almost $40,000 worth of lithographs, paintings, and bronzes. There were additional purchases in other galleries, of course. After all, it was a big house.

Indeed, the mansion was so inhospitable and cavernous that once they moved into it, Priscilla usually confined herself to her three favorite rooms: the kitchen, her bedroom suite, and her bathroom. She decorated these rooms in bright colors to match the vivid Mexican blouses she often wore. The main feature of the master suite was a tremendous fur-covered bed. Stuffed animals and potted plants were sprinkled everywhere, as were a profusion of recording and projection machines. The bathroom was hot pink with a sauna-type tub bordered by green plants.

While she bathed, Priscilla listened to country-western music—Willie Nelson and Jimmy Gatling records and tapes—and sipped orange or cherry Kool-Aid from a crystal goblet. In the mansion's stables she doted on a white mare named Freedom. She also pampered a dozen pets at a time, two or three properly named dogs, and any stray hound or cat that wandered onto the property.

Cullen and Priscilla continued to make grand entrances at gala benefits and the annual parties at the clubs. Cullen would wear a conservative suit, as always, or a modern tuxedo for formal affairs, and she, another of her sexy costumes. Priscilla drank very little, usually lingering over a glass of wine or a beer. She smoked one cigarette after another, always Eve, the pack with the pretty colors. "Cullen and his Barbie Doll," some began to call the couple.

"I can't understand it," one woman observed to another during a fund-raising ball when Cullen sat quietly with narrowed eyes as a group of men flirted with Priscilla and gawked at her exposed cleavage. "It must be humiliating for Cullen, all those men drooling over her."

"I don't think so," another answered. "I think Cullen enjoys it."

Whether it was because of the stags' lust for Priscilla or for other reasons, the marriage began to deteriorate. There were public squabbles when Cullen would turn on Priscilla and bark at her to *shut up*, she didn't know what she was talking about. And there were rumors, especially when Cullen or Priscilla would be seen with blackened eyes, that the husband and wife had violent physical brawls. One story had it that the pilots of the private jet made an unscheduled landing returning from a Colorado ski trip because Cullen and Priscilla were assaulting each other in the plane's cabin. And there were more rumors that Cullen was spending much of his time away from the mansion, seeking other female companionship. But no one really identified the catalyst, if there was one, in the breakup of the marriage. Priscilla later told a friend that she realized she was in trouble with Cullen for the first time when they were talking about the rift between him and his brother William, and Priscilla suggested that maybe Cullen and Ken were being unfair to William. Cullen's reply, according to the secondhand version, was "business is business."

In July of 1974, Cullen and Priscilla were legally separated. Priscilla used her Master Charge card to cash a check for $1500, and hired a divorce lawyer.

Cullen resided for a while in temporary quarters at the Ramada Inn* and then moved into Karen Master's home. He was seen driving around town and at the Petroleum Club at lunchtime. He and Karen visited the Boat Club at Eagle Mountain Lake. He shot some pool, went regularly to Dallas Cowboy football games, and, apparently, enjoyed a placid existence, at least until vexing developments in the divorce proceedings with Priscilla began to plague him. One alleviating factor in the divorce, Cullen told acquaintances, was that he had had the foresight to have Priscilla sign a prenuptial agreement limiting the money she might obtain from his business interests.

Priscilla was seen around town, too, but her life was not as sedate as Cullen's. After encountering friends at her favorite hangouts she would invite them to the mansion to watch television on the big screen and to have something to eat, often burgers or barbecue. Sometimes her guests were from the north side of town, and they wore black leather jackets and had tattoos on their biceps. Some were sufficiently involved in the Fort

---

* The Ramada Inn in Fort Worth is the only motel in Texas with a small cemetery, containing about a dozen graves, in the middle of its parking lot. Another Fort Worth motel provides guests with stalls for their horses.

64

Worth drug scene that narcotics agents began to investigate Priscilla's guests. There were persistent rumors of wild parties at he mansion. It was whispered for a while that a man named W. T. Rufner, with a shady past, had become Priscilla's lover. Then Stan Farr apparently replaced him, and Priscilla and the basketball player were seen together constantly. They shared the master bedroom at the mansion and everyone knew about that. Cullen knew about it, too.

The divorce proceedings were complicated by Cullen's enormous wealth and the premarital agreement, but otherwise the issues were simple. There was no haranguing to be expected about children, as Cullen and Priscilla had none between them. Both parties wanted the divorce, and there were no religious taboos to complicate matters. Priscilla asked at first for the mansion and its furnishings, the Continental Mark IV, and money. Cullen wanted the mansion, too, and knew there would be alimony. It was a question of how much.

District Judge Joe Eidson presided over the prolonged bickering. He was forced on many occasions to make rulings which would, by their nature, have to favor either Cullen or Priscilla. On both sides the lawyers had lengthy—and extremely lucrative—briefs to prepare.

Joe Eidson decided early on to set the temporary support payments to Priscilla at $3500 a month. In the beginning this mollified Priscilla, but her demands skyrocketed when an estimate of the worth of the KenDavis industrial empire revealed that it had more than tripled in value since Priscilla and Cullen had wed in 1968.

At the end of August 1976, Cullen and Priscilla learned of Eidson's decision that the monthly payments were to be increased to $5000. It was a victory for Priscilla and she was in good spirits when she and Stan Farr went to the Swiss House for dinner and then to the Rangoon Racquet Club for a glass of wine before returning to the mansion after midnight to find *the* man dressed in black and wearing a wig.

That decision, of course, was a setback for Cullen. In addition to the increased payments, Judge Eidson had postponed, yet another time, the divorce trial which had already been pending for almost two years. Priscilla's lawyers had requested the extension. She was having problems with her breasts following plastic surgery for silicone implants.

During the last part of 1976 and the first half of 1977, Cullen was involved in a judicial three-ring circus. The trial in which Cullen would be judged for murder had been set for October 11 by Judge Cave, but was not to take place for some months. Cullen's team of lawyers moved to have their client released on bond and his trial conducted under conditions favorable to their client.

Cullen celebrated his forty-third birthday on September 22 in the Tarrant County jail. A week later an appeals hearing on Judge Cave's denial of bond began in Austin, the state capital. Judge Cave postponed the October trial until late February of 1977. There was a motion for a change of venue, based on the argument by Cullen's lawyers that there had been too much publicity in Fort Worth to permit Cullen to have a fair trial. In the meantime, Judge Eidson set the final hearing on the divorce case for January 17. In November there were hearings in Judge Cave's court on more than a hundred defense motions plus a writ of habeas corpus for Cullen.

During December additional motions were filed in federal court by the defense lawyers, and pretrial hearings were conducted. There was bickering about the validity of the premarital agreement in which Priscilla, according to Cullen's lawyers, signed away her rights to much of Cullen's wealth. Priscilla insisted the document was a fraud.

On the last day of 1976 a multimillion-dollar settlement was reached in the case between Cullen and his brother William. One hundred million was the sum bruited as the settlement figure.

The defense attorneys accelerated their efforts to obtain bond so that Cullen could be a free man while awaiting and enduring the February trial. With the assistance of Sam Dash, the former Watergate prosecutor, they went as far as they could: U.S. Supreme Court Justice Lewis Powell refused to hear the case in Washington, as did Justice Thurgood Marshall two days later.

On February 15, 1977 the grand jury in Fort Worth returned capital murder and attempted murder indictments against Cullen. That would guarantee a good show. Cullen was undoubtedly the richest man in America ever to be indicted on murder charges. Would he be the richest man ever to die by lethal injection at the state prison in Huntsville?

The trial began in Fort Worth on February 22 and continued for nineteen days and then came to an abrupt halt.

Judge Cave ruled a mistrial. He had learned that a woman juror, allowed to visit a dying father in Chicago, reportedly was making telephone calls back to Fort Worth to assure her friends that Cullen was guilty, and, that she could not understand why so much money was being spent on the lengthy trial when it would be easy to simply turn Davis over to the sequestered jurors and "let us hang him."

Despite her denial of the accusation, the judge himself now filed a motion for a change of venue, and, in early May, selected Amarillo as the site of the new trial. It was to commence in June 1977.

For most people who knew him, it was preposterous to believe that Cullen could be responsible for the murders at the mansion: *I just can't believe Cullen would do such a thing! Where would he ever get the idea?*

During those days when everyone was debating Cullen's guilt or innocence, there were some who recalled a party on June 11, just ten weeks before the murders on Mockingbird Lane. Members of the Arlington Heights High School class of '51 had gathered for a reunion. It was great to see old friends and to hear a speech by one of their very own who had made it in the world.

Thomas Thompson had been the editor of the *Yellow Jacket*,

the school newspaper. He'd wanted to be a writer since the time as a youngster he was given a toy printing press for Christmas. Later, he had worked for the *Houston Post*, and, eventually, he went to New York where he worked for *Life* magazine for a dozen years. Then he decided to write his first book, the story of two cardiovascular surgeons, Michael DeBakey and Denton Cooley. Then, Thompson found himself out of a job when *Life* folded, so he started a second book, based on a Houston murder story which had come to his attention while doing the research on *Hearts*.

Everyone at the reunion was pleased that Tommy had flown in from Houston for the evening. Why, the only other really famous person to come out of their class was a girl who had become a notorious high-class hooker (and she passed around cards during the reunion). But Tommy had written a *book* and was about to publish another. It was the story of a Houston woman who had died under mysterious circumstances. Her husband had been indicted for the murder, and there had been a trial. The defendant got off when his lawyer reportedly was clever enough to engineer a mistrial. Fortunately for him, he had the money it took to hire that master of the courtroom, Houston attorney Richard Haynes.

Thompson said his new book, entitled *Blood and Money*, would be out shortly.

Everyone was fascinated. One of those who gathered around Tommy Thompson was Thomas Cullen Davis, class of '51.

Fort Worth's citizenry was momentarily dejected when they learned their big show was going on the road. But never mind. There was a great cast: the wealthy Cullen and Priscilla, known as the X-rated Sandra Dee. And *now* you could be sure the facts would come out about what Priscilla had been up to at the mansion after she and Cullen had separated. Cullen's lawyer would see to *that*.

Cullen had hired a new chief honcho for his legal team. Richard "Racehorse" Haynes, often known simply as Race.

Why, he was the courtroom genius who was giving Percy Foreman, Edward Bennett Williams, and F. Lee Bailey such a run for their money. He was almost as famous as they were, at least in Texas. Everyone had heard the story about that case when Haynes drove a spike through his hand in the courtroom. That was to prove his motorcycle gang clients didn't really hurt that girl very much when they crucified her, nailed her to a tree.

In June 1977, Glen Guzzo learned he would be covering the trial in Amarillo for the *Star-Telegram*. Glen was a young reporter who edited a small paper in Detroit for the syndicate which had just recently purchased the *Star-Telegram*; they had sent him to Fort Worth when they bought the paper from Amon Carter's family. Glen heard estimates that the Amarillo trial might last longer than most usually brief Texas murder trials. Perhaps two months. Glen decided to plan on being in Amarillo as long as three months.

Glen had no way of knowing that his beat was to be the longest, most expensive murder trial in the history of Texas.

·5·

THE OLD JUDGE

The journalist visited Fort Worth again in mid-June 1977. He telephoned Judge Willard and, declining an invitation to accompany the old man on his early morning hike around the golf course, went to his home the following afternoon. The two men talked for some time until the Judge, observing through the picture window that the sun was dipping toward the horizon, announced that it was time for a drink. The journalist was taken aback when he saw the size of the Judge's mug; his own was a normal-sized highball glass. The journalist finished the last of his bourbon long before the Judge significantly reduced the level of his excessively large potion of Jack Daniels and water.

"Have another drink, son," the Judge invited. "I'll just make do with this one."

The journalist asked the Judge for his opinion of Judge Cave's decision to declare a mistrial in Fort Worth and to designate Amarillo as the site for a new trial.

The Judge said he certainly agreed with Cave on the change in venue because of the publicity about Cullen's predicament which would make a fair trial in Fort Worth unlikely. And there was no question in the Judge's mind that Cave had ruled correctly in declaring a mistrial after a woman juror had so blatantly flouted the rules of juror conduct when visiting Chicago. Texas is the only state in the country, the Judge said, which does not have an alternate-juror provision in criminal cases; only when a juror must be dismissed because of an unexpected physical disability may the remaining eleven jurors reach a decision. That law needs changing, the Judge insisted.

The journalist asked the Judge for his evaluation of District Attorney Tim Curry's decision to prosecute Cullen only on the murder indictment for killing Andrea, when no eyewitnesses could testify to that tragic event? Why not the charges which alleged that Cullen had murdered Stan Farr, or that he had wounded Priscilla and Gus Gavrel?

The Judge speculated that Curry believed the jurors would be shocked at the thought that anyone could slay a twelve-year-old girl and would be anxious to condemn the perpetrator. But the more important rationale, the Judge was convinced, was that Curry was aware of the propensity of Texas juries—especially in a Bible-toting community like Amarillo—to sympathize with a man who shoots an unfaithful wife or her lover. In the old days the doctrine of "hot pursuit" prevailed in such cases. And sometimes juries exonerated irate husbands who murdered their wives or those who had defiled them long after the trail was cool. In Cullen's case the Amarillo jury would probably suggest a probated sentence if they found him guilty of attacking Priscilla and killing Stan Farr, or pin a medal on Cullen by declaring him innocent. A wily defense attorney like Richard Haynes would be able to evoke in the jury a sneaking nostalgia for the old days in the Southwest when a man was expected to philander, but a wife did so at her own risk.

"Who is Richard Haynes?" the journalist asked.

"Before arriving at that identification," the Judge said, "you have to ask 'Who is Percy Foreman?' Because Haynes grew up in Foreman's shadow down in Houston and has been sprinting for the past twenty years to overtake Foreman as the most famous trial lawyer in Texas." The Judge reflected. "I'm not sure all lawyers would characterize that ambition as lofty. But Foreman *is* a very successful lawyer."

"Was Foreman the man who defended James Earl Ray?"

"Yes, in the matter of the slaying of Dr. Martin Luther King.

Foreman's been practicing for fifty years. Do you recall the Candace Mossler case in '66? She was a Houston socialite of flamboyant aspect, much like Priscilla Davis. Her nephew and lover was accused of killing her multimillionaire husband by stabbing him to death. But Foreman managed to convince the jury that the dead man, despite the thirty-seven knife wounds in his body, was the real villain and the nephew went free. Richard Haynes has adopted and refined Foreman's technique of discrediting any opposition witness, dead or alive, to such an extent that juries forget who is really in the dock.''

"Is Haynes a really great lawyer?''

The Judge thought for a moment, then replied, "He wins cases.''

Richard Haynes's first case as a young lawyer was defending a man charged with the illegal sale of liquor. Haynes became an authority on the subject of intoxication, and subsequently successfully defended more than 150 drunk-driving cases. His fame spread as he became known as a trial lawyer who could stupefy and confound juries with dramatic courtroom tactics. Once he was unable to subpoena a witness he felt vital to the defense, so he cross-examined an empty witness chair with such fervor that he won his case.

"But don't believe all you hear about Haynes,'' the Judge warned. "Everyone believes he once won a case by driving a spike through his hand in the courtroom. That is *horse* shit. Haynes himself has denied the story countless times. He did want to convince the jury that a girl whom a motorcycle gang had disciplined by nailing her to a tree was not really hurt all that bad. He came up with the idea of having a doctor inject a local anesthetic into his own hand so he could nail himself to the defense table during his closing argument. But he didn't really *do* that—didn't turn out to be necessary—although I don't doubt he *would* have, had it been vital. What really got that gang off was his closing argument to the jury. And he's a master at that.''

"Why is he known as Racehorse?"

"From his football days, they tell me. He had the habit of galloping back and forth across the gridiron but consistently failing to go forward. His coach asked what he thought he was, a racehorse?"

"What tactics will Racehorse Haynes use in Amarillo?" the journalist wanted to know.

The Judge predicted that Cullen's lawyer would begin by spending a great deal of Cullen's money on the jury selection. Then, if Cullen has a creditable explanation of where he was and what he was doing at the time of the murders on Mockingbird Lane, he will put Cullen on the stand. Failing that, he will attempt to locate an alibi witness, someone who will swear he or she was with Cullen at the time. And, the one thing you can be sure of, Haynes will do everything he can to portray Priscilla as the great whore of Babylon.

"It should make for interesting testimony," the journalist suggested.

The Judge agreed. "And that should be grist for that book you have in mind. Just what sort of story are you thinking of coming up with, young man?"

"A Texas Gothic, I suppose," the journalist said. "The story of what happens when someone has too much money and doesn't know how to handle it. A sort of Rivercrest tragedy."

"A tragedy?" The Judge sipped what was left of his drink. "I'm not so sure of that. You might consult your Aristotle. I believe it was in his *Poetics* that he said that to have tragedy you must begin with a cast of noble figures. I'm not sure that term aptly describes Cullen and his wife Priscilla."

The journalist explored his thesis further. He told the Judge that when walking with him around the golf course he had considered the enormous wealth represented by the families of inheritors who lived in Rivercrest. The question involved was interesting. Families like Cullen's had forged their great wealth in the fires of early frontiers. Was it possible that the energy and knack for survival necessary to withstand the raw wilderness became twisted into a criminal dilemma when second and third generations emulated their grandparents? When the first settlers in Texas carved out their positions of wealth and power it was sometimes necessary to be antisocial to protect land, cattle, a ranch house, or to guard a well in the days when certain people tried to steal oil when they couldn't find it themselves. Did the sons of those men find it difficult to conform to the regulations of a peaceful society when their boundaries were ennui and country clubs?

The Judge thought about the journalist's exposition. Then he said, "That sounds overwhelmingly *sociological* to me. Maybe, son, you'll find you're writing about a simple case of murder that's unusual and complicated because Cullen happens to be a very rich man. When all of this happened almost a year ago, I saw the development in relatively simple terms as far as the wealth and prestige of this part of town is concerned. It was shocking, but not catastrophic—sort of like we had found a very *large* turd floating in the Rivercrest swimming pool."

The Judge drained the last of his bourbon and smacked his lips delicately.

"Whatever the explanation may be," the Judge assured the journalist, "you can be sure that Cullen's trial in Amarillo will be a spectacle."

·6·

THE AMARILLO TRIAL

The pretrial hearings and jury selection began in Amarillo on June 27, 1977.

Richard "Racehorse" Haynes and his defense team, billeted in the Hilton Hotel, had been working for some time. Phil Burleson and Mike Gibson, the two Dallas lawyers who had originally defended Cullen, were to participate in the trial in those rare interludes—and they would prove to be extremely rare—when Haynes was not on his feet. Steve Sumner, a former semipro baseball player, commanded the defense's investigative task force. During the various civil suits and the aborted trial in Fort Worth, Sumner had employed five full-time private investigators and a half dozen part-time spies to infiltrate Fort Worth's underworld. Haynes had contracted, at one time or another, a number of legal experts.

Richard Haynes was born and spent his childhood in San Antonio, Texas, 200 miles west of Houston. His father was a construction worker and the family never had much money. Richard went to Houston to study law. Twice his schooling was interrupted for service in two branches of the military. He was decorated for saving two fellow marines at Iwo Jima, and jumped as an army paratrooper. He graduated from a little-known law school in Houston and went directly into private practice. He set about becoming as famous as Percy Foreman.

Haynes's reputation as a wily courtroom tactician with a flair for the dramatic spread. In Amarillo, Glen Guzzo of the *Star-Telegram* interviewed Haynes, and the public was intrigued to read of the attorney's flamboyant life-style. Haynes owned three silver automobiles: an Excalibur, a Dusenberg, and a new Porsche, all of which he drove above the speed limit. He flew his own Cessna and liked skydiving. He sailed on the Gulf of Mexico on his sloop. He owned eight racing motorcycles. Once he and a colleague were in a small Texas town with their motorcycles and created a problem for the management of the motel where they were staying. "One night we had a drop or two of Scotch and we did rev up the engines and smashed a hole in the wall. We bought the wall."

Haynes explained his penchant for speed and risk. "God's saving me to save someone else. Or else he would have killed me by now. He's had a lot of chances with me racing on motorcycles and jumping out of airplanes....You know, I'm a speed freak and when I die, it'll be at a high rate of speed, I hope." Haynes had already decided on his epitaph: "I can see it now," he said, "across the tip of my tombstone. 'His fees were outrageous, but he did a good job.'"

His legal fees *were* substantial and increased along with his fame. Haynes said that when asked by the Hearst family to defend Patricia in her bank robbery trial, he quoted a fee higher than that given to F. Lee Bailey, who was given $125,000 and book rights. Once a Houston law student asked Haynes if many clients had retained him a second time. "No," Haynes answered, "I usually take them for all they're worth the first time around."

When the Amarillo trial was underway Racehorse Haynes was known regionally, and was beginning to be recognized nationally. On a national television program he was asked if he considered himself the best criminal attorney in Texas. "It's my belief that I am," Haynes admitted. He paused. Then he commented, "I wonder why you restrict it to Texas?" The flip comment to tv journalist Dan Rather reverberated nationally. It followed Haynes's account of the 1971 case when he had successfully defended two Houston policemen accused of stomping a black prisoner to death. Haynes managed to have the trial heard in a nearby town known for its conservatism and then devoted his energy to selecting just the right jury. "I knew we had that case won when we seated the last bigot on the jury."*

The battery of expensive legal talent from Houston, Dallas, and Fort Worth was augmented in Amarillo by local expertise. Six weeks before the jury selection began, Haynes hired Dee Miller, a former Amarillo district attorney, as a consultant. Miller was never to miss a day of testimony during the lengthy trial. For this silent performance he was to receive the highest legal fee of his career.

Dee Miller's law partner was hired as the architect of the first phase of Haynes's defense strategy. Hugh Miller—no kin of Dee—was a prominent attorney who had been at one time a judge in Potter County. Almost 200 prospective jurors were screened before the final dozen were selected. In capital murder cases in Texas, potential jurors are scrutinized one by one, and the process is vital. Miller used Steve Sumner's investigators as well as local-hire footpads of his own acquaintance. Ray Hudson, Karen Master's father, joined the team; he had lived and worked in Amarillo and had many contacts in town. Karen herself arrived three and a half weeks before the trial to circulate among friends from her early school days there.

The first occupant of the jury box was selected within two days. It would be three weeks before the final juror was approved.

Amarillo, with a population of less than 300,000, was a small enough town to allow thorough investigation of each prospective

* Later Haynes said he was being facetious. During Cullen's Houston trial a journalist asked Haynes if the published anecdotes about him were essentially correct. He did not dispute the quotations but put them in perspective: "You must understand," Haynes said with a smile, "that some of those statements were made drink in hand, at poolside."

juror. Miller compiled histories. Neighbors, friends, former teachers, mailmen, and barbers, were asked to fill out questionnaires. Defense secretaries learned to operate a computer to store and retrieve biographical information. Photographs of their homes went into jury-prospect files. Hugh Miller's task was accomplished on August 17. The result, according to one observer, was that Haynes came up with "a near perfect, hand-picked jury" of nine men and three women.

Presiding over the trial was Judge George E. Dowlen, known by some in Amarillo as "the Cowboy Judge." Dowlen was Boston-educated and a forty-three-year-old bachelor with a reputation for having a lively sense of humor. When he first sat at the bench in the small, fifty-two-seat courtroom, Dowlen inserted a toothpick in his mouth. During the months of deliberation the judge seldom removed the toothpick and its replacements.

Ten days before the jury was selected, Haynes had filed a new request for bond before Judge Dowlen. It seemed a futile exercise as bond for Cullen had been denied several times previously, most recently by Judge Cave in Fort Worth. Tim Curry and his prosecution team—assistant district attorneys Joe Shannon, Tolly Wilson, and Marvin Collins—were dismayed when Judge Dowlen ordered Cullen released on a $1 million bond which Cullen paid with a certified check. The prosecutors read the action as an ominous signal of Dowlen's perception of the case. Cave and the other judges who had denied bond for Cullen had said, in effect, that they believed it possible, even probable, that a jury would find him guilty. Judge Dowlen's decision, the prosecutors believed, revealed that he was not so sure. But Judge Cave in Fort Worth remained the ultimate authority and Judge Dowlen's decision, while allowing Cullen temporary freedom, was subject to Cave's review.

The prosecutors were further dismayed when Judge Dowlen announced his intention to permit unlimited reexamination. This would allow Haynes time and latitude to range far afield in questioning witnesses. Tim Curry and his team sensed, accurately as it turned out, Dowlen would tolerate considerable scope in testimony about sex and drugs. Curry wanted to concentrate on the issue of the dead girl Andrea and the identity of the man in black who shot her. Haynes, from the beginning, wanted to overwhelm the jury with lurid word pictures of the Fort Worth drug culture and Priscilla's role in it. In short, Curry would be trying Cullen, and Racehorse, Priscilla.

The first prosecution witness was Judge Joe Eidson from Fort Worth. The Fort Worth prosecutors intended to convince the Amarillo jury that Cullen's primary motive for the shooting spree was his frustration after almost two years of divorce proceedings. The specific which triggered the murders, they would contend, was Joe Eidson's ruling that the divorce trial again be postponed and that Priscilla's temporary support payments be increased.

Free after more than a year in the Cross-Bar Hotels in Fort Worth and Amarillo, Cullen checked into the Hilton, and when Priscilla arrived to testify they spent the night under the same general roof. After two days of deliberation in Fort Worth, Judge Cave revoked the bond. Cullen got his $1 million back and returned to the Cross-Bar. Perhaps it was just as well. As one of his attorneys put it, "His character was probably better in jail."

A reporter for the *Amarillo Globe News* spotted Priscilla carrying a Bible in the corridors of the Hilton. When they read the story, Amarillo readers bristled. Who did she think she was kidding?

By the time Priscilla appeared at the Potter County courthouse on August 22, the town of Amarillo was solidly pro-Cullen, anti-Priscilla.

Priscilla would have been demure in the witness chair if it had not been for platinum hair dipping provocatively over one eye. Her attire was modest. A beige dress, high at neck and below the knee at the hem. She wore a gold bracelet, and on a chain, a simple gold cross. Some surmised that the ensemble had passed muster by Tim Curry, if not in fact selected by the district attorney.

Curry disposed of one piece of business immediately: Priscilla's relationship with Stan Farr. He knew that if he didn't, Haynes would. Curry asked Priscilla where and when she met the basketball player. She said that Farr had approached her at the rodeo in February two years before, and they had begun seeing each other regularly in March.

"At my home," Priscilla responded when Curry asked where Farr lived at the time of the murders.

When Priscilla's first day on the stand—devoted to her version of the night of August 2—was finished, Haynes was asked why his reexamination of Priscilla was so tepid. "In the early rounds," the Houston lawyer said, "I just like to horse around and see how the other guy reacts. Then I get to the heavy stuff."

The second round and the heavy stuff began promptly the next morning. Those who had waited through the seemingly interminable jury selection and the tedious pretrial hearings were not disappointed. Racehorse Haynes delighted them with an example of his courtroom audacity.

Haynes produced a photograph he wished to place in evidence. It had been enlarged until it was the size of a travel poster. In vibrant color, it depicted two persons: first Priscilla, in a low-cut halter and blue slacks, smiling at the camera; then W. T. Rufner, the electrician with a record of narcotics violations, with his arms loosely around Priscilla. Rufner was grinning and his head was tilted against hers. He was nude except for a single red and white Christmas stocking which he wore on his penis.

The prosecutors bolted out of their chairs objecting to the ribald photograph. They protested that it was not relevant to the charge that a young girl had been slain. In a benchside huddle Judge Dowlen ruled in Haynes's favor: the piquant pose was not to be seen by the jury but was admissible as evidence. He did admonish the gleefully contrite Haynes and ordered that henceforth the photograph must be mounted on an opaque cardboard backing.

In fact, the photograph had been transposed to thin, translucent paper. When he had first displayed it Haynes had held the print in such a manner that light from the fluorescent ceiling fixtures in the courtroom shone through the paper. The jury had a good look.

Asked about the circumstances in which the photograph was taken, Priscilla said she couldn't recall them. Later Haynes questioned Priscilla's vague recollection.

"Have you ever seen W. T. Rufner in a social atmosphere," Haynes asked, "when he was running around without his clothes on?"

"I don't recall that I have."

Haynes persisted. "You have never seen W. T. Rufner naked as a jaybird with his you-know-what in a sock? You do not recognize the man in the photograph as W. T. Rufner?"

"Well, I recognize the face." Priscilla paused, as if trying her best to remember. "I don't recognize the sock."

There were giggles in the courtroom. One delighted spectator whispered to a friend, "Leave it to old Race to come up with a peter heater." The reference was to a quaint knitted garment of phallic dimension available in some Texas novelty shops.

The first exchange about the candy-striped sock occurred in the jury's presence, the second when the jury was absent. Judge Dowlen then, and on many occasions throughout the lengthy trial, dismissed the jury for various reasons while questioning of witnesses continued. Usually the testimony unheard by the jury concerned matters the judge believed might become relevant later, especially if Cullen were convicted and his case taken to the appeals court. Haynes and his team, and Curry and his colleagues often engaged in heated debate about what the jury should or should not hear or see.

Priscilla did tell the jury that Rufner had stayed for several weeks at the mansion. He had been ill, she explained, and it was more convenient to have Rufner there than to make frequent visits to his place. When she did visit him it was at the houseboat where Rufner lived on Possum Kingdom Lake, not far from Fort Worth.

Haynes attempted to introduce into evidence two additional photographs. They were blurred, as though an amateur photographer had snapped the images with unsteady hands. They were described as "sex scenes in a lake." The jury was not permitted to peek at the watery frolics. This time Judge Dowlen ruled, to the relief of the prosecution, that the photographs were inadmissible.

During the period when Rufner resided at the mansion, Priscilla said, he stayed in her bedroom.

"Was Rufner a violent man?"

Not very, Priscilla responded. She did not hesitate to elaborate. Once he tossed a potted plant into the bathtub while she was in it. Another time he disembowled a large teddy bear she had given him as a birthday present, scattering the animal's kapok entrails about the master bedroom suite. Then there was the night Priscilla, Rufner, and some friends were at the Old San Francisco Saloon: She argued with Rufner and he stormed out of the bar. When Priscilla and her companions went out they found the tires of her Lincoln Continental slashed. She and her friends returned to the mansion to find Rufner waiting for them; Andrea had let him in. Rufner became obnoxious and a stocky oil lease peddler named Jerry Thomas, who sometimes walked the streets of Fort Worth in his karate costume, began to "pulverize" Rufner. Priscilla stopped the fight (but not, according to Thomas, who had a dislocated little finger after the melee, until Thomas "beat the shit" out of Rufner). Priscilla denied other acts of violence on Rufner's part.

If Andrea had not opened the door for Rufner, could he have entered anyway? Did Rufner have a key to the mansion? A number of people had keys, Priscilla testified. There was a couple who lived there two or three months after Cullen departed. Delbert McClinton, the country and western singer, had stayed there occasionally with his wife. Then there was a second couple who had keys, at least temporarily. A man named Larry Michael Myers had been a house guest for several weeks, but Myers, a convicted felon, had not been entrusted with a key. Then Stan Farr, of course.

But Priscilla insisted that while her guests had keys, only she and her daughter Dee had the master key to the intricate electronic security system which, when activated, rendered other keys useless.

When the trial adjourned that day Haynes had established that Priscilla had lived in the mansion with a motley crew in part-time residence and that Rufner and Farr had been Priscilla's lovers.

Rufner was identified as having been convicted in 1974 for possession of LSD and pethidine with intent to deliver. He had received a suspended sentence.

Racehorse Haynes was satisfied that the second day's testimony had been more interesting than the first.

The next day the subject was drugs. Haynes was so relentless in pursuing the topic that Tim Curry became furious: "We thought we came up here to try a murder case, not a morals case," he fumed. But the judge permitted Haynes to dwell on Priscilla's dependence on drugs.

The jury listened when Priscilla admitted her frequent use of Percodan, a painkiller. She said that she had first used the narcotic after breaking an ankle during a ski spill in Aspen and had been unaware that it was addictive. It had not been so in her case, in any event.

"Are you saying you are not addicted to the use of Percodan?" Haynes asked.

Priscilla retreated. "No, sir, I don't mean to mislead the jury."

"You *are* addicted to Percodan, aren't you?"

"Yes, sir," Priscilla admitted, "there's a possibility."

"Don't you know it to be a fact?"

Priscilla then made a further admission which was to be headline stuff.

"It's highly possible."

"How many Percodans," Haynes wanted to know, "were you taking a day?"

"Due to my gunshot wound," Priscilla said, "I was taking far more than 100 a week."

"Were you taking more than 200 a week?"

"That may be closer to it," Priscilla said. "I was having to take four every couple of hours."

The jury heard the damaging admissions. When they were out of the courtroom they did not hear Priscilla deny that she had used LSD, cocaine, or heroin, as Haynes had intimated. She conceded that she had tested marijuana as a teenager, but had not used it since. Priscilla insisted that she did not encourage or condone the use of narcotics in the mansion on Mockingbird Lane.

Steve Sumner's investigators had obtained copies of Priscilla's bank statements. Priscilla was questioned about large withdrawals during the September and August before the murders and provided answers that explained her need for cash. Haynes, probing for a withdrawal which might have been used for some sinister purpose, went back as far as April. Why, he demanded, did she withdraw $2500 on a single day?

Priscilla had a simple answer: to pay for a "mini-facelift." The surgeon, Dr. Valentin Gracia, wanted cash. "He doesn't take checks," Priscilla explained. "You pay, even if you have insurance, before the surgery. He takes cash or money orders...."

The court did not convene on Friday, August 26. Amarillo celebrated LBJ's birthday.

Priscilla chatted with reporters over the weekend. "I'm not saying I'm Miss Goodie Twoshoes...." But she went on to protest that she was not the wanton Cullen's lawyers had painted her to be.

Cullen, too, spoke to the press, as he did throughout the Amarillo trial. He supported Priscilla on the narcotics issue, saying that he had never been aware she had used hard drugs. But his opinion of her overall testimony under oath was not equally charitable.

"I don't believe she's telling the truth." Cullen paused. "I wouldn't be surprised if God punished her," he added.

During Priscilla's second week in the witness chair both the defense and the prosecution scored points.

Priscilla recounted an emotional telephone confrontation between Cullen and her daughter Andrea while Davis was still living at the mansion. Her version was that Cullen had insisted Andrea return to the mansion for a visit. He cursed the child, and when Andrea said she wouldn't leave her father, Jack Wilborn, even temporarily, Cullen threatened her. From that time on, Priscilla told the jury, Andrea was afraid of Cullen and refused to visit the mansion until his departure.

The matter of the keys to the mansion came up again. Although Priscilla had previously said that only she and Dee had the vital key to the security system, now she remembered a telephone conversation during which Cullen had said he retained a master key. Another key remained in the possession of the man who had installed the system, another was held by a man who worked at Cullen's office, and a third by the mansion housekeeper.

Tim Curry led Priscilla into the subject of Cullen's marksmanship and his possession of handguns.

"Was he a good shot or a bad shot?" Curry asked.

"A very good shot," Priscilla said. She had observed his target practice at the property on Eagle Mountain Lake.

"How many handguns did he own?"

Priscilla could not remember the precise inventory of Cullen's arsenal. "I don't know. He had several...." She did recall one that he kept under his bed, another in a closet, one that rested on a shelf in his dressing area at the mansion...and two more in his Cadillac.

Two grisly photographs were entered as medical evidence. One was a close-up of the cavity in Priscilla's back left by the bullet which had exited there; the other was a graphic image of the incision in Priscilla's body made at the time of surgery, which ran from her chest to below her navel.

Haynes informed the jury of another murder which had occurred shortly before August 2. An ex-convict named Horace Copeland had been mortally wounded while attempting to break into a Fort Worth apartment. Haynes's investigators had discovered that he was an acquaintance of Stan Farr. Would he have a motive for killing Farr? Priscilla said she knew nothing about Copeland or his demise.

Once again Haynes introduced the subject of sex. He asked Priscilla about the recording and photographic paraphernalia in the mansion which rumor had often described as being used to capture sexual escapades for instant replay. What about the camera mounted on the television console in the bedroom?

"Was that camera to take movie film?" Haynes asked.

"No, sir."

"Still photos?"

"No, sir," Priscilla replied. "It was a closed-circuit camera."

Haynes wanted to be sure that the Amarillo jurors were aware of the unique necklace which Priscilla sometimes wore in Fort Worth. He asked Priscilla what the words on the pendant were.

"It was a name given to me by Judy McCrory and Carmen Thomas," Priscilla said. "It spells out 'Rich Bitch.'"

Priscilla was asked about treasures which she and Cullen had collected for the mansion. She described the jade pagoda which Cullen had purchased for $350,000. The white, onionskin Ming dynasty vase. A replica of the Taj Mahal crafted in India of solid gold and diamonds, emeralds, and sapphires. The chess board of black and white jade with pieces sculpted in white and yellow gold. "I think," Priscilla said, "that he had paid $85,000 for that." She spoke of other treasures and the array of art which adorned the mansion.

Haynes exploited Priscilla's testimony in the first of a series of vitriolic denunciations.

Haynes told the jury, "The motive for fabricating a story against Cullen Davis was this woman's personal greed and desire to obtain the fortune of Davis." He went on to aver that Priscilla had been destitute when she entered the marriage, had spent ten to twenty thousand dollars a month while it lasted, and left Cullen laden with "jewels, furs, and treasures."

Curry attempted to counteract the accusation by convincing the jury that Cullen, not Priscilla, had been the profligate responsible for the wildly expensive mansion furnishings. He reminded Priscilla of an art-buying trip in New York.

"Do you recall a purchase that started with you and your husband in a taxi cab?"

"Well," Priscilla corrected the district attorney, "it was a rent [sic] car."

"What was the nature of the purchase?"

"It was one of many," Priscilla said. "We were on our way to the plane and Cullen spotted a painting in a gallery. So he told the pilot and the copilot who were [sic] driving the car to stop. Cullen went down the row of paintings and he thoroughly enjoyed them all, and he could fill his house with them."

"Did he make more than one purchase?"

"He bought the store out," Priscilla replied matter-of-factly.

"And what was the value of those purchases?"

"Approximately $102,000," Priscilla recalled. "For 115 paintings and bronzes."

"Did you *ever* spend any amount of money, whether it be $10 or $20,000 per month, that your husband didn't know about?"

"No, sir."

As Priscilla's second week of testimony ended she and Curry caught Haynes napping; Curry's exchange with his witness was so rapid that the Houston lawyer was unable to contain it.

Curry, abruptly: "On August 2, 1976, who shot you?"

Haynes sprang from his seat, objecting. The judge sustained the objection, as repetitious of previous testimony—but too late, as Priscilla picked up the cue with a firm, "Cullen Davis."

Curry plowed ahead. "On August 2, 1976, Mrs. Davis, who shot Stan Farr?

Haynes bounced out of his seat again, but again too late.

"*Cullen Davis!*" Priscilla answered emphatically.

Haynes didn't bother to voice the second objection.

"That's all the questions I have," Curry told the court, pleased with the climax of the second week of testimony from his key witness.

During the week there had been a brief, amusing interruption of the proceedings. A young college football player entered the courtroom and stood among the spectators. Priscilla did a theatrically deft double take, and laughed. Cullen, turning from his chair to look back, was amused. The man was wearing a T-shirt upon which had been stenciled in dark blue letters: "Sock It To 'Em, W.T."

The attorneys on both sides grinned. The bailiff escorted the student out. Later the student returned in a plain shirt to watch the trial. His mother, queried by reporters, said that she had seen the shirt and presumed it had something to do with her son's football team.

When the trial continued on Monday morning, September 5, Priscilla began her third week as a witness.

She again denied Haynes's allegations that she had, in the midst of her divorce proceedings with Andrea's father, Jack Wilborn, lured him into sexual encounters. That was not the way it happened, Priscilla insisted. Wilborn had been the offender, forcing his attentions on her, as she had testified previously. Haynes suggested she was not being truthful.

"The fact is," Haynes said, "you lied."

"No, sir. I told the truth."

Haynes was skeptical. "Mr. Wilborn came over and *raped* you?"

"Yes."

"You did not report it to the police?" Haynes asked.

"No."

"And when it happened again, the very next *day*?"

"Yes, sir." Priscilla said that after the second assault she did advise the authorities, "on the advice of my attorney." She confirmed that her lawyer at the time had been Tolly Wilson of Curry's legal team.

One day's proceedings were adjourned early to allow Priscilla to regain her composure. She had glimpsed an extremely grisly photograph of the slain Andrea. The photograph had been left, apparently inadvertently, on a courtroom table, and she had broken into tears.

Throughout her testimony Priscilla never wavered on the essentials of her version of the August 2 murders and the circumstances surrounding them. It *was* Cullen who shot her. He *had* mistreated Andrea to the point that the twelve-year-old was frightened to be with her stepfather. She had *not* presided over sexual orgies or drug experiments in the mansion. And, despite Haynes's repeated insinuations, she insisted that Stan Farr had known about her precarious financial position, and that she had not lavished money on him.

Priscilla was allowed to step down on Tuesday, September 6. She had been in Amarillo for over two weeks and had been in the witness chair for eleven of those days.

The prosecution put a Fort Worth ambulance attendant on the stand. He said that it required four attendants to lift Stan Farr's heavy body into the ambulance. The medic also testified that Gus Gavrel had two small bags of marijuana on his person when he was transported to the hospital. Gavrel would later deny this.

During testimony concerning Priscilla's addiction to painkilling narcotics Racehorse Haynes had suggested that her account of the night of August 2 was flawed, her memory warped by drugs. Tim Curry produced the doctor who attended Priscilla when she arrived at the hospital after being wounded at the mansion. Haynes and the physician sparred in medical jargon, much of which was incomprehensible to the jury. As in previous cases, Haynes impressed the jurors with his encyclopedic knowledge of technical details. The doctor maintained that he had examined Priscilla thoroughly. Her pupils were not dilated, nor were there other signs of drug abuse, light or heavy.

Gus Gavrel testified. While his story differed with that of the ambulance driver concerning marijuana possession, it corroborated Priscilla's version in every other detail, and he identified Cullen as the murderer.

On September 13 the trial was suspended for three days. Juror L. B. Pendleton had to have a wisdom tooth extracted.

Newspaper reports announced that the nurse who had attended Priscilla when she was recuperating had filed suit for slander against her for $2.5 million.

The jury was growing impatient. Judge Dowlen approved their petition to work on Saturdays.

A police officer from Fort Worth testified that the mansion was swarming with police, ambulance attendants, reporters, and photographers early in the morning after the murders. Two friends of Priscilla and Cullen had also been there: Charles David McCrory and Pat Burleson, the karate studio owner.

The nine-foot-high door through which Stan Farr had been shot had been transported from Fort Worth, and was lugged into the courtroom. The jury saw the bullet hole, but the judge ruled inadmissible some undescribed graffiti written on the door. The jury learned the precise cause of Farr's death—bullet through his larynx. He had suffocated in vomit.

Beverly Bass was called. She repeated her version of the

events at the mansion and her unequivocal eyewitness claim that Cullen had been the murderer.

Haynes did not dwell on this, but revealed that his investigators had come up with an episode from Beverly's past which the courtroom tactician slowly unfolded to the jury in tantalizing stages. Beverly had a "personal problem" which Priscilla had helped her resolve. A check had been written for $600. The money was for Beverly, and had never been repaid. The "personal problem" was of a medical nature. Beverly had concealed the "personal problem" in a civil disposition the year before.

Beverly broke into tears. She admitted that Haynes was right: Priscilla had financed an abortion, and Beverly had attempted to keep it secret.

Then Fort Worth police department technicians were summoned and testified that there had been no fingerprints of import found at the mansion. The bloody handprint on the door which Priscilla had seen before the killer attacked her was smeared and unidentifiable. The bullets were accounted for, and the wig and shreds of the plastic bag were found upstairs. The murderer had obviously roamed about the mansion.

Three eyewitnesses had survived the shooting, and it had been the defense's intention to discredit them all. Priscilla had been portrayed to the staid, conservative Amarillo jury as a slut, Gus Gavrel as a pothead, and Beverly Bass as a girl who was obligated to Priscilla for her financing of an abortion.

Things were looking better for Haynes in what many had said was an airtight case against Cullen Davis. This had resulted from his reexamination of prosecution witnesses. Haynes's own witnesses were yet to appear.

Could Haynes present a witness able to provide his client with an alibi, someone who would testify that Cullen could not possibly have been at the scene of the murder? Or would Cullen himself be forced to take the stand?

On September 22, Cullen had a cake for dessert with lunch.

Frosted letters spelled out "Happy Birthday Dad." Cullen celebrated his forty-fourth birthday—his second in jail—with his two sons, Cullen, Jr., fourteen, and Brian, eleven. They had flown in from Dallas where they lived with their mother. Cullen maintained his composure, but the reunion evoked tears from the boys.

Haynes caught an early flight for Houston the same day to be with his son at a football game. His boy had grown into a sturdy linebacker for undefeated Kincaid High. Haynes explained to his colleagues that a friend of his had died recently, and Haynes had been a surrogate dad at a father-son game with that man's boy. He had vowed not to be absent when Kincaid played its father-son game.

Priscilla, before returning to Fort Worth, had a wry response when asked what she thought about the damaging testimony Haynes was eliciting from her own friends. "If they're my friends, why are they up there testifying?"

During a recess Priscilla protested to a journalist. Why, she wanted to know, did the newspapers always play up the fact that she had lower-class guests at the mansion? They never mentioned that she also had entertained the Boy Scouts, the Bluebirds, had been the hostess at a political rally for a Mexican-American candidate, and opened her house for various civic gatherings. She explained why she invited visitors from the wrong side of the tracks. She had grown up dirt poor and understood what deprivation meant. "I have those people at the mansion," Priscilla said, "because I'm trying to *rehabilitate* them."

Soon afterwards, some journalists began referring to the mansion as the Mockingbird Halfway House.

In the evenings and on weekends in Amarillo the media people and the out-of-town lawyers congregated at Rhett Butler's restaurant and bar. Charles David McCrory, hovering anxiously around the trial, was often seen at the restaurant.

In a prediction which would later turn out to be excessively optimistic, one of Cullen's lawyers said, "I think McCrory's painted himself out of the picture."

Pretrial hearings, jury selection, and testimony from dozens of witnesses had stretched the trial into four months. Traditionally Texas murder trials were brief. The weary jurors asked how much longer they would be sequestered, and out-of-town journalists wondered when they would see their families again. When would it end?

"Don't worry," Judge Dowlen promised, "we'll be done before Christmas." Then the judge reflected. "But then I'm the guy who said we would be done by bird season." Bird hunting season starts each year in Texas on September 21. "Deer season, which opens November 12," Glen Guzzo wrote in a dispatch to the *Star-Telegram*, "is now in jeopardy."

Joe Shannon was even more pessimistic when he came up with a suggested slogan for Tim Curry's political campaign for the following spring: "Don't change DA's in the middle of a trial."

There were some diversions, including another involving T-shirts. W. T. Rufner was not going to be upstaged by an Amarillo kid, the young football player who had previously capitalized on Rufner's claim to fame, the celebrated green and red sock. Rufner appeared in the courthouse wearing a T-shirt entitled "W. T. Rufner Socks It To 'Em." In a paper sack he carried a supply of extras which he attempted to peddle for $100. Rufner approached Haynes in the hall, said he had something for him, and reached into a paper sack. Haynes had a momentary vision of Jack Ruby in a Dallas police station. But Rufner was only offering him a sample T-shirt.

Cullen began his second year of confinement with apparent equanimity. During breaks in the trial proceedings he was approached in the hall by supporters and well-wishers. The legendary poker player, T. A. "Amarillo Slim" Preston, paid a courtesy call. Young women, legal groupies, asked for Cullen's autograph. He gave press interviews and posed for photographs, the picture of propriety in his blue and gray conservatively tailored suits, solid color shirts, and sombre ties.

"He is treated with the deference of a statesman here," Glen Guzzo wrote. "He is calm. Always. And he is regarded as a gentleman. Always cool."

The defense legal squad had employed a public relations man to enhance Cullen's image in Fort Worth. Phil Burleson was asked why he was not in Amarillo. "Cullen is our P.R. man now," Burleson replied.

Cullen obviously had good relations with his jailors. He was treated well in Amarillo, usually accommodated in a comfortable cell with a color television, despite an overcrowded jail where other prisoners doubled and tripled up in smaller quarters. Another prisoner in the jail was raped by nine cell mates during this period. Cullen's meals were catered, delivered from the Hilton or Rhett Butler's. During court recesses, Cullen wandered about the halls greeting the multitudes.

Once Cullen was in the Potter County jail's booking office. The telephone rang. Cullen looked about and found that he was alone. He answered the telephone.

Cullen: "Jail."

Outside voice: "Who is this?"

Cullen: "Cullen Davis."

Outside voice, in amazement: "Oh, my God, have ya'll taken over?"

Cullen's loosely supervised excursions were curtailed by Judge Dowlen after the prosecution complained that Cullen had been seen chatting with the mother of one of the jurors. Although the jury was sequestered, visits from family members were allowed. The judge admonished Cullen. But Cullen continued to enjoy special privileges and spoke frequently with reporters.

During one interview Cullen set the record straight concerning how he felt about the mansion. He told Evan Moore (who was covering the trial along with Glen Guzzo for the *Star-*

Telegram) that the Davis property at 4200 Mockingbird Lane was *his* place, not Priscilla's. "Priscilla's characterization of the house as being a dream home I built for her is typical untruth....I did not build the home as a dream house for her. I built it as a culmination of an idea I had many years before I met her....The idea of locating the home where I did had been in the back of my mind for twenty years."

Priscilla was furious when she read the interview, saying that the mansion had been a joint project. She did conclude, however, that Cullen "obviously built this house as a monument to himself."

Cullen talked with Glen Guzzo in late October. He gave Glen an exclusive story—for the first time he would reveal his whereabouts on the night of August 2 of the previous year. Early in the evening, Cullen said, he went to dinner. Alone. Then he had gone to a movie. Alone. He didn't answer Guzzo's questions about which restaurant, what film. Cullen said he went home to Karen Master's place after the movie. He had called their mutual friend, Jim Mabe, between midnight and a quarter after. Mabe had said, "Hell, it's still early; come on over and watch tv." Cullen had declined and crawled into bed with the sleeping Karen.

The jury was not to hear Cullen's explanation. Everyone else read either the headlines on the front page of the *Star-Telegram* the next morning, or the reprint of the story which was picked up in Amarillo and throughout the state.

The parade of prosecution witnesses had filed by the jury. Haynes called his first witness for the defense on Wednesday, October 26.

Tommy Jourden had been a patient in the two-bed hospital room in Fort Worth when Gus Gavrel was wheeled in after surgery. Jourden testified that Gus had said he didn't know who had shot him. Jourden also claimed he had suggested to Gus that he could reap a rich harvest by suing Cullen Davis, and that Gus had done so the same day, asking for $3 million.

But after the defense's questions the prosecution read into the record a litany of petty episodes from Jourden's past. The prosecution had been ready for Jourden.

If Tommy Jourden had been anticipated by the prosecutors, Tim Curry and Joe Shannon were not prepared for Haynes's second witness, or at least for the magnitude of her testimony. Karen Master wore a stylish gray dress with a row of bows and a choke collar. Her blonde hair was expertly coiffed. She was decorative—"stunning," one newspaper reporter wrote—without losing the appearance of decorum that would place her a rung up on the social ladder from the flashier Priscilla. Karen looked and acted a lady.

Haynes guided Karen through a series of introductory questions. She said that she had met Cullen three years before, about three months after he had separated from Priscilla. They had been friends for a year before he moved into her home. Since then, Cullen had provided financial support for her and her two sons, both injured as a result of an automobile accident.

Asked about August 2 of the previous year, Karen said it had begun like any other day. Cullen had gone to work between 7:30 and 8 in the morning. She did not hear from him all day, but his secretary called to say he would not be home for dinner. Karen said she took some sleeping pills and went to bed.

"When," Haynes asked, "was the first time you were aware that Cullen Davis was home?"

"I awoke very briefly at 12:40 A.M." She explained that she remembered seeing the time on her digital bedside clock.

Joe Shannon and Tim Curry exchanged glances. Shannon was frustrated because he could not mention to the jury that Detective Davis, in a notarized statement, had stated that Karen had told him after the murders that she had slept from 10 P.M. until 4 the next morning—and had not seen Cullen during that period.

"Was Davis there?" Haynes asked.

"Yes."

"Where was he?"

"On the other side of the king-size bed," Karen said.

"Did you get up?"

"No, I didn't."

Haynes asked when Karen fell asleep again.

She replied that she had gone back to sleep very shortly thereafter.

"Was he asleep?"

"Yes."

"How was he dressed?"

"He had his shorts on," Karen recalled, "and he did not have anything on his top."

Haynes had a final question.

"Are you in love with him?"

"Yes, I am," Karen said. She turned to the jury and smiled. While the prosecutors had once entertained the queasy notion that Karen might provide an alibi for Cullen at the time of the murders, Karen's grand jury testimony had led them to believe she would not.

Karen was calm when Joe Shannon began to question her. Frequently she turned and smiled at the jury. Shannon asked her if she had been coached by Haynes.

"No," Karen answered. "This is the first time I've had a chance to see the jury. They're very interesting people."

Shannon asked Karen to ponder her grand jury testimony of August 12, 1976, ten days after the massacre on Mockingbird Lane. Her memory was hazy. Shannon refreshed it: She had failed to mention to the grand jury that she was in bed with Cullen. There were gasps in the courtroom.

Nor, Shannon said, did she mention that vital fact to Detective C. R. Davis (no relation to Cullen), the officer who had interrogated her on the morning Cullen had been arrested at her home. Karen conceded the omission.

"Your boyfriend, the man you hoped to marry"—Shannon's voice was heavy with incredulity—"had just been arrested for *murder*, and you did not tell Detective Davis that he was at home in bed with you?"

"No, I didn't," Karen said.

"And, didn't you tell the grand jury on August 12 that you had told them everything that could possibly shed light on the subject?"

"Yes," Karen admitted. "I told them that."

Shannon asked if she had called the detective later in the day; or the next; or the next; or if she had *ever* contacted him again. She answered no to each of the four queries.

Then Shannon read into the record a quotation from Karen's grand jury testimony: "Well, of course Cullen prefaced our conversation with the fact that his attorneys had told him not to talk about the case, and though he said that, I went on and asked him what time he had gotten home, and he said it was a little before 11 P.M."

The excerpt was not as meaningful to the jury as to the spectators in the courtroom. They had read Glen Guzzo's story about Cullen's alibi: Cullen, one week before, had told Guzzo that he had returned to Karen's home that night fifteen minutes after midnight.

Joe Shannon pressed Karen to explain why she had not mentioned to the grand jury or to Detective Davis that she had been in bed with Cullen at the time of the murders.

"At the time, it had no relevance," Karen said. "It didn't seem significant."

The next defense witness was one of Priscilla's friends. W. T. Rufner was ready, even anxious to testify despite speculation that he would invoke the Fifth Amendment if called. The night before, Rufner had been asked what he planned to do in preparation for his testimony. "I'm going to drink a lot of beer tonight," he said. If he did, presumably the brew was Bud, because the next morning in the courtroom he was an apparition in his "Sock It To 'Em" T-shirt, a black cowboy hat, and a red raincoat emblazoned with an advertisement for Budweiser beer. He did say he had brought along a change of clothes in case the judge insisted on a different costume. When he did finally take the stand Rufner was wearing a suit; whether this was done out of a sense of propriety or because Judge Dowlen insisted was not recorded. But Rufner's predilection for beer was recorded for posterity when he was described as "a man who measures time in six-packs."

Racehorse Haynes had suggested to the court that W. T. Rufner was a man who had the motive and means to kill Stan Farr. Rufner claimed he had never met the ex-basketball player and had only seen him twice, both times at a distance. Haynes moved on to Rufner's relationship with Priscilla. Rufner said they had met at a Christmas party in 1974. The following March he had joined Priscilla in Boston where she was visiting Charles David and Judy McCrory. Haynes wanted details of that New England encounter.

"While in Boston, Massachusetts," Haynes queried, "were you paired up together?"

Rufner was confused at Haynes's technique of asking a number of indirect questions before eliciting the final answer he wanted.

"I don't know what you mean by paired up together," Rufner responded, apparently genuinely perplexed. "We weren't *tied* up together."

"You weren't tied up. You did keep close quarters, though?"

"I had a place to sleep," Rufner said. "She had a place to sleep."

"There was not mutuality? You didn't share the same couch, so to speak?"

"Yes." Rufner finally understood. "We shared."

Haynes asked a number of questions which were intended to convey to the jury that Priscilla had lavished money on Rufner, using charge accounts for which Cullen was ultimately responsible. Rufner admitted that Priscilla often used her charge plates to pay for gifts for him.

"And that included clothes?" Haynes asked.

"Yes."

"Shoes, boots?"

"Yes."

"Jewelry?"

"Yes."

Rufner's access to the mansion was established. As an electrician he had admired the complicated electrical circuitry which controlled the mansion's security system and the sensors which could detect intruders; he had escorted other electricians through the house to explain the system. And, yes, he knew the system sufficiently well to thwart it if he had wanted to do so.

Rufner commented that life in the mansion, despite the luxuries and festive atmosphere, was a mixed blessing. "There was mornings when it was total harmony," he mused, and "there was mornings when it was total hell." He decamped after four months, Rufner said, because he felt more comfortable at his own place with his dogs and his mother.

When asked to describe his personal use of narcotics or the drug experiences of others who lived in the mansion, Rufner pleaded the Fifth Amendment nine times after nine questions.

By the time Haynes announced that he had no further questions, the wily attorney had established that Rufner had begun his sexual liaison with Priscilla four months before she had filed for a divorce from Cullen. Priscilla had testified otherwise.

Despite his new business of selling "Sock It To 'Em" T-shirts, Rufner said he knew nothing about the famous photograph; he did *not* recall wearing a sock anywhere on his body other than his feet.

100

Joe Shannon's reexamination reminded the jury that the murder weapon had never been recovered.

"You were afraid for your life," Shannon asked Rufner, "in late 1976 and early 1977?"

"Yes, sir."

"Did you feel you were being made a patsy in the whole deal?"

"Yes, sir."

"And were you afraid that one of these days you would wake up dead?" Shannon went on.

"Yes, sir."

"Had you heard that there was money on the street," Shannon continued, "and there were people who would assist in making *you* a patsy in this double homicide?"

"Yes, sir."

"Did you hear," the prosecutor concluded, "that dead men tell no tales?"

W. T. Rufner welcomed the question since it called for a different response. "I *know* that for a *fact*."

If the previous witnesses had held the attention of the courtroom at the end of the first week of November, Haynes produced a witness who enthralled the jurors; they sat forward on their chairs while he described a party at the mansion. His account provided a titillating panorama of life with Priscilla in her pleasure dome on Mockingbird Lane.

Malcolm "Danny" McDaniel testified that he had attended a birthday party at the mansion two months after Cullen had moved out. Priscilla and W. T. Rufner had been joint hosts. The celebration was in honor of Priscilla's house guest, Sandy Guthrie Myers (who was to be convicted a month later on drug charges).

There were maybe 70 to 100 guests, McDaniel said. You could get anything you wanted from the plentiful supply of stimulants—marijuana, cocaine, pills, and capsules. He himself had selected, first, a "white cross." McDaniel enlightened the jury by describing the amphetamine as something good to "get the system going." Later, when he wanted to sleep for a while, he took LSD. Worked real good.

McDaniel said he watched guests splashing in the indoor pool. Some of them were wearing bathing suits. He went upstairs. When he peeked into Priscilla's bedroom suite he saw a number of people, nude, in the bed. "I was embarrassed," McDaniel said.

At one point he saw Priscilla remove some jewelry from her upstairs safe.

"Did you see Priscilla Davis take anything out of the safe other than jewelry?" Haynes asked.

Yes, it was answered. A little plastic sack. A white substance—coke. Priscilla tossed it to Rufner, who was sprawled on a bed, wearing a necklace from which a small spoon hung. He watched while Priscilla and Rufner sniffed the cocaine...and later LSD.

The picture of debauchery that McDaniel painted would prove to be devastating.

It rankled Joe Shannon that the rules of evidence prevented him, on reexamination, from pointing out why McDaniel could testify with impunity about his own role in the bacchanalia: The witness undoubtedly had been made aware that the sensational festivities he described had occurred more than three years before, and so would cause him no problems because of Texas's three-year statute of limitations on drug offenses. The party had also been celebrated before McDaniel's own conviction on aggravated robbery charges; consequently, his testimony did not violate his ten-year probated sentence.

McDaniel was followed to the stand by a young woman, Becky Ferguson, who said that she had been present at a Willie Nelson Fourth of July picnic in 1974 when Priscilla had been among those sampling a wide choice of narcotics.

The witness giggled when shown the photographs which previously had been described as "love scenes in a lake." Yes, the water nymph was Priscilla, and the satyr, W. T. Rufner.

The next day, a working Saturday for the court now, the witness was Sandy Myers, the house guest who had been feted at the party McDaniel described so vividly. Her husband, Michael Myers, was not in Amarillo as he had by now become an inmate of the Huntsville penitentiary, convicted of robbery.

Much of Mrs. Myers's testimony was taken while the jury was out, when Judge Dowlen ruled it hearsay evidence. She said she had heard W. T. Rufner threaten Stan Farr after Farr had replaced him as Priscilla's favorite: "I'll get that tall son of a bitch and I'll get that cunt." The jury returned to their box, however, to hear Myers relate that she ran into Priscilla by chance in a doctor's waiting room five days before Stan Farr had been shot. On that occasion, she told the jury, Priscilla had predicted, "Something heavy is coming down."

A young witness identified herself as a member of Dee's graduating class at Arlington Heights High School. The 440 seniors had been unable to find a place for their June graduation party and Priscilla had offered the mansion grounds and paid for the barbecue and kegs of beer. The local rock band, the Cahoots, had provided the music. There was a lot of smoking, the witness said, resulting in a "haze" over the revelry.

With the possibility that W. T. Rufner could have been the murderer on August 2 implanted in the jurors' minds, Haynes moved on to surface a second suspect.

Valerie Marazzi Faulkner was a bartender at the Rhinestone Cowboy. She said she had seen drugs used there and that Stan Farr had often been as much as $200 short when the bill for the night was toted up. She connected Farr with Horace Copeland, the burglar who died with a bullet in his head. Ronnie Bradshaw, who operated the Rhinestone Cowboy with Farr, testified that Stan had feared Copeland might harm him and requested that Bradshaw return a pistol Farr had loaned him. Bradshaw said that everyone liked Stan—he was called the Jolly Green Giant—and added that Stan had expressed apprehension that a jealous Cullen Davis might seek revenge.

The jurors were confused, but Haynes insisted these details were relevant. The assertion that Stan Farr was afraid of Copeland was corroborated by a new witness, Charles Baldwin. A few weeks before, Baldwin had turned over to the police a gun he said belonged to Copeland; he suggested that it might be the August 2 murder weapon; ballistics tests disproved this.

A private investigator from Fort Worth, Sylvia Meek, testified that she had been approached by Priscilla Davis in July before the August murders. Priscilla wanted assistance in hiring a full-time bodyguard. The female private eye could not say whom Priscilla might have been afraid of.

Then there was a surprise witness. Kimberly Lewis, nineteen, said she had been Stan Farr's secret lover for five months before the murders and while the Jolly Green Giant had been Priscilla's live-in companion. During one clandestine tryst, Kimberly said, Farr had been nervous and was carrying a gun. He had described Priscilla as "his investment."

As the trial drew to a close, lines began to form early in the morning. Spectators knew the courtroom would be filled once the bailiff opened the doors. Young law students anxious to observe Haynes in action, legal groupies who pursued the lawyer and Cullen during recesses to obtain an autograph, a handshake, or a kiss. The reporters, photographers, sketch artists, and wire-service men. And the curious. Everyone wanted to be on hand for the final testimony and the verdict.

Despite Judge Dowlen's admonition that Cullen should be more closely supervised, he continued to mingle with the spectators during the day, and he gave impromptu press conferences when the court adjourned. Many reporters thought that Cullen was demonstrating an unusual preoccupation with sex. One un-published story had it that Cullen told a group of women onlookers he was anticipating the end of the trial and his freedom because, when that occurred, he was going to screw all of them "up and down." The newspapers reported that Cullen was seen wearing a wristwatch, the hands of which were elongated nude females and the dial inscribed "Time To F——."

On Thursday evening, November 10, Haynes gave jour-nalists the signal that his parade of witnesses was nearing a halt. He described the testimony they would hear the next morning. "It's going to be dynamite. We're going out with a bang."

Haynes indeed detonated explosive testimony the next morn-ing. Arthur Ulewayne Polk took the stand.

"I always collect in person," the nurseryman told the jury. He had made a number of fruitless visits to the mansion to col-lect money he said Priscilla owed him for 677 plants he had delivered for the mansion's interior and gardens. He went to the mansion during the day on August 2. Inside the house he talked with Priscilla on the internal telephone. She had brushed him off again and he resolved on the spot to return and recover the greenery that very night. Polk unlatched a door so that he would have access after dark. He loaded his motorcycle onto his pickup truck. He parked the truck several blocks from 4200 Mock-ingbird Lane and proceeded to the edge of the property on his cycle. Then he dismounted and prepared to make his hugger-mugger foray.

He looked, Polk said, at his digital watch. It was 11:11 P.M. Four aces. Lucky. A time a poker player could remember.

Just as he was about to trespass onto the mansion's grounds Polk saw another figure. At first Polk thought it was a hobo. Then the figure passed close enough for Polk to see him. Or-dinary build. Short, curly hair. "He had big eyes; you could see the white all around the pupils."

Polk said he followed the man up the hill to the mansion. He saw him approach the swimming pool area. "Then he put something on his head," Polk testified. "At first I thought it was a stocking."

The lights of the swimming pool were on. Polk could see the man's face.

Haynes asked the inevitable question.

"Was the man you saw in the swimming pool area Cullen Davis?"

"Definitely not!" Arthur Ulewayne Polk said.

"Had you seen the man before?"

"No."

"Have you seen him since?" Haynes was standing near the chair where Cullen sat.

"No."

"Could you recognize him again," Haynes asked, "if you saw him?"

"Of course."

Polk said that he abandoned his plan to recover surreptitiously his unpaid-for plants, fearing he might be spotted. He went home. When he read the next morning of the murders he decided to remain silent. But he finally spoke out in October of 1977, while the Amarillo trial was in progress. He told a friend, his mother, and a business associate. The last recommended that Polk confide in a lawyer. The attorney—who had lost a close election to Tim Curry for the district attorney's job in 1974—sent Polk to the defense lawyers.

An agitated Joe Shannon confronted the witness.

"How much money have you been paid to deliver this cock-and-bull story?"

"Not a red penny," Polk answered calmly.

Shannon pointed out in caustic terms that it was highly unusual for a man who had been an interloper on the mansion grounds in August 1976 to wait more than a year before surfacing his story. Polk replied that he had not followed developments in the case closely and had not read many of the newspaper accounts about the murders.

The assistant district attorney asked the nurseryman to explain his lack of interest in the biggest crime story in the history of Fort Worth, one in which he now claimed to be involved.

"I wanted to forget about it," Polk said.

"You are aware," Shannon asked, "of accusations that Mr. W. T. Rufner may have committed these crimes?"

"Yes."

"And you are aware of accusations that Mr. Horace Copeland may have committed these crimes?"

"Yes."

"Isn't it a fact, Mr. Arthur Ulewayne Polk, that when Mr. W. T. Rufner wouldn't float and when Mr. Horace Copeland wouldn't float—"

Haynes's objection, sustained, cut Shannon off.

Shannon said further rebuttal would wait until closing arguments.

"What can you rebut?" Shannon wondered later. "Are we supposed to find somebody who said he was out there too?"

Tolly Wilson expressed his fear that Polk's testimony might defeat the prosecution's case.

"It's not the deciding factor," Haynes said. "The fact is the prosecution failed to prove its case beyond a reasonable doubt."

Again, Joe Shannon and Tim Curry regretted that the jury would not learn more about the background of the witness—in this case that Arthur Ulewayne Polk was convicted in 1969 of armed robbery and, in 1968, indicted for arson.

But the prosecution did come up with a rebuttal witness who, while not out on the mansion's grounds on August 2, had been there before. Arthur Ulewayne Polk's estranged wife had worked with her husband in the nursery business and been with him on one occasion when he had tried to collect his bill from Priscilla.

Mrs. Polk told the jury that two months before the murders

Arthur had fallen off a boat into the water. He was wearing that digital watch and, she testified, it had not worked properly for five months after that. If Arthur had read 11:11 P.M. on his watch, it was probably wrong.

Because Judge Dowlen ruled inadmissible a conversation between a husband and wife, the jury did not hear Ms. Polk recount a conversation which she said had taken place several days before the murders. Arthur had been upset when Priscilla reneged on the bill and told his wife that he had sneaked onto the mansion grounds to recover his plants the night before. He had approached the swimming pool area, but approaching cars made him decide to abandon his effort. If this testimony was accurate, it would explain how Arthur was familiar enough with the nighttime surroundings of the mansion to describe them convincingly.

Racehorse Haynes's final witness was Dr. Robert Miller, a pharmacologist and professor, identified as an expert on opiates. He testified that drugs such as Percodan could cause the user to experience illusions, and perhaps fabricate versions of events which never took place. It was quite possible, the doctor said, that such a person could live in two worlds, a socialite in one and a denizen of the underworld in another. The witness said such people were "the Dr. Jekyll and Mr. Hyde, so to speak, of the drug dependency field."

Haynes had a final question.

"Could you have a Mrs. Jekyll and Mrs. Hyde?"

"I would agree to that," the drug expert said. "Yes."

The defense rested.

The testimony concluded on November 14 after 12 weeks, 700 items placed in evidence, and 67 witnesses. The trial had lasted from late June until mid-November. Judge Dowlen had arranged for the final session, when the defense and prosecution would present their closing arguments, to be held in another, more commodious courtroom which could seat 200 spectators.

The opposing lawyers were to be allowed a maximum of two and a half hours each.

Joe Shannon led off for the prosecution on Wednesday, November 16. In an emotional two-hour plea to the jury (which attorneys on both sides were later to characterize as brilliant) he described the "carnage" at the murder mansion on August 2 of the previous year. He repeatedly reminded the jury that they were not seated to pass judgment on the character of Priscilla Davis or the drug-culture scene in Fort Worth. Their duty was to decide if the man in the dock—Cullen listened impassively—was guilty of murdering a twelve-year-old girl. Shannon, and Tolly Wilson following him, described Cullen as a man accustomed to getting his own way and who had the means and motive for attacking Priscilla—"the source of all his problems."

Cullen was as expressionless and calm as he had been throughout the trial.

Racehorse Haynes rose to address the jury. For an hour and a half he spoke with the fervor of an evangelist, pointing out that not one item of evidence pointed directly to his client. He pointed the finger of guilt at Priscilla. She moved, he said, "in a world of scuzzies, scalawags, rogues, and brigands." He felt sorry for Beverly Bass and Gus Gavrel, who had been blinded and trapped into a conspiracy directed by Priscilla. "They were drawn like a moth to a flame by a queen bee."

It was over. Cullen had never taken the stand.

On Thursday, November 17, the judge gave his instructions to the jury. They returned to the courtroom after four hours and twelve minutes of deliberation. The verdict, written on a piece of paper, was handed to Judge Dowlen.

For the first time Cullen was shaken. His face was drained white. He trembled.

"Not guilty," read Judge Dowlen.

Cullen's first quoted reaction was, "I'm glad it's over." And, from Priscilla, "He'll have to answer to God and that's One that can't be bought."

A photographer snapped a photograph of Cullen smooching with Karen, with a jubilant Haynes in the background.

Cullen did not immediately return to Fort Worth from Amarillo because he had social obligations to fulfill. He was host at a round of victory parties, Karen at his side. The first was a celebration at Rhett Butler's the night of the acquittal. Four of the jurors were there, and the food and drink were plentiful. A little later another guest dropped in, and he stayed until late: Judge George Dowlen.

A female bailiff who had been working during the trial kissed Racehorse Haynes. The triumphant lawyer grinned and said, "I think this is illegal." The bailiff said, "Oh, it's all over. We don't have to worry about being legal anymore." It was a good party. Gary Cartwright, a writer for *Texas Monthly*, later wrote of the celebration:

"There was hugging, kissing, laughing, crying, toasting, and a good word to say about nearly everyone. With the obvious exception of the prosecutorial team, the whole cast turned out—judge, jury, bailiffs, press, Cullen's bodyguards, even a few select groupies. To express his appreciation, Cullen picked up the $650 tab. In the glaring lights of cameras, Cullen and Haynes did the kind of number you would expect from a couple of rookies who had just combined on the winning touchdown. They danced around each other talking jive, slapping palms, and bumping asses."

Before the trial, Cartwright had written about the murders at the mansion in *Texas Monthly*, and he was obviously sympathetic to Priscilla; he hadn't changed his mind. He quoted Haynes from a television broadcast just after the verdict.

"...then, in an incredible display that I'm sure he later regretted, Racehorse went before the live cameras and talked about Priscilla. In an evangelical crescendo, he proclaimed: 'She is the most shameless, brazen hussy in all humanity. She is...a liar. She is a snake, unworthy of belief under oath.'"

Then Cartwright described a question put to Cullen by a wire-service reporter who had covered the trial.

"One night after the acquittal, AP writer Mike Cochran asked out of the blue, 'By the way, Cullen, what movie *did* you see that night?' There was a long, bone-chilling silence. Then Cullen answered, 'That will have to wait for the next trial.'"

·7·

THE OLD JUDGE

"*Circus maximus!*" The old Judge leveled an accusing finger in the general direction of Amarillo. "A goddamned *circus maximus!*"

The Judge was agitated. He strode back and forth before the picture window in his living quarters. After a few paces he would slam one fist into the palm of his other hand and repeat his exhortation to the journalist—"*Circus maximus!*"—before turning on his heel. Finally the Judge slumped into his chair and rubbed his face wearily.

The Judge repeated to the journalist his dismay about the events which had occurred in Judge Dowlen's courtroom during the long weeks of testimony. The parade of dubious witnesses. The process which seemed to be riveted to Priscilla and the sordid company she kept in the mansion rather than addressing the issue of who killed Andrea. And, the post-trial social episode involving Judge Dowlen which disturbed the Judge. "There was no reason in the world Judge Dowlen shouldn't want to relax after the trial, and to drop *in* at Rhett Butler's for a drink. But I do find fault in his not dropping *out* when he saw Racehorse Haynes and Cullen and all that gang."

The Judge was sufficiently concerned, he told the journalist, that he had complained to the Texas State Commission on Judicial Conduct down in Austin.

"Cullen's trials aren't over," the journalist remarked. "There are still the indictments for the death of Stan Farr, and the attempted murder charges in the cases of Priscilla and Gus Gavrel.''

"I'm not so sure," the Judge retorted. "That decision will be up to Tim Curry. I wouldn't be a *bit* surprised if Curry decides not to prosecute the remaining cases.''

"Why?"

"A number of reasons," the Judge said. "The Amarillo expenses must have seriously depleted the district attorney's budget. There's other work to do; crime detection and punishment must go on. But the principal reason Curry may decide not to further prosecute Cullen is that it might be illegal. The doctrine of collateral estoppel. Sort of a second cousin to double jeopardy. That poses problems in trying Cullen for crimes related to one of which he has been acquitted. I cite the U.S. Supreme Court case of *Ashe* v. *Swenson*, which laid the foundation for collateral estoppel. In the early '70s, in Florida, a gunman robbed a group of men who were playing poker. He was tried for robbing *one* of the poker players and acquitted. Then a *second* poker player sued, and the case went to Washington. The doctrine that resulted holds that the gunman, acquitted of robbing *any* of the poker players, could not be tried for stealing from the others—because there was only one robbery, not five or six separate ones.''

The journalist still did not understand how that related to Cullen's situation.

"It can be argued," the Judge said, "that all the shootings at the mansion that night were part of the same incident, and thus collateral estoppel applies. Richard Haynes would protest further prosecution on that ground. One the other hand, Tim Curry could argue that Gus Gavrel's wound was suffered in a separate incident. According to the testimony, Gavrel wasn't even *at* the mansion when the first shootings occurred. Tim Curry might have done better to charge Cullen only in Gavrel's case and to settle for the prospect of something less than a death sentence. Whatever the merits of that speculation, Curry must

113

decide what to do now. He might well figure that further prosecution would be fruitless.''

The journalist remarked that the tone of the Judge's comments indicated he was convinced that Cullen had been guilty.

''As a man not in possession of all the facts,'' the Judge said, ''I should not presume guilt or innocence. I appreciate the reasons that jury could not arrive at a conclusion which was beyond a reasonable doubt. But in my own mind it disturbs me mightily that Davis was acquitted without appearing on the stand. That bothers the shit *out* of me. The principle that a defendant does not have to testify comes out of English law and was based on a respect for civil rights. That's sound and rational when it applies to *political* persecution. I'm not so sure it's good law when it applies to *criminal* prosecution. Why shouldn't a defendant take the stand in the face of a criminal charge?''

The jury must have weighed Cullen's absence from the witness chair, the journalist remarked.

''Undoubtedly,'' the Judge said. ''But don't forget that they were never reminded of the fact. If Shannon or the other prosecutors had even *intimated* to the jury that Cullen was not defending himself the judge would have correctly declared a mistrial, or an appeals court could have deemed it reversible error. But it bothers me that Cullen didn't testify in his own defense. It's been my experience that a lawyer for an innocent client can't *keep* that client from the witness chair. An innocent man will tell his lawyers to go to hell and he will *insist* on jumping into that chair. He wants to stare into the jurors' eyes and proclaim his innocence.''

There will always be speculation, the journalist surmised, that with all his money Cullen might have paid handsomely for those ex-convict witnesses who had so many sordid things to say about Priscilla.

The Judge nodded.

And, the journalist went on, there may be suspicion that Cullen was able to buy Judge Dowlen.

"What's that?" The old Judge was shocked. "Don't you entertain that notion for one minute! I've known all sorts of judges, son. I've known incompetent ones. Sleazy judges. Drunk judges, and senile ones so palsied they should have been put to pasture. And certainly I've known prejudiced judges who have dealt unfairly with blacks and reds and Mexicans. But I've never known a *dishonest* judge."

The journalist raised a skeptical eyebrow.

"Oh, I know they exist," the Judge conceded. "I've read about them, and others have told me about them. But I repeat, son, *I* have never known a dishonest judge! That is an *important* observation."

The journalist rose from his chair. He told the Judge that he was going to New York soon and would seek a contract to write a book about Cullen's trial. At the door the journalist reminded the Judge that he had not answered directly when asked if he thought Cullen was guilty.

"Knowing whether Cullen is innocent or guilty," the Judge said, "would only resolve another murder case. The thing that matters, son, is the integrity of the law, the conduct of the process. That's what *matters*! Disraeli defined justice as truth in action. And I'm still trying to locate the truth in action during that *circus maximus* out in Amarillo."

·8·

THE LULL BETWEEN

During the weeks following the trial *Star-Telegram* readers in Fort Worth waited anxiously for each edition as it came off the press with the details of Cullen's acquittal.

Racehorse Haynes was advised of Priscilla's statement that God couldn't be bought. "If God finds out that Priscilla is even remotely interested in Him," Haynes retorted. "He will strike her down in a minute."

Other defense attorneys commented. Hugh Russell, who had so expertly managed the investigation which preceded jury selection, said, "If Cullen was a poor man, he would have been convicted." Mike Gibson made a statement inferring that Judge Dowlen had sympathized with Haynes: "I think Cave [who had presided over the aborted Fort Worth trial] had his fill of ol' Haynes, where Dowlen never got enough of Haynes." Steve Sumner was candid: "A lot of people may have seen this as a chance to get back at [Priscilla]. And to be honest we exploited that." Sumner also expressed his concern about Cullen's future safety. "There are so many nuts," he said, "it wouldn't surprise me one bit if there are attempts on his life."

District Attorney Tim Curry and his assistant Joe Shannon reiterated their belief that the trial had placed in judgment Priscilla's morals and the Fort Worth drug culture, and not the issue of the death of Andrea Wilborn. Both said they could understand, however, why the jury might have been reluctant to find Cullen guilty beyond a reasonable doubt. Tolly Wilson made a statement to a reporter about the wig cast aside by the murderer which conjured up speculation about a kinky side of Cullen's background. "I think if we went into other times he's worn women's wigs," Wilson said, "it would make very interesting testimony."

Judge Cave refused to comment, adding, "I'm a judge." Judge Matthews, who had stirred a controversy by releasing Cullen on only $80,000 bond after his arrest, felt vindicated: "I knew from the beginning he was just not guilty."

The majority of Fort Worth policemen polled on the Amarillo acquittal disagreed with it, believing Cullen culpable.

When a reporter approached Stan Farr's mother to tell her of the verdict she burst into tears and couldn't make a coherent statement. Gus Gavrel's parents, at their leather-cleaning business on Camp Bowie Boulevard, would not comment. Andrea's father was bitter. "I just want the world to know what a heartless, cruel person he is...." Wilborn expressed his fear that Cullen would "run around loose."

Cullen told Glen Guzzo, who was again the conduit for a startling statement, that he "probably" knew the killer's name, but would not reveal that identity to anyone.

Within a matter of days after the trial, the *Star-Telegram* conducted a telephone poll asking readers whether they believed the jury in Amarillo had been right or wrong. The special phone lines burned with two thousand calls in the first five hours. Fourteen hundred forty-eight citizens agreed with the Amarillo jury; about five hundred believed they had been wrong. The three-to-one majority opinion among callers persisted until the poll closed after six thousand votes. Some citizens berated the newspaper, saying the poll was shabby journalism. One of them was a Fort Worth woman named Oswald, who complained: "I question the right of the *Star-Telegram* in requiring the public's opinion, since a verdict was reached according to our Constitution by a...jury. I consider again the exploitation of another human being's rights. Cullen Davis had a trial. Why continue

117

the exploitation?'' Ms. Oswald's son, Lee Harvey, had grown up in Fort Worth.

Following the Amarillo trial there was a meeting of the Texas State Commission on Judicial Conduct in Austin. Judge Dowlen was not subpoenaed, but he was "invited" to come down to the capital. The commission wanted to ask the judge some questions in response, it was said, to pressure from a number of Texas attorneys who evaluated Dowlen's performance and found it to be low on the scale on which justice is expected to be weighed.

Judge Dowlen was candid. "I made a mistake," he told the commission, "by even being with that group for one minute." He was referring to the festive crowd at Rhett Butler's which had celebrated Cullen's acquittal. The commission concluded that no sanctions were in order as it appeared that Dowlen just happened to be in the building. "The party following the trial was regrettable," the commission reported, "but it appeared to the commission that the judge was a victim of circumstance."

Media accounts of the party, the commission added, were exaggerated and, a committee spokesman pointed out, Judge Dowlen paid his own expenses for his travel to Austin from Amarillo.

The Potter County sheriff was temporarily suspended from office and a petition filed to remove him permanently for "gross ignorance of his official duties" in permitting Cullen to roam about the premises during the trial and for providing liquor to the sequestered jurors. When Tarrant County received the Potter County bill for the whiskey, payment was refused.

Glen Guzzo anticipated the end of his coverage of the murder mansion trial and his five long months in Amarillo.* But there was a final chore. He interviewed a number of new sources about the trial and most of the jurors who had made the decision

---

* Guzzo's *Star-Telegram* colleague in Amarillo, Evan Moore, retired from journalism two weeks before the trial ended to become a cowboy in Happy, Texas.

in Amarillo. His report was a twelve-page special supplement in the *Star-Telegram*.

Guzzo wrote that the jury had decided (a) that the murderer might well have been intending to kill Stan Farr, (b) that Priscilla was a slut whose testimony was dubious, and (c) that there were discrepancies in testimony about vehicular traffic around the mansion on the night of the murder...all of which created doubts in the minds of the jurors.

If the killer had gone to the mansion to kill Farr, he could have been Cullen—or W. T. Rufner—or the deceased Horace Copeland.

Most jurors believed that Gus Gavrel told the truth about the events of the night of August 2; they did, however, feel that he was not truthful when he said he had recognized Cullen, and had not been in possession of marijuana.

The jurors did believe Beverly Bass. Contrary to the expectations of the defense and the fears of the prosecution, the jury did not seriously entertain Arthur Ulewayne Polk's wild story. They simply could not put credence in his assertions that he concealed his information for so long. It hardly mattered, the jurors later said, for the majority of them had made up their minds before Polk went into the witness chair.

What *did* affect the jury's conclusion that Cullen was not guilty—they did not, they repeated afterward, say he was innocent—had to do with the movement of automobiles onto and around the mansion grounds on the night of the murders.

The prosecutors had presented evidence that Cullen had driven his Cadillac to the downtown parking lot used by Mid-Continent, switched to a pickup truck, and driven away in it, to return sometime after 11 P.M. to recover the Cadillac. Believing this to be indisputable, the prosecutors did not make any special effort to explain why witnesses might have mentioned other vehicles. Two witnesses, who had no reason to be biased, mentioned that "late model" automobiles had been spotted on the

119

grounds before the murders. The jury found this nocturnal traffic on the drive up from Mockingbird Lane to be confusing, and it suggested the possibility that someone driving something other than a truck might have been the killer. The jurors never learned that shortcut traffic across the 140 acres of the grounds was not unusual. At that time the main gate near the Colonial Country Club was seldom closed, despite a sign which read: "Private Property—Do Not Enter." It was the habit of some who lived in the neighborhood to go through the Mockingbird Lane gate and take a second road across the grounds to another gate on Hulen Avenue, a wide thoroughfare which bordered the grounds on the west. The shortcut saved several minutes for those who knew about it.

On their first ballot the jurors had voted ten for acquittal and two for guilty. The two who initially branded Cullen guilty were highly regarded by their fellow jurors. The first was a quiet, Bible-reading postman, who had been elected foreman. The second was an FAA radar technician, the only other member of the jury to have been nominated as foreman. The postman and the radar man changed their votes in deference to the will of the majority.

One juror told Guzzo why he voted for Cullen's freedom. "I figured he was no angel if he was tied up with Priscilla. I'm sure that at one time or the other he didn't have the best morals in the world. But I don't judge a man on that account—until you get to the level of Priscilla. The way she lived, that don't cut it. I get down on liars and dopers. You can't trust many dopers."

Glen Guzzo's analysis of the Amarillo trial contained a prediction which was prophetic to a degree the reporter could not have imagined at the time he wrote it: "The mystery will extend to future episodes...."

Cullen and Karen returned to Fort Worth after the round of victory parties in Amarillo. Cullen drove directly from the airport to his office and, later, to a welcome-home gathering of his acquaintances. The guests pumped his hand and slapped his back. He was received as a conquering hero or a famous movie star. "It was chilling," one observer said. "Some of those people thought Cullen was guilty as hell, but that didn't keep them from shaking his hand and telling him what a great guy he was."

The chairman of the board and the president of the Fort Worth National Bank sent Cullen a huge floral arrangement with the salutation "Hooray!" The bankers had reason to cheer: the interest on Cullen's extensive loans at the bank could more conveniently be paid from Cullen's office than from the prison in Huntsville.

Cullen and Karen flew to Aspen for a skiing vacation. Cullen had made the reservations for the holiday season months before.

When they returned to Fort Worth they were confronted with another legal squabble, which also was to be adjudicated by Judge Joe Eidson. Karen's former husband, Walter Master, had been granted temporary custody of their two boys while she and Cullen were on the Colorado ski slopes. The question of which parent should have permanent custody was unresolved. Now Walter Master wanted custody because of Karen's "adulteress relationship" with Cullen. In the court papers filed by Master he accused Karen of neglecting the children, leaving them with baby sitters while she enjoyed the good life with Cullen. He asked for custody and support payments.

"Unfortunately neither party has shown what I would believe to be desirable qualities on the parts of parents," Judge Eidson said, but he awarded custody to Karen.

A number of people in Fort Worth commented on the demure ladylike impression Karen Master had left on jurors during her Amarillo testimony and the sedate role she had assumed in Fort Worth after the trial. Now she was active in good works and dressed attractively but conservatively. Some remembered an August 1975 item in the *Star-Telegram* about Cullen's inviting friends to an "electronically equipped" van where a "sports film" was shown as entertainment. The star of that film had been Linda Lovelace, and Karen had been one of the viewers. A photograph taken about that time revealed a Karen who resembled Priscilla, with long blonde hair and a tight sweater.

Then, in 1976, just before the murders on Mockingbird Lane, Karen had accompanied Cullen to a class reunion of Arlington Heights High School, and Karen had worn a white gown with a plunging neckline.

One observer drew an analogy between Karen and Priscilla. "Both were high school dropouts, both were blondes, both products of surgical sculptings, both friendly while suspicious, both knew how to get into it with a guy who has millions—and both, I'm sure, can be extraordinarily mean if necessary."

Cullen and Karen sent a Christmas greeting to their friends, a long poem written for them by a friend, Cathie Carroll. The blue foldout card was decorated with a dozen family and religious sketches. It was signed by Cullen, Karen, and the two sons of each. Cullen, Jr., and Brian Davis, and Trey and Chesley Master.

The long poem was entitled "Something Special." The first seven stanzas read:

> We started to send out "pre-made" cards
> With a verse whose meaning stood so tall.
> But the card, we quickly realized,
> Just couldn't really say it all.
>
> "When we count our blessings at Christmastime,
> We think of friends like you."
> It's lovely, yes; and yet *this* year
> It's not enough—it just won't do!
>
> And since we have a "private poet"—
> A friend to whom a "gift" was given,
> We humbly bare our hearts to her,
> And, this "Something Special" has been written:
>
> It's been a nightmare—*all* of it.
> So many problems, toils and cares—
> And now we're facing Christmastime
> With a load we feel too great to bear.

Some 16 months ago a friend,
Whom we'd seen little thru the years,
Told us to read Psalms 56—
Assured us we were in her prayers.

So many times we've marvelled at
The trust that David had in God.
We've seen ourselves in his same shoes:
Yet sleeplessness and fear withstood.

We've cried 'til we could cry no more—
God promised He would save each tear.
Our enemies have seemed so great—
Yet they've been made the truth to hear.

There were twelve more stanzas.

The Fort Worth *Social Directory* had gone to press during the Amarillo trial; when it appeared, Cullen's name had been dropped from the exclusive list, presumably because the editors feared listing a convicted felon in the sacrosanct pages.

Cullen returned to his work at Mid-Continent and, to a limited degree, to Fort Worth social circles. There was a photograph in the *Star-Telegram* of Cullen and Karen at the home of Charles and Anne Tandy shortly after the Amarillo trial, but that inclusion was misleading. The reception was to thank those who had contributed to a local charity, and the act of giving had entitled Cullen to a ticket for the party.

There was another photograph of Cullen and Karen at the Tandys' in May 1978, and that was meaningful. It was Charles Tandy's birthday party, and the invitation had been personal, which meant that Cullen had his foot back in society's door, that he and Karen were once again acceptable. It was predicted that Cullen's name would reappear in the *Social Directory*. Tandy was one of the richest men in Texas. In diversifying his family's leather business, Tandy had acquired nine electronic supply shops in Boston in 1963 which he expanded into a chain of 6500 domestic Radio Shack stores and 480 outlets overseas. Tandy was reputed to be worth hundreds of millions of dollars by 1978, and his $850,000 salary made him the highest paid executive in

Texas. His wife Anne was from one of Fort Worth's oldest families and extremely wealthy in her own right.

So, along with watching tv, going to the movies, and shooting some pool, Cullen was occasionally seen in Fort Worth's restaurants and bistros. Karen was usually with him. They were an attractive couple. "What a sweet smile," one woman said to another after meeting Cullen. And even the most discriminating had to admit that Karen was dressed fashionably. Karen persuaded her friend to write another poem for her, this time dedicated to Cullen:

> That crisp October day we met
> I knew you'd be a special man.
> I guess because I'd waited
> For a lifetime to hold your hand.

Perhaps Karen's ghost-laureate lacked the essential elements of greatness as a poet. Cullen himself had not been known for literary talent, and there was little indication that his repartee was scintillating as he reentered society. A columnist in the *Star-Telegram* reported that Cullen was introduced to a young lady at a private party shortly after his acquittal. Someone said to the woman, "I want you to meet Cullen Davis."

"My God," exclaimed the woman, raising the back of her hand to her brow, "what do you say to Cullen Davis?"

"You could start," Cullen said, "by saying hello."

Cullen reiterated his previous declaration that he considered the mansion on Mockingbird Lane *his* property and that he intended to marry Karen and to move into the big house. Asked about Priscilla, Cullen snapped, "She's a guest." And he would remind the listener of the prenuptial agreement Priscilla had signed.

Judge Eidson had ruled that Cullen was not to trespass on mansion property, but did permit him one visit to inspect the house and its furnishings in the company of his lawyers. According to one story, Cullen opened the downstairs safe to inventory the contents. There were only two items in the vault. Two photographs, two faces staring out of the safe at Cullen: Andrea and Stan Farr.

Priscilla had become a semirecluse in the mansion. Guards kept watch around the clock, and she seldom ventured out except for visits to her lawyers or to the beauty parlor at Neiman-Marcus. Dee and Beverly Bass were off at Texas Tech University, and Priscilla's most constant companion was a man named Rich Sauer, a real estate salesman, who had been Stan Farr's best friend. Priscilla did frequently entertain visitors, and they returned to the mundane world to relate stories of life inside the mansion.

One visitor had asked Priscilla about the Fort Worth perception of her as a usually underdressed and overexposed hussy who shocked society. Hadn't the *Star-Telegram* photographer fixed her public image for all time with his picture of her with Stan Farr at the Colonial National Invitational Tournament in 1975? "There are about sixteen trillion younger, prettier girls than me," Priscilla said. "But I'm the only one anybody remembers wearing a croptop. I don't see what I did that so many other girls didn't do." Priscilla conceded that her attire had often been flamboyant. "It got to be a game," she said. "I never thought people would hate me for it."

A journalist from the Houston *Post* interviewed Priscilla in the mansion. Standing at the side of the indoor swimming pool Priscilla mentioned that she seldom used the pool. "Bleach blondes and chlorine don't mix," she explained. There was another room in the mansion that Priscilla did not often utilize: the game room, with an electronic football game, a bean-bag chair in the shape of a fielder's glove, and Cullen's three pool tables.

In the main hall the renowned chess set rested under the painting of Cullen and Priscilla. Not far from the winding, polished stairway was Cullen's library. On a desk was a mounted drawing of a noose, and under it an inscription:

Depend on it, Sir, when a man knows he is to be
Hanged in a fortnight, it concentrates his
Mind wonderfully.
                              SAMUEL JOHNSON, 1709–1784

Downstairs Priscilla preferred the brightly decorated kitchen,
and upstairs her bedroom and dressing quarters. The bedroom
was populated with stuffed animals, and the dressing room and
bath were gardens of potted plants. (Priscilla had finally paid
Arthur Ulewayne Polk for his plants, despite the fact that she
believed the nurseryman had overcharged her atrociously.) In
the bathroom a glistening chandelier hung over the whirlpool,
sunken marble tub. There was a bidet, uncommon in Fort
Worth.

In the bedroom there was a fireplace and a deep white carpet.
The cover on the motor-adjustable oversized bed was, it was
revealed, silver fox. The oversized video screen above the three-
machine television console loomed over the bed. There were
photographs of Stan Farr and, on a table, a copy of Rod
McKuen's *The Gentle Giant.* In a vast, mirrored closet were two
of Stan's giant-sized suits, a pair of his jeans, and his extra-
length golf clubs. Also in the closet was Andrea's suitcase, still
unpacked from the night she returned to the mansion from the
Bible school in Houston.

Because Priscilla grew up in Houston, she was asked about
her youth. She had lived with her two brothers in the Galena
Park area of Houston in a modest, green, ranch-style house on
Benson Street. Priscilla's father had been a geologist and rodeo
rider, and he had a fire in his heel. "He just kind of wandered
off...." Priscilla's mother had been, perhaps, overprotective,
but she saw to it that the children were introduced to dance and
music. Priscilla took ballet lessons and was disappointed when
she failed to make the grade as a cheerleader. Her body
burgeoned and boys ogled her; her schoolbook photographs
show her as a handsome girl with black hair. Priscilla dropped
out of the eleventh grade. At sixteen she married Jasper Baker,

an ex-marine. He threw his hat in the door a few times during the two years the marriage lasted. After it dissolved, Priscilla worked in the service department of Montgomery Ward's store. Then, "I went to lunch one day and never returned." When she was eighteen she married Jack Wilborn, age forty, a visiting used-car salesman, who introduced Priscilla to a more affluent life in Fort Worth. One day she was playing tennis at Ridgelea Country Club, and Cullen and his then wife Sandra were playing nearby. Cullen and Sandra were arguing. Priscilla and her partner challenged the feuding couple to a game of doubles. Afterwards, Priscilla and Cullen met secretly and became lovers. The day after they returned from a clandestine New Year's trip to Acapulco, they shared a room at the Green Oaks Inn. Jack Wilborn and Sandra Davis and private detectives stormed into the room to photograph Cullen and Priscilla together. The two divorces followed, and Cullen and Priscilla married the day Stinky died.

One prominent Fort Worth woman said she wasn't sure whether or not Cullen was guilty, but as for Priscilla, "Well, anyway, she deserved it." A few staunch friends stood by Priscilla in the aftermath of the Amarillo trial when two out of three persons in Fort Worth believed that Cullen was innocent of the charges for which he had been tried. Judy McCrory, soon to remarry after her divorce from Charles David McCrory, was steadfast. Others came to the mansion for long evenings of watching tv on the big screen. Some of them were roughnecks befriended by Priscilla before the Amarillo trial.

Another Fort Worth woman became a friend of Priscilla. She hadn't known Cullen: "I wouldn't know Cullen if he kissed me." She found life in the mansion to be much more placid than she had expected. After all those rumors about wild parties she was prepared to witness some sybaritic residue of frolic in the huge house. But, she said, "The only thing I ever saw on the big television screen was 'Roots,'" and all the camera and recording equipment wasn't even working. Priscilla was usually dressed in jeans and a Mexican shirt, and she drank Kool-Aid more often than beer or wine. Sometimes Priscilla wore her hair in braids, knotted with tiny pink bows, and her only jewelry was the massive diamond ring given to her by Cullen.

What about Cullen, Priscilla was asked. Do you sometimes feel like you'd like to kill him?

"Sure," Priscilla responded. "I'd like to put a gun to his head and ask, just before I pulled the trigger, '*Why*?'"

"What about the rumors about you? What about all the guys who tell everyone in town they've screwed you?"

"I'd like to get them on the stand," Priscilla retorted dryly.

Priscilla was justified in perceiving the rumors as unfair and one-sided. Since the beginning the newspapers had referred to Stan Farr as Priscilla's lover. Never did they describe Karen Master as Cullen's lover. And an ugly rumor about Priscilla's having been a call girl continued to float, despite the lack of evidence. An even uglier rumor that Dee had been Old Stinky's child persisted, again without basis. There were never any rumors that *Karen* might be Stinky's child—even after it was reported in the *Star-Telegram* that Karen's mother had been an employee of Stinky's at Mid-Continent when she was pregnant with Karen.

No one had ever denied that Priscilla was a voluptuous woman. Priscilla was still proud of her body. Once when a woman visiting the mansion speculated that her figure must have been sculpted by Dr. Valentin Gracia, the plastic surgeon, Priscilla protested. The mini-facelift, the improved nose, and the implants in her breasts, yes, but no tummy or bottom lifts. Priscilla stripped in her hot pink bathroom to prove her point, challenging the guest to inspect her body for scars.

Even so, Priscilla's facial beauty was fading. She had remained serenely beautiful, if pale and drawn, when she testified from her wheelchair. But the effects of her wounds and the recurring complications from the breast surgery and from a duodenal ulcer began to take their toll. She increased the patina of makeup to cover the lines. One unkind man was quoted in a Texas magazine as saying that "Priscilla had the look of a woman who has spent too much time in bowling alleys."

In addition to beauty, Priscilla lost another prized possession. In one of the rare excursions she made outside the mansion she went to a party at a friend's home. Her "Rich Bitch" pendant of gold and diamonds was in her purse, and someone stole the necklace and her credit cards during the party.

John Makeig, a young *Star-Telegram* courthouse writer, was one of the reporters who covered the murders on Mockingbird Lane in 1976. Later, Makeig reviewed all of Fort Worth's murder cases for that year.

Makeig wrote, "1976, as one detective jokingly puts it, was a 'vinage year' in Fort Worth for murder.

"The year's crop began at 1:45 A.M., Jan. 1, with a knifing at a bar during a squabble over a woman and it ended at 4:45 A.M., Dec. 31 with a stabbing murder during a drunken argument over a girl's old handwritten poetry.

"It included the notorious Cullen Davis mansion murders, the accidental shooting of a woman at her 'going-away' party, and a vicious kidnapping-killing that landed two heroin addicts on Death Row.

"A *Star-Telegram* analysis of homicide and court records for 1976 . . . shows that 65 people died here of shootings, stabbings, and beatings.

"It shows that the police responded to the 65 killings by 'arresting' 66 persons and 'clearing' 96 percent of the year's homicides.

"And it shows that 20 of the 66 persons were sentenced to serve time in prison, mostly for terms of 5, 10, and 15 years.

"Of the 20, two got death sentences and only five got prison sentences of 25 years or more. . . .

"To get a fuller perspective on who commits murders here and how they are handled by the courts, one must look into specific cases.

"For example:

"——Clifford Chance Rubell, 30, had been harassing a 28-year-old woman for four years. A month before his Nov. 4, 1976, death, she had shot him in the shoulder as he was using a plank to cave in her front door. A half-hour before he died, he called her from a bar to say Nov. 4 would be her last day."

"Consequently, she got her .22 pistol and shot him through a screen door as he arrived.

"The result: Grand jurors no-billed [decided there was no case] her 14 days later.

"——Harlin Glen Mayes, 28, had what turned out to be a fatal habit of becoming obscene and belligerent when drinking. On the night of Oct. 1, 1976, he made the error of becoming drunkenly obnoxious in the home of a 50-year-old welder named Lee Roy Howard, who got into a fight with Mayes and stabbed Mayes six times with a handy ice pick.

"'He kept shouting all kinds of nasty stuff...in front of my wife,' Howard told police. 'I told him to cool off and go to bed.'

"The result: Howard pleaded guilty to voluntary manslaughter and was placed on probation for 10 years.

"——Sammy Lee Chopp, Jr., 25, got into a bad argument March 28, 1976, with his common-law wife, Billie Ruth Johnson, 24. She was mad because he'd been staying out late drinking. A furor developed and she shot him with a .22 pistol. A police report says after shooting him once, she stood over the body and shot him again.

"The outcome: She was charged with murder but pleaded guilty to voluntary manslaughter and was given a nine-year prison sentence.

"——John Petty, 74, was getting a divorce from his wife, Ruth Petty, 54, on Sept. 27 when they got into an argument....A police report says he shot the woman, who was

Cullen Davis, 1950, when he was a student at Arlington Heights High School in Fort Worth. (Two Texas writers graduated from this school: David Atlee Phillips and Thomas Thompson, author of *Blood and Money*.)

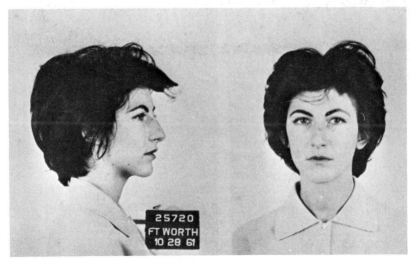

25720
FT WORTH
10 28 61

Mug shot of Priscilla Lee Childers Wilborn Davis when she was booked for shoplifting by Fort Worth police in 1961.

The Davis mansion at 4200 Mockingbird Lane, and a partial view of its grounds, where two people were killed and two wounded on August 2, 1976. *(Fort Worth Star-Telegram.* Photo by Ron Heflin)

Cullen and Priscilla.

Cullen and Priscilla making an entrance to a society gala in Fort Worth. *(Fort Worth Star-Telegram.* Photo by Tony Record)

Priscilla and Stan Farr, the six-foot-nine-inch ex-TCU basketball player, at the Colonial Golf Club Invitational Tournament, 1975. On the night of August 2, 1976, Farr was killed by a man dressed in black and wearing a woman's wig. *(Fort Worth Star-Telegram.* Photo by Gene Gordon)

Karen Master, leaving the Tarrant County Court House after the hearing which awarded Ms. Master custody of her children. (Photo by Gene Gordon)

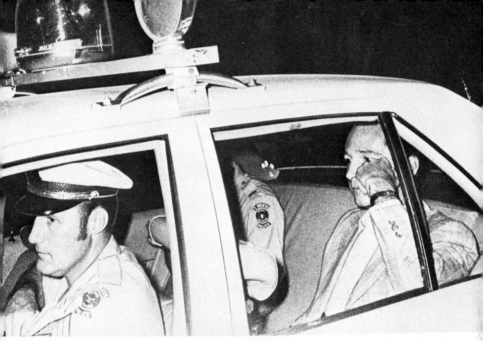

The morning after the murders at Mockingbird Lane Cullen Davis was arrested and whisked off to the Tarrant County Jail. *(Fort Worth Star-Telegram.* Photo by Gene Gordon)

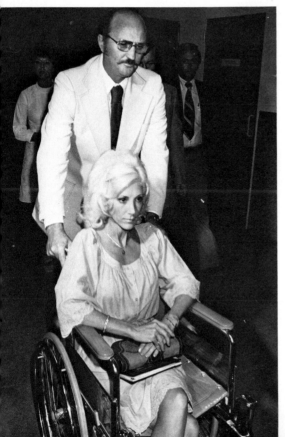

Priscilla, after recovering from the shot which went through her chest, appeared in a wheelchair to testify before the grand jury which indicted her husband, Cullen Davis, for capital murder. *(Fort Worth Star-Telegram.* Photo by Ron Heflin)

Priscilla rarely ventured outside of the Davis mansion after the trial in Amarillo. *(Fort Worth Star-Telegram.* Photo by Al Panzera)

Karen Master. At the time of the murders, Cullen Davis was living with Ms. Master and her two sons. *(Fort Worth Star-Telegram.* Photo by David Breslauer)

Cullen and Karen celebrate Cullen's acquittal after the longest murder trial in Texas history. Richard "Racehorse" Haynes, Cullen's lawyer, is in the background. (AP, Wide World Photos)

Following the Amarillo trial, Cullen and Karen rejoined Fort Worth society. In May 1978 they attended a party given by Charles Tandy, the owner of Radio Shacks and one of the wealthiest men in Texas. *(Fort Worth Star-Telegram.* Photo by Willis Knight)

A drawing which hangs on the wall of the Master residence: Cullen, Karen, his
two sons, her two sons, and family members. (David Breslauer)

Priscilla in the mansion after the Amarillo trial. The boy on the left is her son Jack Wilborn, Jr. The girl in the pictures, center and left, is Andrea Wilborn, the twelve-year-old who was murdered in the mansion on August 2, 1976. *(Fort Worth Star-Telegram.* Photo by Al Panzera)

From a nearby van the FBI photographed Cullen Davis as he met with Charles McCrory, who had promised to arrange the death of Judge Eidson and "a bunch of people."

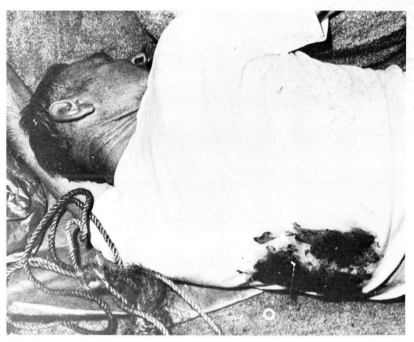

FBI photograph of Fort Worth Judge Joe Eidson, who presided over the divorce between Cullen and Priscilla for almost four years. Fort Worth law officials persuaded the judge to play dead in the trunk of his automobile. The "blood" is catsup.

Richard "Racehorse" Haynes in his Houston office at the time Cullen's second trial began in Houston. *(Fort Worth Star-Telegram.* Photo by Gene Gordon)

Witnesses in the Houston trial: 1. W. T. Rufner after being removed from the courtroom for using profanity in answering questions by the chief defense lawyer. (AP, Wide World Photos) 2. David McCrory. *(Fort Worth Star-Telegram.* Photo by Ron Heflin) 3. Pat Burleson. *(Fort Worth Star-Telegram.* Photo by Ron Heflin)

1

2

3

After FBI informant McCrory testified that William Davis was on Cullen's list of victims, William began to erect a fence around the Rivercrest mansion where Cullen grew up and where William now lives. Shown is the gate of the still-unfinished fence.

on crutches, with a .22 pistol. When officers arrived at the scene, the report says, Petty walked up and announced: 'I shot my wife.'

"The result: Petty pleaded guilty to a reduced charge of voluntary manslaughter and was placed on probation for 10 years.

"——Joe Green Carter was very drunk—triple the Texas standard for intoxication—on the night of Sept. 24 when he went to the Jack-in-the-Box on West Berry. He was drinking in the parking lot and became irate with a security guard. Air Force S. Sgt. Leslie Lee Brice, 28, told him to stop acting outrageously. He began taunting Brice, who was armed and frightened. Finally, to protect himself, Brice drew his pistol.

"'Joe, I've known you for a long time,' Brice told him. 'I don't want you to do this. Back off.'

"'Shoot me,' Carter said, charging forward and getting killed.

"The outcome: Brice...stood trial for murder and was found not guilty....

"——Felix Alexander Ramirez, 26, had just returned to Fort Worth from Mexico with $2000 worth of illegal pills and been selling them on the South Side. On Jan. 3, according to one version of his death, Ramirez was murdered in the Enchanted Flame Club on Evans Avenue when he tried to stop a fight between two other people. Another version had it that someone was irate because he was dealing bad-quality dope. Whatever, he was shot to death.

"The police quickly rounded up a handful of suspects, including one man who had just finished serving two years of a five-year sentence for murder, but never got enough evidence to charge anyone.

"The result: It was only one of three similar crimes that went unsolved in 1976.

"——Jerry Ray Renfro, 29, was a door-to-door salesman who stopped at a truck stop on NE 28th on July 20. While there, he met some attractive women who offered him a chance at cheap sex. He left with an ex-convict named Betty Haire and she took him to an apartment in the Riverside Village apartment complex. When they finished a sex act Dwight Lamar Sanders, 21, entered and a short while later Renfro died of stab wounds.

"The police finally arrested Ms. Haire and Sanders for the brutal killing and, typically, they blamed each other for what had happened.

"The outcome: Betty Haire agreed to testify against Sanders and murder charges against her were dropped. Sanders pleaded guilty to murder and was given a 50-year sentence—the fourth highest sentence handed down for a 1976 murder.

"——Willie McCullough, Jr., 48, was at the Happy City Bar on Aug. 14, 1976, drinking and flashing money around, attracting attention. Three young women, acting at the behest of a 29-year-old convicted thief, decided to relieve McCullough of his money by promises of sex or whatever was necessary. So they lured him out to a vacant lot where the thief shot McCullough in the head.

"The outcome: The thief was identified and arrested, but charges ultimately were dismissed by prosecutors, who said they had only 'accomplice testimony' to use in court. . . .

"Other homicides included several killings that grew out of child custody and visitation rights fusses, a homosexual murder, the killing of a 16-year-old who kept going into a woman's apartment and trying on her underwear, and a man who earned the Carnegie Hero Fund Medal for dying while preventing the murder of a man he liked.

"But mostly, the 65 deaths become a gray blur of feuding relatives and hostile neighbors, bad drunks and men who went around picking fights, naive children playing with shotguns and young thugs looking for older people to 'roll.'

"And in all but a few cases, it could be argued that the victims provoked the disputes which led to their deaths.

"It is certain, however, that 52 of the 65 murders were committed with pistols. (Six others were done with knives, one with an ice pick, and three with shotguns; three people were also beaten to death.)''

Makeig added to his survey, ''Only two defendants were acquitted of murder charges—Brice for killing Joe Green Carter and Cullen Davis for the alleged murder of 12-year-old Andrea Wilborn....''

Five months after the Amarillo trial, in the spring of 1978, Tim Curry had said nothing for the record about the status of the remaining three indictments against Cullen: Farr's murder and the woundings of Priscilla and Gus Gavrel. It was not an easy decision for Curry. Even his own staff in the district attorney's office had conflicting opinions as to whether Cullen should be tried for the three offenses. One prosecutor said, colorfully mixing his metaphors, ''If Davis is guilty, he should be punished for it. But something went wrong with the system in Amarillo, and if that system doesn't work and if the state has fired its best shot and missed, then I think they ought to throw in the towel.'' A Fort Worth judge not involved in the case said, ''Just as a practical matter, it's a dead horse. But I'm glad I don't have to make the decision.''

In addition to the upcoming divorce case, Cullen's trial docket was loaded with another tribulation: Priscilla's attorneys filed two additional civil suits charging Cullen with the murder of Andrea and Priscilla's own wounding. Priscilla asked for ''far in excess of $10,000'' in each suit.

By midsummer of 1978, Jack Wilborn had been besieged by three heart attacks and undergone open-heart surgery. Beverly Bass, age twenty, complained she was depressed and felt forty. Gus Gavrel, on crutches, was despondent because of the slow progress of recovery from the bullet the doctors had elected to let remain in his spine. He said he sometimes went to a ball game, but usually just sat around the house. The divorce proceedings were in their fourth year. Judge Eidson established a new trial date for mid-August. Karen Master, anticipating that event, had something to say about Priscilla: "Everybody we know expects her to come up with more of her deviousness and lies. But I don't think a jury here is going to believe her any more than the jury in Amarillo did."

In early August, Priscilla's lawyers, in a formal hearing, confronted Cullen with approximately 2000 questions they needed answered in order to prepare for the divorce trial. Cullen's legal team—Racehorse Haynes was still in command—presented a 251-page deposition to Judge Eidson, who allowed Priscilla's lawyers to question Cullen. Finally, the remote, inscrutable multimillionaire was on the stand. Although Cullen refused to say anything about his activities on the night of August 2, 1976, he did provide information about his personal and corporate wealth.

Cullen was asked about total sales for KenDavis Industries during 1977. "One billion, twenty-nine million dollars, plus change" was the response. During the ten-year period after Cullen and his brothers had inherited the family enterprise, the net income after taxes had been something between $175 million and $200 million. Profits in 1976 had been good: $60 million after taxes. Earnings declined in 1977 to $38 million. (Priscilla's lawyers were suspicious. Were Cullen and Ken draining profits to reduce the amount of settlement money available to Priscilla?) Prospects were brighter for 1978; in the first six months of the year profits had been $25 million. Now there were 101 companies and subsidiaries in, or affiliated with, Kiii.

Stinky's boys had watched and nurtured the financial eggs in the Davis family basket. Since Stinky's death KenDavis Industries' assets had grown by $652 million to a current value of $800 million.

How much of that did Cullen own, personally? The tycoon couldn't be precise, but did say he held 47.5 percent of the Mid-Continent stock, and sizeable blocks of Great Western Drilling and the other major corporations.

The subject turned to Cullen's relations with Priscilla. What did he have to say about her allegations that he had physically abused her?

It was true, Cullen replied, that ". . . he had struck Priscilla on possibly three occasions."

"Did you once break her collarbone?"

"I don't know whether I did or not," Cullen said. "She says I did and maybe I did. But I don't know whether I did or not."

Cullen acknowledged the incident in California in 1974 about which Priscilla had testified. He said he "threw her down on the bed and she fell on the floor." Another time, he added, in the mansion's pool room, "I put her down on the floor and twisted her arm until she told me what I wanted to know."

Concerning his stepdaughter Dee, Cullen said he had occasionally found it necessary to administer discipline. In the early '70s he had used "either a board or a belt" on Dee's bare bottom. Was she rather severely beaten? "On the rear end, yes," Cullen said, adding that no medical attention had been necessary. He confirmed he had slapped Dee in the Rivercrest house and, then, killed a kitten. He denied ever striking the younger Andrea and could not remember if he had spanked her.

Yes, Cullen said, he had invited friends to see *Deep Throat* in his van during a golf tournament.

He was asked about any sexual relations with women other than Priscilla during the 1968–1978 decade. Cullen responded, "I think they all came after the separation." He harked back to the days before his marriage to Priscilla and confirmed that someone had broken into a motel room they shared and attempted to photograph them.

Cullen testified that he had never smoked marijuana nor snorted cocaine and had attended only one party where other guests had, and that was limited to marijuana.

Cullen's medical record was unveiled. He had undergone major surgery for a spinal fusion, an operation which often alleviates a disc problem in the lower back; he had also had a

135

hernia operation and a vasectomy. There had also been cosmetic eye surgery.

While the *Star-Telegram* had reported that Cullen stayed at the Schick Hospital, which specializes in psychiatric treatment, after the murders at the mansion, it had not previously been known that Cullen had consulted other therapists. Cullen testified that he had visited Fort Worth psychiatrist Blaine McLaughlin on "one or more" occasions.

"What was the nature of your visit?"

"I'll be darned if I know," Cullen responded.

Cullen toted up his financial expenses since he had moved into Karen Master's home three years previously. He had paid all household bills and doled out $3000 to $5000 a month in allowance to Karen. He had bestowed a number of gifts on her including jewelry and fur coats, one a natural muskrat valued at between $5000 and $10,000. He had also given Karen a Cadillac and two dogs, and had paid medical bills for a porcelain cap for one of her teeth and for undisclosed cosmetic surgery.*

There had been wild speculation about the legal costs Cullen had incurred during his various trials and hearings. On this matter Racehorse Haynes refused to comment, but during the pretrial divorce hearings Cullen said the Houston lawyer's Amarillo fee had been a quarter of a million dollars. Phil Burleson, the Dallas attorney, had received $1.25 million, from which his firm paid other lawyers and investigators' expenses. Karen's father, Ray Hudson, had been paid $45,000 for the period he worked for Cullen in Amarillo, and Cullen still owed

---

* As the result of a 1971 automobile accident in which her two sons were severely injured Karen suffered head injuries and lacerations. This operation may have been in relation to those injuries. Purely cosmetic surgery, however, is common among those in Fort Worth who can afford it. Eye tucks, mini and major facelifts and breast enhancement can be obtained by consulting one of the fourteen plastic surgeons listed in the yellow pages of the Fort Worth telephone book. During medical testimony in Amarillo it was revealed that the bullet which passed between Priscilla's breasts was deflected in its trajectory. This stimulated speculation and amusing anecdotes to the effect that Priscilla's silicone implants saved her life. Professional pathological opinion, however, discounts this.

$300,000 to $400,000 in legal fees to his several attorneys. Cullen's total legal tab to date, he estimated, was about $2 million. Fort Worth had learned more about Cullen than was previously known when he was forced to answer questions candidly in Judge Eidson's court.

Little had been heard from William Davis, Cullen's younger brother, since the report that his suit against Cullen and Ken, Jr., had been settled out of court. Details of that transaction came to light in a sixty-page deposition and testimony by the youngest Davis at the hearings. William said that his position as a corporate equal to Cullen and Ken, Jr., in the Davis enterprises deteriorated long before the 1976 settlement. William had been stripped of his "directorships and officerships" at a meeting of the board of directors in 1971. William claimed he had been "squeezed out" of power.

"And how was that done, sir?" the question was read.

"I was voted off the board by the majority of the stockholders."

William referred to stockholders Cullen and Ken, Jr., who owned nearly two-thirds of the KenDavis Industries at that time. William had not voted as he was not present at the meeting of the board.

By the beginning of August 1978 it was generally believed that District Attorney Tim Curry was not contemplating further trials for Cullen based on the charges of killing Stan Farr and wounding Priscilla and Gus Gavrel. By Texas law he would have to pursue the charges if Cullen requested "a speedy trial," but Cullen did not exercise that option. And Judge Eidson had ruled that the events of the night of August 2, 1976, the night of the murders at the mansion, were not to be discussed during the divorce trial.

In any event, the divorce trial would begin on August 10, and it promised to be a great show. Anticipation of the exciting event enlivened the conversation at the late-summer cocktail parties and dinners in Rivercrest and Westover Hills, and in Ridgelea and the Tanglewood area near the Colonial Country Club. The impending trial even aroused almost as much speculation as the Dallas Cowboys' standing in the National Football League.

The lines had been drawn by the opposing forces. Cullen made public statements branding Priscilla an adulteress. Priscilla's lawyers and Racehorse Haynes and his stable of assistants were reaching the boiling point in their relations with each other, bickering and shouting during the pretrial encounters.

Cullen was a Davis and everybody knew Stinky's son wouldn't want to give up property. It was obvious that Cullen wanted his mansion. Priscilla, it was learned, was willing to let him have it, but on her terms. She wanted selected items among the furnishings. She wanted the white Lincoln Continental Mark IV with the red carpeting inside. She wanted all her personal effects, including Freedom, the white mare. She wanted six months to arrange her affairs before vacating the mansion.

And, she wanted $20 million. Cullen had offered $5000 a month for twenty years, a total of $1.2 million.

What happened next took everyone by surprise. Priscilla's lawyers wanted yet another postponement. During the pretrial hearings they had accumulated such a pile of documents about Cullen's financial status they needed time to study it. They wanted to ascertain if Cullen and Ken were concealing profits.

Judge Eidson granted the extension. The divorce trial scheduled for August 10 was rescheduled for September 18.

So, during the month of August 1978 there was not much going on in Fort Worth. The big event would be the preseason game at Texas Stadium when the Dallas Cowboys played the Houston Oilers on the third weekend of the month. Everybody would be out for the game, the more affluent fans in their "skyboxes." Most of the private observation lounges had two television sets—one to watch the instant replay of the game unfolding on the field, the other to keep abreast of games being played elsewhere. Cullen and Karen would be in Cullen's skybox, with its thick carpet, satin brocade walls, and mirrored ceiling and bar.

So the social persiflage was mostly football chatter, except for the exchange of gossip which hadn't really abated since the murders on Mockingbird Lane two years before. Juicy gossip about Stan Farr and Priscilla, and her new companion, Rich Sauer, circulated, as did rumors about Stinky, and about Karen and Cullen.

Star-Telegram reporter Glen Guzzo, after two years covering the Cullen Davis beat, was ill during the third weekend of August 1978. That Sunday while recuperating in his apartment he recalled a midnight conversation he had had two summers before with his boss, the managing editor of the morning edition. "Things are just too quiet for this town," the editor had commented. Then he made a prediction: "I have a feeling a big story is about to break—and I'll bet it will be on the police beat."

Guzzo's editor had been prescient in 1976. But now, two years later, it appeared the Cullen Davis story was fading away.

·9·

THE OLD JUDGE

The old Judge stood near his mailbox and read the letter he had just opened. It was from Maryland. The closing paragraphs read:

...and the publishers have decided that, on balance, they believe the book is not worth the candle. After so many months without any signal that Cullen will be prosecuted on the remaining murder indictments the story is losing some of its reader appeal. The divorce case and the various civil suits still pending will be of much interest in Fort Worth, but they will not catch national attention. Consequently, I am busy writing an espionage novel.

Thanks again for giving me so much time in our long discussions about Cullen's case....

The letter was signed by the journalist.

The Judge thrust the letter into his pocket. He turned to the dog sitting obediently at his feet.

"Come along, Oliver. I have a bone of immense proportions I've been saving for you."

·10·

THE WIRED CANARY

On Monday, following the third Sunday of August 1978 there were double-bannered headlines in the morning *Star-Telegram:*

CULLEN DAVIS BACK IN JAIL
PLOT TO KILL JUDGE CHARGED
Pistol, $25,000 seized in arrest

"Millionaire Cullen Davis was in Tarrant County jail without bond Sunday night, charged with soliciting the murder for hire of Tarrant County District Judge Joe H. Eidson, the judge presiding over the divorce case involving Davis and his estranged wife Priscilla.

"Davis—who last year was acquitted after the longest and one of the most spectacular murder trials in Texas history—was arrested Sunday after a police informant, wired for sound, showed Davis a counterfeit photo of Judge Eidson's 'body' stuffed into a car trunk, the Associated Press reported."

Eidson had posed for the photo at the request of police, the story continued.

"The AP said it had learned from sources that the informant also showed Davis the judge's driver's license before collecting an alleged payoff of $25,000 in $100 bills...."

The startling story went on to say, "In addition to the pistol and money, officers Sunday also found a 'hit list' of persons presumably to be murdered. Eidson headed the list, which included Priscilla Davis, Beverly Bass, Gus Gavrel, and District

Judge Tom Cave, who had refused to free Davis on bond after the shootings at the mansion....''

It had all begun when an informant had approached the Fort Worth FBI bureau on August 17, the previous Thursday. He told the federal agents that Cullen Davis had contacted him to arrange the murders of a bunch of people. The FBI wired the informant for sound and monitored a meeting that afternoon between him and Cullen. What the FBI men heard was enough for them and local authorities to plan a second encounter between the informant and Cullen. On Friday the informant was instructed to summon Cullen to a meeting at 9 A.M., Sunday, two days later.

A top secret post was manned at the federal courthouse by District Attorney Tim Curry, Fort Worth Police Chief A. J. Brown, and U.S. Attorney John Sweeney. That headquarters was to supervise the surveillance conducted by police officers, FBI agents, and Texas Rangers.

Two FBI agents taped a microphone about the size of a pencil eraser to the informant's left shoulder. A wire led from the microphone to a small gray recorder which the Bureau men taped to the informant's back. The FBI agents also stowed a pocket-sized beacon in the trunk of the informant's automobile. It was a continuous-signal transmitter which could be monitored by the police, allowing them to locate the automobile if surveillance failed.

A total surveillance breakdown was unlikely. When the informant approached the location of his rendezvous with Cullen, a van with four FBI men inside was parked nearby. They would be eyewitnesses to the meeting; they would be able to record the conversation if the equipment strapped to the informer's body performed as it should. A camera in the van was set up to videotape the encounter. There was a communications link between the van and the command post downtown.

Given the circumstances of the meeting, it was assumed Cullen would take evasive action to be sure he was not being trailed. The lawmen in the several automobiles involved in the operation would have to stay out of sight.

Cullen and the informant met. They talked briefly. There was an exchange of material. The informant dropped something in the trunk of Cullen's automobile, and they parted.

Tim Curry and the officials in the courthouse were advised by radio of the development and ordered that Cullen be apprehended.

Policemen and FBI agents in a fix-winged aircraft circling overhead observed as Cullen drove away from the restaurant and began to wash his trail. "Washing," in Fort Worth police jargon, is the process of shaking surveillants by a series of double turns, U-turns, and other measures. Cullen performed four such evasive actions but the skyborne policemen kept him in view, reporting his position by radio to others on the ground.

Cullen parked at a Kentucky Fried Chicken restaurant and entered an outside telephone booth. As he was leaving the booth an unmarked sedan bearing a flashing red light drove up and three officers with pistols and a shotgun jumped out. "Hold it there, Cullen!"

Cullen raised an arm as if to conceal his face. Then he surrendered quietly. He was handcuffed and placed in a police car which was to whisk him once more to the Cross-Bar Hotel.

"He didn't say anything," Police Lieutenant A. M. Patterson said. "To me, that was a little unusual. Normally they say, 'Hey, what the hell are you arresting me for?' or something like that. Cullen didn't say a thing."

Another arresting officer, Morris Howeth, read Cullen his rights—for a *second* time: he had been the arresting officer when Cullen was detained while attempting to board his jet—on another Sunday, in another August precisely two years before.

The authorities released an affidavit signed by the informant. It was a shocker.

My name is Charles David McCrory. I am 40 years old. I live at 3017 Bigham, Fort Worth, Tarrant County, Texas.

Within the last four days, Thomas Cullen Davis had a meeting with me in person, during which he discussed with me hiring a hit man to kill the judge presiding in his (Davis') divorce case. I know this judge to be Judge Joe H. Eidson, a Tarrant County Judge who presides in domestic and family matters. Davis had already discussed with me the amount of money necessary to hire such a hit man for this purpose.

During the conversation I had with Davis within the last four days, he wanted me to get a silencer for a .22 caliber pistol which I had brought to him (also at his request). I agreed to supply him such a silencer, and he left the .22 caliber pistol with me. During this meeting with Davis, Davis was driving a white over blue 1975 4-door Cadillac, Texas License Number CNM-144.

On Sunday, August 20, 1978, I again met with Thomas Cullen Davis, who was again driving the white over blue 1975 Cadillac mentioned above. On this occasion [sic] at around 8:50 a.m., I delivered to Davis (at his request) the .22 caliber pistol described above, with the homemade silencer attached. I did this in cooperation with the federal and local authorities to whom I had previously reported this matter. I placed the .22 caliber with the silencer attached into the opened trunk of Davis' Cadillac at Davis' request, and the trunk lid was closed with the gun inside.

Davis thereafter left our meeting place (at the parking lot of Coco's near the intersection of Hulen and Loop 820 in Tarrant County, Texas) in the 1975 Cadillac. He did not remove the pistol from the trunk before driving off.

The above statement is true and correct.

The telephone lines crackled in Rivercrest, Ridgelea, Shady Oaks, and the Tanglewood area near the Colonial Country Club.

Charles *McCrory!* Charles David *McCrory!*

Why, he was Cullen's pool-playing buddy, the one he met at the Pink Elephant—they used Cullen's money to buy the place so they could shoot whenever they wanted. Priscilla and W. T. Rufner had shacked up with the McCrorys in Boston, before McCrory and Judy were divorced. Judy had become Priscilla's best friend; she was at the mansion the night they

144

heard about the verdict from Amarillo. McCrory had gone to work for one of Cullen's companies.

The reaction to Cullen's arrest in Fort Worth ranged from outrage to grim satisfaction. Kay Davis, Cullen's niece and Ken's daughter, was an attractive young woman who had become an executive at KenDavis Industries. "A goddamned frameup," she snapped. One young man was astonished when his mother, a cultured Rivercrest matron he had never before heard swear, announced, "They finally got the son of a bitch!"

Priscilla's penchant for holding impromptu press conferences at inopportune times had long vexed her lawyers. This time they apparently had the volatile Priscilla under control; her reaction was not available. Speaking for his client, attorney Ronald Aultman told a reporter, "She is, of course, disturbed about it. She was disturbed for her own personal safety. She didn't express any opinion about how this will affect the divorce." For his own part, Aultman added, he would just as soon go ahead and get it over with. And he saw no reason that Judge Eidson should turn the case over to another judge.

A somewhat distraught Judge Byron Matthews telephoned the *Star-Telegram*. He said he had heard that Cullen was interested in "getting me killed, too." He had been warned by more than one person that "Cullen cussed me and said we [Matthews and Judge Cave] were in a conspiracy to keep him in jail and he was mad about that." Judge Cave, characteristically, reacted in a low key. While he was aware that Cullen was unhappy with him, he had not been threatened and had heard no rumors that he was in jeopardy.

Jack Wilborn said he had received an anonymous telephone call immediately after Cullen's arrest; the unknown informant claimed that this wasn't the first time Cullen had tried to arrange Judge Eidson's demise.

The *Star-Telegram* received another call that Sunday from a man who wanted to put something on the record before others did. Mayor Pro Tem Jim Bradshaw said that he and his wife had been among a Saturday group which had watched a Dallas Cowboy football game from the Davis skybox at the stadium. They had drinks elsewhere after the game, and Cullen and Karen dropped the Bradshaws at their home about 2 A.M. on Sunday morning.

"It's just so odd," Bradshaw said. "It's the first time we've ever been out with them." He added that his association with Cullen had only commenced about three weeks previously, when Cullen telephoned to say that he had just purchased Jet-Air, the aircraft sales company. Bradshaw had met Cullen personally for the first time a couple of days later, and Cullen had said that he might be interested in buying Bradshaw's auto parts business.

"I don't know why I called to tell you this," Bradshaw told the *Star-Telegram*. "I guess I just wanted somebody to know when it all came out."

Some readers believed Bradshaw's telephone call indicated he suspected that he had been euchred. Karen Master responded to the speculation that the mayor pro tem of Fort Worth had been invited to watch the Dallas Cowboy game from Cullen's skybox as part of an alibi arrangement.

"It's ridiculous," Karen told Dallas reporters, "to suggest that I would invite the Bradshaws to the game so they could testify to an alibi for Cullen. They are longtime friends and I would certainly do nothing to put them in an embarrassing position."

Racehorse Haynes was relaxing Sunday afternoon on his forty-foot sloop when he was called on the marine radio with the news that Tim Curry had released Charles David McCrory's statement at a press conference earlier that day. Haynes lost no time in flying to Fort Worth to reassemble the team which had defended Cullen in Amarillo—Phil Burleson, Mike Gibson, and Steve Sumner.

Even so, Haynes knew nothing of Cullen's latest predicament. "Is this the same McCrory who was involved before?" he asked at the airport. It was confirmed that McCrory was the ubiquitous figure who had been a minor participant in Cullen's tribulations in recent years.

Haynes reflected. "It's curious," he allowed.

Haynes and his team moved quickly to seek Cullen's freedom on bond. It was the seventh bond request Cullen's lawyers had sought, but it was not to be the last. The hearing was set for the following Tuesday. A visiting judge, Arthur Tipps, was to come from nearby Wichita Falls to preside. Tim Curry was to ask that bond be denied under a new state law denying bond to persons accused of felonies while out on bond for another crime—the murder of Stan Farr and the wounding of Gus Gavrel and Priscilla were still to be officially resolved.

And Tim Curry would have another opportunity to install Cullen as a permanent guest at the big Cross-Bar Hotel in Huntsville: a solicitation of murder charge, with a second charge of possession of an illegal weapon—a silencer—could bring a sentence of ninety-nine years.

On the first day of the bond hearings, Tuesday, August 22, the courtroom was packed. "You could have sold tickets for $50," one spectator said. It turned out to be an exciting show for the nonpaying audience. The first act involved intriguing testimony by McCrory. The second act was even more dramatic: The judge permitted the prosecution to play in court the tape recording of the meeting between McCrory and Cullen in a motel on the Thursday before Cullen's arrest on Sunday.

The transcript released to the public was bowdlerized, with "bleeps" screening the obscenities. The conversation began as McCrory presented Cullen with a gun:

McCrory: I've got a little present for you.
Davis: Well, that's nice.
McCrory: Just what you ordered. They haven't got—
Davis: What the doctor ordered.

147

McCrory: They haven't got the silencer made yet but, uh, they're working on it.

Davis: When will it be ready?

McCrory: Uh, just a few days. Don't point that at me.

Davis: Huh?

McCrory: Don't point that son of a bitch at me. No, you have...uh, the bottom.

Davis: Here?

McCrory: You have to pull this back. Is that sweet?

Davis: All right!

McCrory: That is sweet. Now, do you want the uh, do you want all this taken off, the numbers?

Davis: Well, can you get 'em off?

McCrory: Uh, I don't know whether they get 'em to where they can take 'em off. If I was you, I would rather have it with 'em just like it is.

Davis: Yeah.

McCrory: Cause that's out of the, out of the factory. Uh, you don't have to worry about it. They got to do a lot of work on the front end of it. Take all that off, make a silencer go on it.

Davis: Huh?

McCrory: They got to do a lot of work on the front end of it to make a silencer go on it.

Davis: They have to modify this to—

McCrory: Oh, yeah.

Davis: Before that thing will go on there?

The next segment of the tape was to be used to allege that Mc-Crory had told Cullen that he had rummaged around in the underworld and arranged for the services of a professional assassin who worked for Murder Incorporated. McCrory referred to his imaginary hit man as "the man" or "the shooter."

McCrory: Yeah. Uh, we got somewhat of a problem. The man is here to put the judge away. Uh, he is ready, just found out that he was a judge and he wants a lot more fucking money. Uh, I just threw my hands up and said, I...that's the most money you can get. And he said, "Well, fuck you, that's a judge and it's gonna bring more heat." Uh, I said, well, the money's, you know, there. But he wants, uh, the son of a bitch wants $100,000 to uh—

Davis: Bullshit.

McCrory: Well, I told him bullshit, too, Cullen, but goddamn, there's not anything I can do when it's in the fucking paper every day. You know, he's on tv, he's in the paper, uh, what else can I do?

Davis: [unintelligible; possibly, I don't know.]

McCrory: Well, now, Priscilla is a different story. Uh, that's, you know, he'd rather do Priscilla than the judge. Uh, I don't know. He says he can do it easy.

Davis: Huh, like hell.

McCrory: Well?

Davis: Priscilla's always got somebody around her; the judge doesn't.

McCrory: The way...you know the way we talked about doing it he doesn't see that to be any problem. That fucker's busted. This whole goddamned car's a fucking ...did you get to talk to Art?

Art Smith was the president of Air-Jet. It had been through Cullen's intercession that McCrory had obtained employment with the aircraft sales firm which Cullen had purchased a short time before. McCrory was concerned that his frequent absences from the job would make his boss suspicious.

Davis: Today? No.

McCrory: He's a hot son of a bitch at me.

Davis: [unintelligible]

McCrory: You're gonna have to alibi for me for the last two days. You're gonna have to just tell him, you know, he was workin' for me.

Davis: Why weren't you there?

McCrory: Well, you know, uh, I had shit that I had to get done. You can't get this kind of shit done, Cullen, with uh, havin' to be stuck under his fucking thumb twenty-four hours a day. It's impossible. Now, wipe that son bitch, take the clip out and wipe it down. You handled the clip too, so wipe it down, too. Now, the, uh, does it make any difference to you what color the silencer is or you just want one with a fucking silencer, period?...the brown beret cap to drop by the judge. Shit man, where do you find one of them mother fuckers? If you're gonna blame it on the Brown Berets, where do, where in the fuck do you find one of their caps? There's not any.

Davis: Beats the shit out of me.

The Brown Berets is a Los Angeles-based organization of Mexican-American political activists which has twenty-six chapters in Texas. The local groups have a history of some violence and subsequent involvement with Fort Worth courts. Thus a brown beret—the cap is recognized as the insignia of Brown Beret members—found near a dead Judge Eidson would cast suspicion on Hispanics Eidson or other Fort Worth judges might have dealt with harshly in court.

McCrory: Give me a price on Priscilla.

Davis: [unintelligible]

McCrory: He says he'd rather do Priscilla than the judge so if you give me a price on, you know, Priscilla and I'll just, uh, lay it in his lap, unless you want to talk to the mother fucker.

Davis: Who's that?

McCrory: The shooter.

Davis: Well....

McCrory: I think you'd be making, well fuck, you may not, he may trust you more than he trusts me.

Davis: Now, you're supposed to be handling that.

McCrory: Well, I can, fuck, I can understand your point. I don't. I'm doing the very fucking best I can, Cullen. I have had my hands tied in a lot of ways trying to do things. I mean, I have busted my goddamn ass working for Art. I have really busted my ass, uh.

Davis: You just can't keep being absent.

McCrory: Well, I know that.

Davis: Like that, uh, I can't fade* that, all that, and uh, nothing happening here either. Nothing's, absolutely nothing's happening. Go back to the original plan.

McCrory: What do you mean the original plan?

Davis: Uh, get the other one, you know, who we started this out with.

McCrory: You mean Priscilla?

Davis: No.

McCrory: Oh, Bev?

Davis: Yeah, with—

McCrory: Boy, you gonna bring more fucking heat down on you, Cullen, you have that son of a bitch killed. I promise you, you gonna have heat. Well, you know what you're doing. I'm sure you've thought it out. I'll do whatever you want done, uh. You still want all three of them at once?

Davis: Do it either way, whatever, whatever's there.

McCrory: Well.

Davis: You know what's better.

McCrory: You know what's gonna happen, uh, is that fucking old man, uh, is gonna, he's gonna grab up his shotgun. You know the son bitch is nutty as a fruitcake. Well, can you handle this deal with Art, or what's, you know...I think...

Following the taped insinuation that the "original" plan had been to kill Beverly Bass and Gus Gavrel, the man McCrory described as "nutty as a fruitcake" was Gus Gavrel's father.

* To fade, in Texas gambling jargon, is to cover a bet, especially in dice games.

Gus Gavrel, Sr., was indeed perceived in Fort Worth as a strong-minded man who would not hesitate to grab up his shotgun if seeking revenge. McCrory reiterated his concern about his supervisor. He then spoke of obtaining narcotics, which the prosecution later alleged Cullen wanted dropped at the scene of Gus Gavrel's murder to give investigators the impression the crime was drug-related. Cullen's remarks indicate that he believed there would not be further prosecution for the woundings of Priscilla and Gavrel and for Stan Farr's murder. The tape continued:

Davis: Art hasn't talked to me, uh.

McCrory: Well, I know but—

Davis: [unintelligible]

McCrory: When I talked to him, you know, the last two days, uh, I told him that I was traveling for you. I was workin' for you, doin' stuff for you and uh, that, uh, you told me you would get in touch with him. He said, well, I was out all day Wednesday so he probably, uh, he knew that I was gone all day Wednesday, so—

Davis: You said two days, didn't you?

McCrory: Well, he was gone Wednesday, though. But see, I was out of pocket, uh, Wednesday and Thursday both. I mean I told you to begin with, that, you know, I had to make trips, you know. The only place that I'm gonna be able to get the goddamned dope, uh, I've gotta go to Mexico and pick it up, uh, if we're going to redo her. Uh . . . you sure that's the one—

Davis: That's the one that makes sense to me right now due to the current circumstances.

McCrory: What happened in that deal?

Davis: Just put off. They wanted it put off, so it's put off.

McCrory: All of a sudden—

Davis: Put off.

McCrory: Does it fuck you with them not lettin' them bring everything up in trial, just no contest thing or what?

Davis: Not particularly. Uh, just shorten it.

McCrory: That bitch.

Davis: Although I'm not really sure who got the better end of the . . . that judge's ruling.

McCrory: (laughs) I think they had to fuck theirself [sic] to fuck you a little bit.

Davis: Yeah.

McCrory: Okay.

Davis: I think they got the better end of the deal but I, it really didn't matter.

McCrory: What if he does all three of those and just goes right on? This is the reason, that's the reason I told you you may want to talk to him. He, uh, wants his fucking money and uh, he wants it immediately and then I don't have the money to pay him, so—

Davis: Immediately?

McCrory: Just as soon as he gets the job done, he wants to be paid.

Davis: Well, I will. . . . He will be.

McCrory: Okay.

Davis: You just get in touch with me anytime afterwards that you want to and it'll . . .

McCrory: Well it's got to be immediately afterwards, that's the problem 'cause I don't have the fucking money.

Davis: You just call me and it's, you got it.

McCrory: Okay, how are we gonna do that now, if he moves tonight or tomorrow night on her, how do we, what do we do? I mean how are we gonna get money exchanged? You know how much fucking spying and everything I've done on her already. I'm, you know, hot as a pistol as far as, I've got to be out of the picture somewhat when she goes, uh, down.

Davis: Well, you know when it's going to happen you can always cover your, get yourself covered real good.

McCrory: Uh, when are you gonna be covered?

Davis: I'm, uh, I'm covered all the time.

153

McCrory: You're staying covered.

Davis: I'm staying covered. I'm not, I'm not taking any chances. If I wasn't gonna be covered, I was going to let you know. Anytime that I'm not gonna be, I'm going to let you know. That's the way we're gonna work that deal, uh.

McCrory: Hey, now we're friends. You're not gonna do something stupid with this fucking gun are you?

Davis: No, I'm gonna give it back to you right now.

McCrory: Well, I know but I'm talking about with the silencer and all that shit.

Davis: No.

McCrory: I don't know what the fuck you want with the silencer myself.

Davis: [unintelligible]

McCrory: Self-protection, my ass.

Davis: [unintelligible] . . . I'm protecting myself. . . .

McCrory: Yeah, okay, uh, what else . . . are you gonna cover me with Art?

Davis: Well, I will this time, but I can't keep, you know, you can't just take off a day or two every week. It's not gonna work.

McCrory: It's not every week but goddamn when it's just like I told you before, when stuff comes up, uh.

Davis: Well, what did you tell him, exactly?

McCrory: I told him that I had to go out of town for you. I'd been working—

Davis: Which days was that?

McCrory: That was Wednesday and Thursday.

Davis: Who were you shacked up with?

McCrory: None of your fucking business . . . (bleep) . . . Uh, well, this man's good, Cullen, he's uh, supposedly one of the best, and, uh . . .

In the transcript printed in the press the expletives had been denoted by "bleep." In this instance, however, the bleep represented a sequence of dialogue deleted from the transcript. After McCrory told Cullen it was none of his business whom McCrory had been shacked up with, McCrory continued. "Hell, I'm entitled to a little pussy too. No, nobody really, huh, no I, shit, I, I tell you what I haven't had any. I don't even get any at home, much less any strange pussy." Cullen responded: "Shit." After this digression he returned to the subject of the methodology of murder:

> Davis: Well, you just, uh, whenever you need the money, well, uh, whatever day that is, you just call.
>
> McCrory: Okay, you definitely want her to go down before the judge.
>
> Davis: Yeah, I want—
>
> McCrory: Why? I don't understand it.
>
> Davis: Well.
>
> McCrory: I mean I'll go along with whatever you say, but, uh, what are you gonna do if the son bitch wants to do, you know, they're awful close together. Uh, if he grabs that judge up and puts him in his car, knocks him out and puts him in his car and takes him off, uh, which is what he said he'd do, uh, there's gonna be a helluva stink but not near as much as if he left that son bitch bloody and bleeding in his driveway. Or, walk in the house and have to blow up the judge and his wife and anybody else that might happen to be there.
>
> Davis: Well, he's not gonna be wandering in there if there's anybody else there. He's gonna, he'd know what he's doing better'n that. Do the judge, then his wife and that'd be it.
>
> McCrory: Yeah, but he ain't gonna leave any witnesses?
>
> Davis: Or if he, or he might catch the judge, uh, coming in the house or something like that.
>
> McCrory: No, the judge goes out and remember, the judge goes out and waters his, turns his fucking water off. That's when he's gonna get him. Uh, but he doesn't want to leave him there, he wants to hit him, uh.

155

Davis: What good's—

McCrory: Snatch him up and take him off.

Davis: What good's that gonna do?

McCrory: Well, it's, man, there's a lot of difference, a lot of difference. Not near as much heat. Uh, you know they can't prove much unless they find a body.

Davis: Well.

McCrory: You know that's what he's gonna do with her. If it's her by herself.

Davis: Let's plan on gettin' all three of 'em over there.

McCrory: It's a hard son of a bitch, but, uh.

Davis: It's the best way.

McCrory: Oh, I know it is. Shit yeah, but if he does that, Cullen, he's got to, I don't know who all, man I have never been able to figure out all that investigation shit, there's always a bunch of fucking people at that house.

Davis: Uh.

McCrory: The only time he can do this is the daytime. He's got to go in there in the daytime, or catch 'em in that, uh, big motor home.

Davis: M-m-m.

McCrory: Now, he says he . . . there's a possibility of blowing up that motor home with butane . . . with all of 'em. Let me go talk to him and see what he wants to do, uh, and uh, I'll call you in the morning.

Davis: Okay.

McCrory returned an apparent consideration of alibis, and how he would signal Cullen so that Cullen would be aware when the hired killer might strike, and arrange his whereabouts accordingly.

McCrory: And I'll just tell you, I'll tell you I'm going out of town and that means, if I say I'm going out of town that means that uh, he's going to work. Far as any more money, I'll just tell him you can't do it. You got to do the job first, right.

Davis: Got to be on the same—

McCrory: All right, let's get the fuck out of here, I've got things to do, people to see.

Davis: All right.

McCrory: You're looking better.

Davis: If I'm—

McCrory: Been getting any sun?

Davis: Yeah.

McCrory: Look like it.

Davis: Uh, remember you can, it's all right to tell Brenda that you're going out of town—my secretary.

McCrory: Well, tomorrow morning, you'll be at home won't you?

Davis: Uh.

McCrory: Saturday?

Davis; Oh, well yeah, in the morning.

McCrory: Okay, that's what I thought.

Davis: I'm talking about anytime that you have to call my office—

McCrory: Well, when I call Karen—

Davis: But, not on weekends though.

McCrory: Hey, now are you planning on being shacked up with any other gal anytime soon?

Davis: No.

McCrory: Like—

Davis: No, if I was I'd—

McCrory: What'd she do, run you off? The girl friend run your ass off?

Davis: Hell, no. What girl friend? What girl friend?

McCrory: [laughs] Hey, you don't have to worry about me, I'm not going to tell anybody.

Davis: Talk to you later.

McCrory: All right. Hey, if he works, if he goes to work, uh, and gets her like tonight or tomorrow night, don't leave me hanging 'cause that mother fucker will kill me, Cullen.

Davis: I've got it, it's—

McCrory: Okay, just don't leave me hanging.

Davis: I won't.

McCrory: All right.

Davis: Go back to plan, plan—

McCrory: Well, now, he may take a bunch of them off, that's what I want to know.

Davis: Hm?

McCrory: He may take a bunch of them off at once. Uh, I mean he's that kind of person and he may just waste the shit out of a bunch of 'em and get a bunch of it over with at once.

Davis: Well.

McCrory: If, all right now, all right.

Davis: That suits the shit out of me.

After telling Cullen that the shooter might get rid of a bunch of people at one time, McCrory returned to the subject of Priscilla as a victim.

McCrory: All right, now there is something I need to . . . come here just a second. There's something I need to ask you. How much money is he going to get if he gets Priscilla? I mean you've got, man . . . I've got to tell him something, if you want the bitch dead then you got to tell me how much it's, you know. I can't, uh. . . .

Davis: [unintelligible]

McCrory: I mean he says he can do 'em all you know, he says shh, you know.

Davis: One at a time.

McCrory: I know, but tell me something.

Davis: Uh, I'll have to think on that one.

McCrory mentioned another candidate, Cullen's brother William, who owned a resort home in New England.

McCrory: What, uh, you know Bill's in Connecticut?

Davis: Huh?

McCrory: You know Bill being up in Connecticut and every-thing, she's not going to get any help from him.

Davis: My brother?

McCrory: Yeah, you see all those security guards, all those security guards uh, that he was paying for are no longer over there.

Davis: Yeah, I, I, I knew there weren't any around there anymore.

McCrory: There's one at night.

Davis: Hm?

McCrory: There's one at night.

Davis: Every night?

Davis: Well.

McCrory: Fuck, don't you know, aren't you paying for him?

Davis: Huh?

McCrory: Aren't you paying for him?

Davis: Fortunately, that's one, one I'm not, one thing I'm not paying for.

McCrory: Okay, well.

Davis: All right, go back to the original plan.

McCrory: Done.

Davis: Talk to you.

McCrory: All right.

It was here, McCrory was to testify, that he and Cullen parted company. McCrory's final words came after a long pause, while he watched Cullen drive away. The two words were spoken into the microphone taped to his body for the benefit of the FBI: "Mission completed."

Charles David McCrory was known as a romantic loser with a reputation for telling tall stories and switching allegiances. Hardly a creditable witness. But the twenty-three-minute tape had two voices on it, and most of the people who knew Cullen believed the second was his voice.

The day the tape was played, McCrory testified to fill in the gaps. Cullen, grim, stared intently at his one-time "trusted friend" while McCrory recited the damning litany. Karen Master, immaculately clad, sat not far from Cullen in the crowded courtroom. McCrory outlined the sequence of events which began, he said, when Cullen broached the idea that Mc-Crory investigate Dee Wilborn and Gus Gavrel and ended when Cullen decided he wanted fifteen people eradicated.

McCrory's marriage to Judy had dissolved but he and Cullen had remained friends after McCrory remarried. Broke—"Isn't everybody when they get divorced?"—McCrory and Cullen had gotten drunk one night and Cullen became aware of his pal's need of employment. In early June, Cullen telephoned and asked McCrory to meet him on the parking lot at Coco's Famous Hamburgers, saying he had a job for McCrory.

Cullen wanted, McCrory testified, to know the source of supply for drugs used by Beverly Bass and Gus Gavrel, and whether Gus's father knew about it. He also wanted McCrory to check out his suspicion that Priscilla's lawyers in the divorce case were conniving with Judge Eidson. Cullen gave McCrory $5000 to finance his investigation.

Prosecutor Tolly Wilson interrupted McCrory's testimony to ask him if he had known the full extent of Cullen's wealth. The witness said his newest wife had asked Cullen one evening why he spent so much time in "crackerboard" houses such as the McCrorys' modest dwelling.

"He replied that if he only talked to other rich people, the only person he could talk to was Howard Hughes, and he was dead."

McCrory and Cullen planned clandestine meetings. The signal for a meeting would be the use of an alias Cullen had chosen for McCrory: Frank Johnson.

On June 12, some two and a half months before, Cullen had arranged for McCrory to become the assistant to Art Smith, president at Jet-Air. McCrory's attempts to unearth information about Beverly, Gus, and Priscilla's attorneys were fruitless. Then: "We started talking about the future proceedings against him," McCrory said. "He wanted to know if I knew anyone that could get rid of somebody for him, and what it would cost. . . . He said Bev Bass was the only witness that the jury believed in Amarillo."

McCrory said he didn't think Cullen was serious until, later, Cullen said he had thought about it and "decided to go ahead and hire someone to kill Bev Bass. And I was to do the hiring."

A threat from Cullen accompanied the assignment. "If you cross me this time . . . I'll have you and your wife and your whole damned family killed, and don't think I won't do it." Cullen added, "I know some things you don't. She [Beverly] has to die." Then despite his reservations about McCrory's trustworthiness, "I have other people who could get it done, but you're the only one I trust."

The warm August courtroom was becoming stifling as Mc-Crory continued his damning testimony. Most of the male spectators and lawyers removed their coats. Cullen did not. He continued to stare at McCrory. The witness said he and Cullen had discussed the expense involved in the murder not only of Beverly Bass but of two other persons Cullen added to his list: Gus Gavrel, Gus's father, and Judge Eidson. McCrory said, "[Cullen] felt very, very sure that Judge Eidson was going to try to break him financially. . . . Judge Eidson was in cahoots with—in bed with, as he said it—Priscilla's attorneys."

A week later, McCrory testified, he met Cullen again at Coco's Famous Hamburgers and at that time Cullen said he wanted a total of fifteen people killed. Augmenting his previous hit list, Cullen ticked off the candidates: Judge Tom Cave, W. T. Rufner, and his own brother William. "He didn't want to tell me the names of the rest of them right then," McCrory added. While the tapes had mentioned William, McCrory's testimony was the first indication that Cullen had discussed the disposal of his own brother.

McCrory dreamed up and henceforth employed the story that he had been able to contact a hired killer out of a Kansas City branch of Murder Incorporated. "I told [Cullen] it would cost so much money that even he couldn't afford it." After reminding McCrory that he would need to know in advance of any action so that he would be covered with an alibi, Cullen said, "I'll spend what it takes."

McCrory's testimony filled out the chronology of a series of meetings with Cullen throughout the summer of 1978. In June, McCrory said, Cullen gave him $50,000 in cash to be laundered in Las Vegas so the bills would be untraceable. McCrory and his wife had spent five days at the gambling tables of the Nevada gambling city for that purpose, and the prosecutors presented two airline tickets as evidence.

In July, McCrory claimed, Cullen had asked him to procure a .22 pistol with a silencer. At that time and during other encounters Cullen also had some suggestions as to how the murders could be carried out with a minimum risk of disclosure. In one scenario he suggested that a sugar substitute of the white powdery kind mixed with cocaine or heroin be left at the spot where Beverly Bass was to be killed. Or, her body could be cut up and the pieces scattered so the corpse could never be identified. Maybe Judge Eidson could be kidnapped while he was watering his lawn. Then a brown beret and a Mexican-American driver's license could be left wherever the body was dumped to make the judge's death appear to be a political assassination. And perhaps in William's case, a contrived scuba-diving accident could be arranged while William was enjoying his favorite sport at his summer home in New England.

By mid-August, Cullen had become disturbed that none of the murders had actually occurred despite McCrory's assurances that a hit man was stalking the victims. McCrory testified that Cullen threatened again "to kill me and have my wife and children slaughtered."

On Thursday, August 17, McCrory said, he decided to contact the FBI. The FBI agents decided that the case fell within federal jurisdiction—because of the kidnap threats against Judge Eidson and William Davis—and they instructed McCrory to arrange another meeting with Cullen the next day. On Friday, McCrory, wired for sound, met Cullen at Coco's. The recording of that conversation resulted in the tape which had just been played in the courtroom.

Before the end of that Tuesday's bond-hearing session the prosecution played a second, brief tape. It was telephone conversation which the FBI had recorded the previous Friday night.

Karen Master, in the courtroom, listened as the ring of the telephone at her home was followed by a recording of her voice. "Cullen's here," she had answered. "Hold on just a moment." The remainder of the conversation between McCrory and Cullen involved the couple's plan to attend the Dallas Cowboys-Houston Oilers football game on Saturday night. The conversation ended with McCrory saying, "Hang loose and stay covered."

McCrory was a dubious witness, and his testimony could be attacked. But how was Haynes going to explain those tapes with Cullen's voice on them?

What about a defense based on temporary insanity? There was considerable speculation that Haynes would have no other option. Cullen dismissed the idea himself when speaking to reporters before the tapes were played. There would be no insanity plea, he said, and his attorneys did not contemplate a psychiatric examination. Steve Sumner confirmed, cautiously, that defense lawyers had no such plans "at this time."

After the devastating tapes had been played, Phil Burleson reiterated that there was no basis for speculation that Cullen would plead insanity. "We have found nothing," the Dallas lawyer said, "to suggest that he is mentally unbalanced."

One observer, not quite so sure, quipped: "If Cullen doesn't plead insanity now, he's crazy."

The person, the past history, and the present credibility of Charles David McCrory now became a matter of importance.

163

The facts which had come to light about McCrory's involvement with Cullen and Priscilla since the murders on Mockingbird Lane in August of 1976 were hazy. His role in the developments of the next two years was confusing.

In 1976, McCrory and his then wife Judy had dined with Priscilla Davis and Stan Farr the night before the murders. He had been at the mansion after the shootings, mingling with police officers and reporters. He had testified eight months later, in April of 1977, at pretrial hearings and during Cullen's trial in Fort Worth before Judge Cave had declared a mistrial.

Six days after the mistrial Richard Haynes requested that Judge Cave grant Cullen freedom on bond. In support of the motion, Cullen's defense team presented an "affidavit" purportedly based on statements by McCrory which linked Priscilla to drug use at the mansion, suggested that Priscilla had tried to bribe McCrory to support her version of the shootings, and discredited the testimony of Gus Gavrel, Jr. The "affidavit" carried no legal weight—it was unsigned.

The same day McCrory disclaimed the statements attributed to him. He told a *Star-Telegram* reporter that the "affidavit" which supposedly reflected his views had been "written, edited, rewritten, and reedited by Haynes, Cullen, and others."

One week after repudiating the unsigned "affidavit" presented to Judge Cave by Richard Haynes, McCrory signed an affidavit which was legal—this time for the district attorney's office. McCrory had abruptly switched his allegiance from Cullen to Priscilla, with the newest affidavit contradicting the previous one.

Further, McCrory's new prosecution affidavit hinted darkly that Haynes as well as Cullen's other defense lawyers had tried to bribe him. At a conclave at the Green Oaks Inn in Fort Worth just before Haynes presented the original, unsigned "affidavit" to Judge Cave, Cullen's attorneys had shown him the document and asked him to sign it. "I told them I would not sign it," McCrory said, "because it was not truthful." Then he added, "Mr. Burleson suggested that I have another drink."

164

McCrory further swore, in the prosecution's affidavit, that Haynes had noticed a ring McCrory was wearing, which looked like a diamond.

"I told Mr. Haynes that evening that I wished the diamond were real. Mr. Haynes said that he had confidence in me and that some day it would be real."

Whatever the facts concerning the origin and validity of the first, unsigned "affidavit," Judge Cave reacted strongly to the manner in which Richard Haynes and Burleson attempted to use it during the bond hearing after the Fort Worth mistrial. He cited Haynes and Burleson for contempt of court—a charge which could have led to fines or, theoretically, jail sentences. Cave said that the two lawyers "knew at the time [the papers] were filed that certain of the statements attributed to David McCrory were false and not true, yet [they] deliberately filed or allowed it [the affidavit] to be filed with the other papers in the official records of this case."

As a part of the official records, the highly damaging allegations about Priscilla's conduct became public knowledge. The publicity was one of several developments which prompted Judge Cave to rule that Cullen's subsequent trial be moved to Amarillo. (The contempt charges against Haynes and Burleson were not pursued on the grounds that in defending themselves the lawyers would be forced to reveal information which could be detrimental in Cullen's various civil cases.)

Despite McCrory's reluctance to verify scandalous stories about Priscilla, Racehorse Haynes subpoenaed McCrory to testify for the defense when Cullen's Amarillo trial began in June of 1977. McCrory appeared in Judge Dowlen's chambers during pretrial hearings, but invoked the Fifth Amendment when asked about specific statements. Apparently this diminished his appeal as a defense witness and McCrory was not called to the stand during the actual trail. McCrory said, "I think I've about eliminated myself as a witness." And defense lawyer Mike Gibson had remarked, "I think McCrory's just about painted himself out of the picture."

But now—one summer later, in August of 1978—McCrory had painted himself back into the picture. He reappeared dramatically, a central figure in the bizarre development which stunned Fort Worth. Charles David McCrory was important now; he was no longer a shadowy minor character. The drifter who had failed consistently in business and in his private life would now play a leading role in a major drama: the determination of whether or not T. Cullen Davis would become the richest man in America ever to be tried for murder—twice!

But could McCrory carry off his new role? Could he be trusted, whether commenting in a legal document or during testimony under oath? Who would believe Charles David Mc-Crory?

Some began to believe him on Wednesday, August 23, the second day of Cullen's bond hearing in Fort Worth, when the prosecution played a third tape recording. It was an encounter between McCrory and Cullen which had taken place on Sunday morning, August 20. Cullen believed a hit man from Kansas City had been busy murdering Judge Joe Eidson.

> The following is a transcript of a taped conversation placed in evidence Wednesday in the bond hearing for T. Cullen Davis.

> I am a special agent, Joseph B. Gray, with the Federal Bureau of Investigation, Dallas, Texas. It is August 20, 1978. The time is 8:12 A.M. I have just installed a Nagra tape recorder on the person of David McCrory, and I have personally inspected that recorder previous to its installation and found it to be in working order.

The introduction by the FBI man was in flat, matter-of-fact tones. But then the unemotional voice of the federal agent was followed by the recording of the meeting between McCrory and Cullen the same Sunday morning at Coco's. The spectators listening in the courtroom were mesmerized. The dialogue between Cullen and McCrory was agitated; the two men kept interrupting each other; it was exciting real-life talk about murder and mayhem. The radio from McCrory's car provided a dramatic musical background for the macabre conversation:

Davis: Just paranoid.

McCrory: Goddamn!

Davis: Come on.

McCrory: I got some...hey! I got something here. I've got something here. I don't...well.

Davis: Goddamn, you just won't let a body sleep, will you?

McCrory: Don't go anywhere. I gotta go. I got problems.

Davis: Dang, you keep—

McCrory: Uh, who do you want to go next? I never have gotten ahold of him to change any plans. Uh, I've got more fucking pressure on me right now than you can imagine.

Davis: Okay, what are you going to do with these?

McCrory: I'm going to get rid of the mother fuckers.

Davis: That's good. Glad to hear it.

McCrory: All right, who do you want next?

Davis: Uh, the ones we talked about...the three—

McCrory: Bev, Bubba, all right.

Davis: Yeah.

McCrory: All right. I gotta go.

Davis: Okay, uh...just a minute.

McCrory: You going to get in the trunk?

Davis: Uh huh.

McCrory: I got something for you to put in the trunk.

Davis: Okay.

McCrory: I'm going to go ahead and get your stuff out.

Davis: Is this the place to do it?

McCrory: Yeah.

Davis: I believe I forgot my glasses.

McCrory: Your glasses?

Davis: My sunglasses.

McCrory: Is that it?

167

Davis: Yeah.

McCrory: Wait, wait a second.

Davis: Mm huh.

McCrory: Wait just a second. I'm a scared mother fucker. I don't mind telling you. When you kill a man like Judge Eidson...hey, there is going to be more heat caused than you can imagine. Hold on, leave the trunk up. Come here.

Davis: Goddamn, pretty.

McCrory: Okay, now you got it, leave—

Davis: You got it...look at that mother fucker.

McCrory: All right, but leave it alone.

Davis: I will.

McCrory: Okay, I got to get out of here.

Davis: Bye.

McCrory: Now, you want, you want Beverly Bass killed next, quick, right?

Davis: Aaay, uh.

McCrory: Now, I don't want to make another mistake. You sure?

Davis: Yeah.

McCrory: 'Cause he's going to operate again tonight.

Davis: Oh...well—

McCrory: Hey, the man is good. He's the best I've ever seen.

Davis: Just one problem. I haven't got the money lined up.

McCrory: How long will it take?

Davis: I'll try to get it this week. I can get it in two days.

McCrory: I don't know whether I can keep him here two days or not, Cullen.

Davis: Uh, how far does he have to go? Halfway across the country?

McCrory: He's out of...he's out of New Orleans...he says. Fuck, I don't know. That is just what he told me. All right, I gotta go.

Davis: You talk to him and ask him how he would—

McCrory: Thanks for not letting me down.

Davis: What?

McCrory: I'm trying to do you a good job.

Davis: Well, I'm wondering whether—

McCrory: Uh, I know you were, but I've done everything I could. I've done everything humanly possible. Uh, but man, for God's sake, I can't afford to be fucked up now with Jet-Air. I don't care if you got to tell Art, look, uh, uh, I mean just do whatever is necessary.

Davis: All right, well just don't uh, give me too much pressure.

McCrory: I'm not going to give you any more pressure than I have to.

Davis: All right.

McCrory: All right. But call him and uh, straighten it out.

Davis: What's the deal? He hadn't called me.

McCrory: I know, but he's...he will. I was off...I was out of pocket...

Davis: He didn't fire you, did he?

McCrory: Wednesday and Thursday...no, but he was talking like he was going to.

Davis: Well...I had told him...I'll talk to him, but I'll...I'll have to tell you what I told him. I told him that, uh, treat you like he would any other employee.

McCrory: Okay.

Davis: And, so don't give me too much pressure in that regard. I can't say you are going to be gone a day or two every week or so.

McCrory: Well, look, fucking murder business is a tough son of a bitch.

Davis: You better—

McCrory: Now, you got me in this goddamn deal—

Davis: Give me—

McCrory: What?

Davis: Give me a little advance notice.

Then was heard on the clearly audible tape—the meeting was also being photographed by the FBI men in the van—the exchange which was to be headlined, discussed, and debated:

McCrory: I got Judge Eidson dead for you.
Davis: Good.

McCrory went on to query Cullen:

McCrory: I'll get the rest of them dead for you. You want a bunch of people dead, right?
Davis: All right.
McCrory: Am I right?
Davis: All right, but I—
McCrory: Then—
Davis: You know I—
McCrory: Help me too, okay?
Davis: I've got to have an alibi ready for Art.
McCrory: Okay.
Davis: When the subject comes up.
McCrory: All right, I'll...
Davis: So, give me some advance warning.
McCrory: I will. I gotta go.
Davis: Ask him about, does he want to leave and come back, or do it and then wait three days for the money.
McCrory: He won't wait for money.
Davis: Well—
McCrory: Look, if he kills all three of those people, he's going to walk.
Davis: Yeah. Well, I don't blame him but I just...I've got to get it, so—
McCrory: Okay, you talking about [inaudible] of...
Davis: Better to leave and come back...
McCrory: You're talking about a [inaudible]...yeah, you talking about a lot of money. Figure it up, well, I'll talk to you about it later. Okay? I, I don't...got to get to him, right now. Bye.

[McCrory closed his car door and was departing]

McCrory: I have got the money. He has got the gun. I have to drive to the front...something so he won't get suspicious right now.

This is Special Agent Joseph B. Gray of the FBI. The time now is 9:03 A.M., August 20, 1978, and I am about to remove the Nagra recorder from David McCrory that I installed earlier today.

The three national evening television news programs appear simultaneously in Fort Worth at 5:30 in the afternoon and each carried the T. Cullen Davis saga which almost instantaneously had become a national, even international, story. World media had briefly noted Cullen's acquittal in Amarillo but thereafter the adventures of the Texas tycoon had faded quickly from prominence. Interest was renewed when the telephone calls and clandestine meetings with Charles David McCrory were revealed by the FBI recordings. The scenario was more intriguing than a fictional cops-and-robbers television script. The newscasts had been on for only a few minutes on Wednesday, August 23, when the telephone lines in the western section of Fort Worth began to hum.

He'll stay in the Cross-Bar Hotel now. Not even Racehorse Haynes will be able to convince a jury that those tapes and pictures are faked. Yes, Cullen's going to spend all his birthdays in the slammer from now on!

Cullen was once again confined to Fort Worth's jail. When arrested on Sunday he was wearing a pullover shirt and slacks; now, on Wednesday, he was wearing prison garb. He was billeted in a five-by-eight cell in the Tarrant County Criminal Courts Building. The cell was equipped with a bed, lavatory, and toilet. A mirror hung on one wall and a fluorescent bulb illuminated the space. Like all prisoners, the sheriff said, he would be allowed to bring in a television set.

The stories of Cullen's comfortable accommodations in the Potter County jail, where he was treated like an honored guest, were recalled, and now the Fort Worth sheriff went to some lengths to explain that was not to be the case this time.

At noon on Monday, August 21—the day after Cullen's arrest—he lunched on the regular jail fare of fruit drink and bread, lima beans, mashed potatoes, and chicken-fried steak.* "That's better than *I'm* eating," the sheriff groused. He made it clear he would bend no rules. The sheriff denied Cullen permission to have catered meals delivered to his cell, as he had in Fort Worth and in Amarillo. "If I permit things like that, it's a question of where things are going to end. Some guy may start asking for quail under glass. Everybody is going to eat the same here."

The sheriff reported that he had talked with Cullen only once since his second arrest. "I really didn't talk to him any. I just said, 'Hello,' and he said, 'Hello.'" The sheriff added, "He didn't show much expression. He never does openly show any emotion. He was just like he always was."

Cullen was allowed to make telephone calls and to be visited by his attorneys and business associates. Ironically, the sheriff's rules would permit Cullen to have visits from his legal spouse, Priscilla, whom he did not want to see. They would not allow him to visit with Karen Master.

Karen remained loyal to Cullen. She was permitted to chat with him during the first day of the bond hearing. She smiled as Cullen entered the hearing room, which he acknowledged. During a recess she embraced Cullen and spoke to him briefly, trying to encourage him. Later she told a reporter that she was upset and depressed and, after reading a transcript of one of the FBI-monitored meetings between Cullen and McCrory, she admitted that "Race will have a lot to work with." But Karen recalled that things had looked dismal before the acquittal in

---

*Chicken-fried steak is considered tasty but not fashionable in the wealthy sections of Fort Worth, and is a delicacy in the southwest generally. It is usually beef, but can be batter and breadcrumb portions of veal or pork. Massey's Restaurant in Fort Worth boasts in advertisements that it serves the best chicken-fried steak in Tarrant County, then adds…"Probably the Universe!" Massey's also features "fries"—bull's testicles.

Amarillo and promised to stand by Cullen in his newest predicament.

Karen had been a credible witness in Amarillo, despite her previous failure to mention to the grand jury that Cullen was sleeping at her side when the murders occurred on Mockingbird Lane. Her appearance as a lady had gone unchallenged.

Now the public learned more of Karen's life, past and present.

A *Star-Telegram* reporter's exclusive interview with Karen was splashed over the morning edition of the paper and then continued in the evening paper. There was a reproduction of a painting featuring portraits of Cullen and Karen and their four children, Cullen's two sons and Karen's two boys. There were snaps from Karen's scrapbook: a baby picture at eight months; on a pony as a child; and wearing a fireman's hat after winning a trophy as Miss Flame at a firemen's beauty contest when she was seventeen. A contemporary portrait, at twenty-nine, demonstrated her "flawless complexion and a Marilyn Monroe kind of innocent look."

Karen's conservative but designer-fashioned wardrobe was described, and her beautifully coiffed hair. It was short; Karen explained that it was naturally a light brown but had been overbleached during a ski trip with Cullen and she had to crop it when it became brittle. "I was afraid Cullen wouldn't like it short, but he was lying here on the couch one day, and told me he liked my hair short because it made me look like Mitzi Gaynor."

There were other photographs of the good-looking woman whom the reporter had managed to identify as resembling a film star twice within the space of three paragraphs. There was a photograph of Karen conversing in sign language with her deaf son Chesley, seven years old, and two photographs of Karen and her second handicapped son Trey, age nine.

"I would like a jury to hear what my son Trey has to say about Cullen Davis," Karen told the interviewer, "because there isn't a jury in the world that would convict him after that. He is the only father image my two have ever had—and if Chesley could only talk. They worship the ground that Cullen Davis walks on. Cullen has the patience of Job with Chesley.''

The exclusive interview recounted that before Karen was born her mother had worked for and known Stinky Davis. She was a secretary for Mid-Continent Supply when she was pregnant with Karen, who was born in Fort Worth in 1943. When she was eight her father, Ray Hudson, and her mother separated. Karen and her mother lived with Karen's grandparents after Hudson moved west. Karen attended local high schools and sold shoes after school at Thom McAn's. Offered a full-time position at the shoe store, she worked days and attended night high school until she graduated. During one period Karen held three jobs: days at the shoe store, lunch hours at a boutique, and at a department store at night.

Her relationships with her father and stepfather were equally good. She visited Ray Hudson in Amarillo and at his ranch in Arizona during her teen years. She called Hudson ''Big Daddy'' and her stepfather ''Daddy.''

''Mother got out her old albums and there were photographs of company picnics,'' Karen said, ''with Cullen when he was fifteen or sixteen years old.''

Shortly after her eighteenth birthday Karen married Walter Master. Their first son Trey was born while his father was overseas. Three years later Chesley was born.

In 1971 the Masters were returning from Sunday services at the Assembly of God Church. There was a head-on collision with another car. Karen was seriously injured, suffering a fractured skull, a broken jaw which caused temporary facial paralysis, a burst eardrum, and an arm fractured in three places. She was in the hospital five weeks before she learned of the severity of her sons' injuries. Trey, age four, would have brain surgery ten times and be required to wear a shunt—a tube which relieved pressure on his brain by drawing accumulated fluids away from the cranium to his stomach. Chesley, four months old, was so battered in the accident that he was brain-injured and became deaf, epileptic, and hyperactive. Seven years later he was still attending special classes for the multiply handicapped.

Walter Master and Karen were divorced eighteen months after the accident.

Karen attended Texas Christian University to learn everything she could about caring for handicapped children. The schedule of school and part-time work was so demanding that she compromised by auditing courses at the university when her father, Ray Hudson, began to provide some financial assistance. She augmented this income by working as a "Kelly girl" and occasionally at the First National Bank. Karen taught some classes at the Speech and Hearing Clinic.

A young woman in the office of a brain surgeon who had operated on Trey arranged a blind date for Karen with Cullen Davis in late 1974, a few months after he had been separated from Priscilla. Cullen had been dubious, believing at first that he was being paired up with the sister of his former wife Sandra, whose name as irony would have it was Karen Masters. That misconception disposed of, Karen and Cullen began to see each other frequently.

Karen said that she had no idea who Cullen Davis was when she first began to go with him. When her mother asked her about her new beau, Karen told the *Star-Telegram* reporter, she replied that "He and his brother have some kind of little parts business."

"Karen, sit down," her mother said. "I have something to tell you."

"That was the first time I knew Cullen was a wealthy man," Karen averred. "Now at family get-togethers Mother and Cullen talk business and old times at Mid-Continent."

Karen described life with Cullen after he moved into her home in 1975. She loved to cook and prepared most of the

175

meals. The family had breakfast together each morning. She drove in the car pool to the boys' schools, and Cullen went to his office. During the day Karen was a volunteer worker with the local chapter of the Texas Association for the Deaf, and she was elected state president of the organization in 1978. She attended dance or exercise sessions. She made it a point to be at home at 4:30 P.M. to prepare the evening meal so that it would be ready when Cullen arrived from the office, usually at 6:30 or 7:00 P.M. On Sunday, Karen worshipped at the Trinity Episcopal Church where Trey was an acolyte. "The Episcopal church teaches the love of Christ," Karen said, "and its teachings have met my needs better than any other—but I have attended other beautiful churches and taught Sunday School in some of them."

In the evenings Cullen and Karen would "eat and watch television. Or we go to the movies. Cullen is a great movie buff. We have seen every movie in town—except the X-rated movies. Contrary to those stories, he doesn't want to see the X-rated shows."

In addition to her increased concern for Cullen after his second arrest, Karen expressed another apprehension. "The only fear I have for my children is that their father will try to take them away from me again." Walter Master had taken the boys after Cullen's Amarillo trial. They returned to Karen's custody after a court hearing.

Karen said she found it impossible to believe that Cullen could be guilty of the allegations in Amarillo and the new charges against him now. "I believe in his innocence," she said. "So does everyone else in my family. It's beyond our comprehension how this thing can happen. When a man can take on responsibility for two handicapped children—especially a deaf child—work with them, and have the patience of Job, it's heartbreaking to have someone think he would even think of killing a child—much less be capable of any kind of a crime."

The newspaper interviews revealed that Karen had never been inside the mansion on Mockingbird Lane, and that she was not sure she would want to live there. "I would be foolish to say that material things don't matter, but Cullen and the boys and I have a beautiful family life, and I wouldn't trade that for any material thing. If Cullen decided he wanted to live in that house, as long as I could take the love shared with the children and Cullen it would be okay with me."

Meanwhile, Karen concluded, she was confident she and Cullen and the children would someday lead a normal life in Fort Worth.

"I'll keep my mind busy now," Karen said. "I don't intend to let those deaf children down."

Priscilla Davis was asked by a journalist to comment on Karen Master's remarks about her sons. Priscilla contended that Karen was "jeopardizing their lives" by living with Cullen, and intimated that Karen must be aware of that. "She knows the truth about Cullen and Amarillo," she said. "He got away with murder. And he thought he could do it again. Cullen Davis thinks differently from other people. Anytime he does something and gets away with it, he'll try again."

Describing her reaction to Cullen's arrest, Priscilla said she intended to keep a low profile: "I don't want them to say, 'if it hadn't been for Priscilla. . . .' " But her desire for a low profile didn't keep Priscilla from reiterating her accusations against Cullen. She said she felt he had become convinced he could "get away with murder on a big scale after his attorneys pulled the wool over the eyes of the jury in Amarillo." She added that she knew he was capable of cold-blooded murder "since he marched Andrea down to the basement, looked into the eyes of that little child, and shot her in cold blood. Anybody capable of that is capable of anything. . . . I thought until the end the jury would see through the garbage thrown up by Cullen's attorneys . . . all that garbage about drugs and sex and everything they used in an attempt to discredit me and divert attention from the main issue."

Priscilla admitted that she had been concerned about her personal safety long before being advised that her name was on Cullen's hit list. She said that she maintained a security squad at the mansion; William Davis, Cullen's brother, had paid for the guards at first, and now she did.

Priscilla was asked if she thought Cullen was insane.

"Well, they say there is a very thin line. Has he crossed over?" Priscilla reflected. "I can't say."

A newsman asked Jack Wilborn for his reaction to the latest development in the case of the man who had been acquitted for the murder of Wilborn's daughter Andrea. Wilborn recalled his frustration at the Amarillo trial. "It was strange to me that, as many witnesses as they had to testify for him, not one was from the restaurant or the movie [where Davis claimed he was the night of the murders]. There was not one single person who corroborated that he was at the restaurant or the movie; not a customer or employee of either establishment testified that he was at either place. . . . The true character of Davis was never allowed to be established at that trial. . . . His whole history is one of vindictiveness and the beating of women and children."

Wilborn expressed surprise that his name was not among those on Cullen's hit list. He said that Cullen had threatened eight years previously "to have me fixed so I would never walk again."

Wilborn provided his psychological assessment of Cullen's character. "He is like a child. He wants everything and if something doesn't go his way, he goes wild. . . . I think he feels he is above being trapped. . . . He thinks he can do what he wants to. . . . He believes money is the answer to everything. I have felt all along that all of this has been over money. . . . He worships money. The first remark he ever made to me was 'You're not getting any of my money.'. . . I think the divorce situation began getting into his money, [and] that triggered the whole thing."

"The divorce situation" had become involved and messy during the four years (since 1974) Cullen and Priscilla had been separated; Cullen's latest detention made it even more complicated.

During the extended haranguing between Cullen's lawyers and Priscilla's, Judge Eidson had directed each party to formulate and deliver to him the settlement position it believed fair. Division of property was the issue, with ownership of the mansion on Mockingbird Lane a major bone of contention. That property Cullen insisted on retaining. As for money, Ronald Aultman, Priscilla's attorney, proposed that Priscilla should receive alimony of $5000 per month—the temporary support stipend she was then receiving—for twenty years. That would total $1.2 million over two decades, but Priscilla declared it was not reasonable. Further, Cullen's long-term offer was based on the proviso that the payments would continue only so long as Priscilla was alive. Priscilla and her attorneys saw this stipulation in an ominous light, especially after McCrory's testimony that Cullen wanted Priscilla dead.

The Texas Family Code calls for a fair and equal distribution of property in divorce settlements. But the Priscilla-Cullen case had as an added consideration the premarital agreement Priscilla signed waiving future benefits from any of Cullen's inherited wealth or the profits from KenDavis Industries International. Priscilla continued to insist that the document was a fraud, perpetrated when Cullen insisted she sign the agreement without explaining accurately its conditions.

As the top figure on Cullen's hit list, Judge Joe Eidson's position in the divorce was tenuous. The judge had the sole responsibility of deciding if he should remove himself from the proceedings. Cullen's attorneys insisted that he do so. Priscilla's lawyers believed he should remain on the bench.

Could Judge Eidson be impartial despite the fact that Cullen was presently facing indictment for hiring a murderer to kill him?

The *Star-Telegram* reviewed Eidson's four-year record of decisions in the convoluted case. The survey showed that in fact most of the judge's rulings had favored Cullen. He had released Cullen from the obligation of paying for Priscilla's nurses while she recuperated after being wounded at the mansion. Eidson had ruled that Cullen did not have to pay for the security detail at Priscilla's home. He had agreed that the murders at the mansion were not to be mentioned at the divorce trial. Further, he had permitted Cullen to expend monies destined for Priscilla's support in the payment of taxes instead; had allowed Cullen to sell a uranium lease to raise cash; and he had permitted Cullen to pay additional taxes with money held in escrow pending the outcome of the divorce. Eidson had denied Priscilla's request that Cullen's brother Ken be a party to the divorce suit; he had refused her request to keep secret a deposition made in the case and, again, had ruled that Cullen could borrow money for current expenses. Of the nine rulings, the one prohibiting mention of the murders on Mockingbird Lane during the divorce trial was the one which most offended Priscilla's lawyers. As in the Amarillo trial, they felt, there would be no opportunity to impugn Cullen's character.

Judge Eidson had ruled in favor of Priscilla in ordering Cullen to increase temporary alimony payments, in agreeing several times to a delay in the divorce proceedings, and in refusing to allow Cullen to sell a particular block of stock coveted by Priscilla. He had also issued a temporary restraining order which prevented Cullen from visiting the mansion.

Priscilla's lawyers wanted Eidson to stay on, contending that Cullen's attorneys had the attitude: "We don't have this judge in our pocket, so let's shop elsewhere." Another observer claimed that Eidson should remain on the bench. "Otherwise, any man who doesn't like a judge can go out and threaten his life and get a new judge."

Cullen's attorneys were insistent that Eidson step down. They were also adamantly opposed to further delays. Another delay, said one, "would be an utter disgrace and the severest blow I can imagine to the integrity of the judicial system in this country."

Some Fort Worth citizens who thought Cullen guilty believed Judge Eidson shared some blame—Cullen would not have been driven to his desperate acts if the divorce proceedings had been

briefer. Others, whatever their feeling about Cullen's guilt or innocence, did not approve of Eidson's posing for a fake
photograph for the FBI. It was beneath a judge's dignity, they
said, to stoop so low as to crawl into the trunk of a car.

Judge Tom Cave had also been involved with Cullen's misfor-
tunes and had been on Cullen's list. Armor-plate was installed
behind the wood panels of his podium soon after Cullen's arrest.
Henceforth Cave would preside from behind a bulletproof
bench.

In Cullen's cell in the county jail a pipe leaked, dripping
water onto his white prison coveralls. Cullen was then moved
from his isolation cell to quarters shared with another prisoner.
There had been glimpses of Cullen during the bond hearings,
but the public had nothing in the way of a current assessment of
him. An enterprising reporter from the Fort Worth bureau of the
Dallas Morning News mailed a letter to Cullen's cell mate, asking
that he respond to a series of written questions.

"I don't know why I was chosen to share a cell with Cullen,"
the man wrote, "other than perhaps somebody noticed we have
similar educational backgrounds." The prisoner was a forty-
one-year-old college graduate with a degree in English; he was
serving a one-year sentence for possession of a forged check.

"We get along very well," Cullen's cell mate wrote. "He is a
quiet, reserved, and intellectual man, and I never once saw him
become upset with anyone. . . . Cullen is a congenial man, and
not in the least arrogant. I have known people, in the past, who
were well off and let you know it immediately. Cullen is not one
of these. He is very unpretentious and impressed me as a man
who liked to have fun. He laughs a lot . . . we laughed a lot
together."

The correspondent said that Cullen denied all the charges that
had been made against him.

During the eleven days they spent together the prisoner said he
and Cullen played quiz games about authors, movies, and capitals. "I beat him on the states but he blitzed me on foreign

capitals.'' They played chess and checkers some fifty times. Cullen won nearly every game. ''He has a very acute and perceptive mind, and is an excellent tactician. . . . He gets along well with the other inmates and myself as well. He is an avid Cowboy fan and was disappointed when Los Angeles beat them.''

Cullen Davis, the imprisoned football fan, waited out August, for him the cruelest month. It was in August of 1968 that he had married Priscilla, an act he later described as the worst mistake of his life. August 1976 he was arrested after the murders in the mansion. He was languishing in the Potter County jail in Amarillo in August 1977. And this August, in 1978, found him again in jail—while Haynes and his legal team were attempting to persuade visiting Judge Tipps that Cullen should be free during his bond hearings and the grand jury deliberations.

In a current August edition of the *Fort Worth Star-Telegram* Glen Guzzo reported an intriguing story. Two months before the shootings at the mansion in 1976, Priscilla had reported to police that she was missing some personal items after a burglary. A few days later two young boys playing on the banks of the nearby Trinity River had found a Colt .45 automatic equipped with a silencer. The boys turned the gun over to the Tarrant County sheriff. It had been recently cleaned, inside and out, and had no fingerprints on it. The sheriff ordered a trace to be run on the weapon to determine its owner.

While awaiting the results of the trace, the sheriff had been approached by one Roy Rimmer, Jr. Rimmer had reported a robbery at his home in 1972. Now, he told the sheriff, he understood that a weapon similar to the one stolen from his home four years before had been recovered. A check revealed that, in an inventory of missing items at the time his house had been burgled, Rimmer had reported the loss of seven weapons—but not a .45 automatic with a silencer. ''We just missed it, apparently,'' Rimmer explained, ''in listing all of the stuff that was stolen.'' In any event, Rimmer decided the gun in the sheriff's possession was not his.

Then the results of the sheriff's trace came back: the owner of the handgun was one Roy Rimmer, Jr. A prisoner in Huntsville was interrogated. He admitted to the robbery at Rimmer's home, but denied taking a Colt .45.

Rimmer, it turned out, was a friend of Cullen. During the Davis divorce hearings he was called to court. The subject of the illegally equipped handgun found near the mansion arose. On the advice of his attorney, Rimmer refused to answer questions about the silencer. But he did tell Priscilla's lawyers that he owed Cullen several million dollars in business debts.

It was strange—so many rich people with so many guns.*

Cullen's cruel month of August passed, but the beginning of September was no better for him. On the first day of the month—after seven days of testimony and eleven witnesses—Judge Arthur Tipps denied the motion for Cullen's bond. Cullen turned to Racehorse Haynes and asked, ''What's next?''

What was next, a week later, was a grand jury indictment of Cullen on two felony counts: soliciting the capital murder of Judge Eidson, and possessing an illegal silencer. The first indictment was in four parts, allowing a trial jury four possible findings if Cullen should be convicted. The maximum sentence a jury could hand down was identical for all four options: each was punishable by life imprisonment or five to ninety-nine years in prison. The second indictment, that of owning a silencer-equipped .22 Ruger pistol, could bring two to twenty years, or a fine of $10,000, or both.

Judge Eidson, certain to be called as a witness in Cullen's murder trial, stepped down as arbiter in the divorce case.

---

* In 1977 the U.S. Securities and Exchange Commission charged Roy Rimmer with violation of antifraud laws. The SEC document confirmed that Cullen had made multimillion-dollar loans to Rimmer. During a 1979 divorce hearing, Priscilla's lawyers were not allowed to introduce evidence possibly linking Cullen and Rimmer to the purchase of a .38 calibre revolver in 1975. The .38 revolver used by the man in black during the mansion murders in 1976 has never been found.

Retired Judge John Barron was brought in from nearby Bryan, Texas, to replace Eidson. Barron rescheduled the divorce trial first for November 6, then later for December 4. A jury would resolve the matter; in Texas, litigants in divorce contests may request a jury trial when custody of a minor child is not an issue, and Cullen wanted a jury. Perhaps he had been persuaded by now that Texas jurors, properly selected, were inclined to be a bit less concerned with legal technicalities and less stuffy about evidence—as well as less strictly accountable for their actions and decisions—than judges tended to be.

Depositions were still being taken and hearings conducted in the divorce proceedings. Each new revelation concerning the squabbles and sexual adventures of Cullen and Priscilla set off a new round of clucking amongst more staid Fort Worthians.

In a sworn statement, just before Cullen's most recent arrest, Priscilla contended that her marriage to Cullen had broken up because he was an adulterer and wife beater. She identified the women she claimed had been Cullen's lovers, one of whom was a woman who traded sex for Cullen's badge permitting entry into the Colonial Country Club golf tournament. Priscilla swore these liaisons had occurred before their separation, and that Cullen had boasted of them to her.

On the other hand, Priscilla vowed that she had not enjoyed extramarital sex until after the separation. She admitted that W. T. Rufner had been her first lover. During the hearing concerning Priscilla's deposition one of Cullen's civil lawyers, Cecil Munn, put a number of questions to her about nudity with obvious reference to W. T. Rufner and the picturesque photograph introduced as evidence in Cullen's Amarillo trial.

"Prior to separation," Munn asked, "were you ever in a circumstance where other men were nude in your presence?"

"Not to my recollection," Priscilla said.

"Virtually nude?"

Priscilla asked for clarification: "Swimsuits?"

"Or Christmas stocking?" Munn prodded.

"I don't remember *that* at all," Priscilla said.

"You don't remember what, Mrs. Davis?"

"What you suggested," Priscilla said.

"Obviously," Munn stated, "you're alluding to a photograph of your friend, W. T. Rufner, taken in the nude with the exception of a Christmas stocking over his genitals, in which you appeared, are you not?"

The spicy exchange ended when Priscilla's lawyer, Ronald Aultman, instructed his client to refuse to answer such questions.

Priscilla had testified earlier about Cullen's vile temper and the frequency with which he had pummeled her about the face and shoulders. She expanded her list of complaints. "He beat me up and broke my nose." She described a lively frolic in the snow at Aspen when Cullen "all of a sudden . . . just went *bam* and busted my lip." Then there was the night Cullen was in a foul mood because the waiter at the Carriage House restaurant had served the wrong kind of rolls. Once home, the enraged Cullen had pushed her down a flight of stairs. On another occasion Cullen "got mad at me and he threw his pudding on me."

And Priscilla once again described the now famous incident after the Steeplechase Ball when Cullen couldn't find his keys. "Cullen took the board and threw it down in the mud and everything. I was down trying to pick them up." Then Cullen had cursed her. The parking lot attendant had said, "You better go, lady, before he beats you up."

Priscilla was asked about her past job experience. She said she had been "a job counselor for an employment agency" before she and Cullen were married. Before that, in Houston, she had worked in the mail room of the Gulf Oil Corporation and, for a while, in the Montgomery Ward "servicing department."

"Have you ever rendered a service of any other kind," she was asked, "at any time for money?"

Priscilla arched an eyebrow. "Basically," she replied, "I've been a housewife."

185

The telephone lines buzzed in the golden ghettos of Fort Worth. *Isn't it juicy? People will pay attention to Fort Worth now—did you see both* Time *and* Newsweek *had full-page stories last week? You can forget Dallas! Cullen and Priscilla are becoming folk figures like Frankie and Johnny. Have you heard the song they're singing down in Granbury?**

Priscilla seemed to relish the notoriety from within her sanctuary at 4200 Mockingbird Lane. Cullen wasn't averse to publicity either. He sent a message, indirectly, to his high school classmate, Thomas Thompson, author of *Blood and Money.* He hoped Thompson would write the first book about T. Cullen Davis. Thompson did not grasp the opportunity, explaining later to another writer that he had already written his Texas Gothic.

There were some in Fort Worth who were seriously concerned about Cullen's upcoming trial, recognizing it as an event of import. There was spirited discussion about his chances of acquittal or a mistrial, and what either would mean to the large number of people who had been involved, one way or another, in Cullen's life. The circulation of the morning and evening *Star-Telegram* increased dramatically. Fort Worth's major radio station reported on Cullen's situation almost hourly. †

Fort Worth lawyers attempted to anticipate the strategy Richard Haynes would employ in defending Cullen in his second trial. Most assumed that Haynes would claim Cullen was a victim of a conspiracy, and that Cullen had been framed by three persons—not an unrealistic assumption considering the testimony during the bond hearings which revealed that a series of meetings had recently taken place between Priscilla and Pat

---

* "Priscilla's Place" was being sung in soft-shoe tempo by a male trio at "4 Doors Down" in the nearby town of Granbury.

† Most radio stations use music or chimes to signal program breaks. For decades WBAP used a clanking cowbell—and still does in early morning programs—in deference to inhabitants who refer affectionately to Fort Worth as "Cow Town." WBAP compromises neatly to suit musical tastes: Every other hour is devoted to solid country music.

Burleson, the karate-studio franchiser. When McCrory had decided that he must inform the FBI about Cullen's murder-for-hire plan, he asked Burleson for advice. Burleson had suggested that McCrory tell his story to an FBI agent who had taken karate lessons from Burleson and, thereupon, arranged the meeting. Burleson, as it turned out, was meeting Priscilla frequently during this period; he had been at the mansion at the very time Cullen was being arrested on the latest charge. That was a suspicious series of circumstances Haynes would certainly exploit.

Another recent development was considered by the local lawyers as a plus for the prosecution. Tim Curry announced that because of the press of official business in the DA's office, he would be unable to travel from Fort Worth to act as chief prosecutor at the upcoming trial. But a new assistant prosecutor in his office would go. Jerry Buckner was the only lawyer in Fort Worth who had ever won a courtroom battle with Racehorse Haynes. After Cullen's Amarillo trial and before Cullen's most recent arrest, Haynes had defended Sylvia Meek, a Fort Worth private investigator, on the charge that she had shot and killed a business competitor during a squabble over ownership of a lie detector. Buckner plea bargained, offering a ten-year probated sentence. Haynes did not accept that, and the case went to trial. Sylvia Meek was convicted, and the jury recommended a ten-year probated sentence. It was the only time during 1978 in Fort Worth that someone found guilty of murder did not serve time. Ms. Meek had been one of Haynes's witnesses in Cullen's Amarillo trial. Although she lost her own case, she was fortunate to have had a defense lawyer of such renown accept her relatively minor case, and to have avoided prison.

The issue of a fair trial for Cullen arose. The decision was in the hands of Judge Tipps, the out-of-town judge who had presided over the bond hearing.

Before Cullen's Amarillo trial, Glen Guzzo, the *Star-Telegram* reporter, had been called as a witness during the change of venue deliberations. Guzzo was called again to testify about the extent of publicity surrounding Cullen's latest situation. "It's my opinion...that you cannot select twelve jurors in Tarrant County who can be fair and impartial." Guzzo said he had talked with hundreds of Fort Worth residents in recent months and found a large majority still convinced that Cullen was innocent.

Then, suddenly, the chances of convicting Cullen *anywhere* diminished. Jerry Buckner, the only attorney in Fort Worth ever to have convicted a Haynes client in a Fort Worth courtroom, abruptly resigned from the district attorney's office to enter private practice, explaining that an uncle had offered him a lucrative partnership. Some thought it strange that a young attorney should retreat from the scene on the eve of a trial which could have made him famous.

Judge Tipps pondered the change of venue during the third week of September; a number of Texas cities were mentioned as potential trial sites—Austin, Corpus Christi, Abilene, and Lubbock. Probably, however, Tipps would select one of the larger cities because it would have commodious courtrooms and travel accommodations for visiting lawyers and news people. San Antonio, perhaps. Or Houston.

On September 21, Racehorse Haynes and Cullen waited for Judge Tipps to decree where Cullen's next trial would be held.

"If it's Houston," Haynes said, "I'll be smirking." Haynes was alluding to the irony of the possible selection of that city where he lived and worked and had many friends in legal circles, both on and off the bench.

Moments later Judge Tipps announced that he had selected Houston.

Glen Guzzo anticipated a long beat out of town covering what had now become known among members of the press as Cullen II. Glen called Houston for a telephone interview with Wallace C. Moore, the Harris County district judge whom Tipps had appointed to preside at the trial.

Judge Moore admitted that he knew little about Cullen's case, but he did describe himself as a close personal friend of Racehorse Haynes.

·11·

THE OLD JUDGE AND
THE JOURNALIST

"So *now,*" the old Judge said, "your publishers find the T. Cullen Davis book to be worth the candle?"

The journalist and the Judge were at the halfway mark in an early morning hike around the Rivercrest golf course. The journalist was in Fort Worth gathering additional material about the Davis family. He had joined the Judge several times for the morning rounds.

"How's the book coming, son?" The Judge bent down with cupped hands at the drinking fountain at the sixth tee while his dog lapped water from them.

"It's not easy," the journalist said, "to resist the temptation of turning a book about Cullen into one about Fort Worth." Returning home after three decades, the journalist was only beginning to appreciate what kind of town Fort Worth was and is now. The affluent mini-culture represented by the huge mansions bordering the golf links was worth a book in itself. It would be intriguing to identify and describe the elusive line which divided the old from the new and the East from the West. The Amon Carter Museum with its fine Remingtons, for instance, next to the Kimbell Art Museum with its superb collection of European masterpieces.

The Judge agreed. "Now certainly this hat," he said, touching the brim of his Stetson, "is a symbol of the West. Do you know where Stetson hats were first manufactured, son?"

The journalist didn't know.

"In Philadelphia," the Judge said. Then he commented on

189

old wealth and new riches in the local society. "Fort Worth is really a small town and, where it matters, a closed corporation in social terms. If you want to get lost in a big city where social mobility prevails, move over to Dallas or down to Houston. Around here, son, money can get you so far and no further—at least until it has been sanctified by several generations of responsible, if not reasonably genteel, conduct on the part of the family. There aren't many places like Fort Worth left to provide people with an understanding of this type of vanishing society. And, since they built that big airport between here and Dallas, Fort Worth as we knew it may not be around that much longer. Maybe its time passed long ago and we just didn't know it. But imagine living in a"—the Judge mouthed the offensive word with distaste— "*Metroplex!*"

The journalist told the Judge of a problem: he was finding that most people who knew or were associated with Cullen refused to talk about him. They were reticent because, in his judgment, they were frightened. He told the Judge about entering a commercial photography shop in Fort Worth with a copy of the 1951 Arlington Heights High School yearbook. He asked that Cullen's class picture be reproduced. The clerk looked down and saw the name Cullen Davis under the boy's photograph. The clerk closed the yearbook, gave it back to the journalist, and moved his head from side to side negatively. The clerk said nothing; he just kept shaking his head. He didn't want to be on Cullen's list.

The Judge chuckled.

People who had known Priscilla talked freely about her. Those who agreed to an interview about Cullen requested anonymity and asked that nothing appear in the book which could be traced back to them.

The Judge's chuckles turned into hearty laughter. He put his hand on the journalist's shoulder. "Son, you have a problem you're not aware of in interviewing people. The word is getting around town that you're not really writing a book."

The journalist didn't understand.

"People are saying you *can't* be writing a book, because you don't take notes when they talk to you."

"That's true," the journalist said. "That comes from my intelligence experience, when I found that taking notes inhibited people I was questioning. Then, and now, I've always jotted down notes after an interview. If I'm not writing a book, what does everyone think I'm doing?"

"That is what amuses me," the Judge said. "They think you're an investigator working for Racehorse Haynes!"

The journalist was genuinely surprised and expressed skepticism, but the Judge insisted it was true.

"Well, Mr. Investigator," the Judge asked, as they continued their walk, "what have you learned?"

The journalist said he had learned that the Judge had been correct when he theorized that Stinky Davis had had a profound effect on his sons, especially in training them to appreciate money and to keep a firm grasp on property. Curiously, however, Stinky told his sons little of his Pennsylvania past. When Stinky died the medical information about his death was recorded by the physician, but his family background, according to the death certificate, was provided by Cullen. In the space requesting his mother's maiden name, the notation was "Unknown."

"Is it true," the Judge asked, "that Cullen married Priscilla the day his father died because the first son to marry after Stinky's death was to inherit the house?"

The story was not true. Cullen and Priscilla had applied for their marriage license two days before Stinky's heart attack. Stinky's will divided his money and property equally between his three sons. It was true that Cullen and Priscilla were married on the day of Stinky's death. He died a few minutes before four in the afternoon, and they went on with evening wedding plans because everything had been arranged. The journalist shrugged. Perhaps that was understandable.

"Understandable perhaps," the Judge grunted. "But it does seem to me to be . . ." the Judge paused, seeking the word. Then he finished: "undignified.

191

"What about all those stories about Priscilla?" the Judge asked.

The journalist said he had heard countless anecdotes about Priscilla which portrayed her as a prostitute, as Stinky's mistress, or as the organizer of orgies at the mansion on Mockingbird Lane. Beyond what had already come to light during the Amarillo trial, evidence of the allegations did not exist. Many Fort Worth men intimated, and a few boasted, that they had bedded Priscilla, but not cited place, date, or circumstance. Priscilla's sexual history fell short of promiscuity. She didn't pretend to be Rebecca, nor that the mansion was Sunnybrook Farm, but she slept with one man at a time. After Cullen it had been W.T. Rufner, then Stan Farr. Now she was seen only with Rich Sauer. In the main, people remembered Priscilla kindly. Everyone the journalist had talked to who really knew her—including those who disapproved of her life-style—sort of *liked* Priscilla.

"Not counting the murder business in 1976, does either Priscilla or Cullen have a criminal record?" the Judge asked.

"Priscilla was booked once," the journalist said, "for shoplifting. That was in 1961, when she was twenty years old. She was accused of taking a dress and a white jeweled sweater from a store on Camp Bowie."

"What about Cullen and wigs?" the Judge asked. "Tolly Wilson made some murky reference to that after the Amarillo trial."

"Wilson was probably referring to the time when Cullen wore a wig during an impromptu public appearance at the Albatross Club. And, then, at a party—here in the Rivercrest house—Cullen put on a wig and did a belly dance. But most men wear a wig, for one reason or another, more than once. So that's not really a valid connection. And I haven't found anything to indicate that Cullen is kinky, or that he ever associated with deviates."

"Mental illness?"

"Cullen's certainly impetuous," the journalist said. "Several people claim he bought his private jet because he became furious after losing his luggage on a commercial flight. He has a reputation for abusing women. But mentally disturbed . . . ?'' The journalist paused. ''If he's guilty as charged I suppose that only some mental quirk can explain what he has done. Maybe he has a Nixon-like complex which allows him to convince himself that he has the right to thwart his enemies. Perhaps Cullen described himself on the tape when he said to McCrory, 'Just paranoid.' ''

''What about that story you told me before,'' the Judge said, ''about Cullen listening to some writer talk about his book—and Racehorse Haynes getting a murderer off—just before the shootings at the Mockingbird Lane place?''

''That connection is tenuous, too,'' the journalist said. ''I talked to several people who were at that high school reunion, and they remembered Tommy Thompson describing the murder case in detail, and talking about Racehorse Haynes. They speculated that Cullen got the idea he could get away with murder then.''

''Well?''

''Then I talked to someone else who was there. He said that the details of the Houston trial were not mentioned, nor was the name of Racehorse Haynes. The man who told me should know—Tommy Thompson.''

''Do you believe Cullen is guilty?'' the Judge asked.

The journalist said he wanted to reserve judgment on that.

''In your book, son,'' the Judge said, ''it appears to me you have the obligation to let your readers know what you believe. If you think Cullen is crazy, you should say so. If you think he's guilty—no matter how the verdict goes in Houston—you should say that, too.''

The Judge fell into silence as they continued their walk. He slowed the pace of his stride and pulled thoughtfully at his pursed lips. The two men and the dog turned the corner of the road which lead to the Davis Rivercrest mansion where William now lived.

The journalist broke the silence. "Judge, I've made an informal survey among people who know something about Cullen's case. The consensus is that Cullen has a fifty-fifty chance of being acquitted. I find that hard to believe, given the evidence on the tapes."

"It's quite possible that he will be acquitted," the Judge said. "Or, that there will be a mistrial or a hung jury."

"But even Racehorse Haynes will find it impossible to explain those tapes," the journalist said.

"In 1973," the Judge recalled, "there was a similar case right here in Tarrant County. The county commissioner then was George Richardson; people called him Skeet. Skeet was approached by three men. It was alleged that the trio attempted to bribe Skeet so he would vote their way on a lucrative contract for some voting machines the county was about to buy. Skeet went to the district attorney. A microphone was concealed on his person, and at the next meeting between Skeet and the three men the conversation was recorded. There was a trial, and the tape was the prosecution's main evidence. But the lawyer claimed that the talk on the tape meant nothing, that his client had been framed, that he was not a conspirator at all. All three of those men were acquitted, son." The Judge sighed; he seemed weary. "Despite that incriminating evidence those men went free."

The Judge looked at the journalist.

"Do you know who that lawyer was, son?"

"I can guess," the journalist said.

"That's right," the Judge said. "Richard Racehorse Haynes, up to Fort Worth from Houston.

"During Cullen's trial in Houston," the Judge explained, "Haynes will have to decide early on if he should claim the tapes were fabricated or tinkered with in some way. Before doing that he'll have to consider the reputation of the men who made the tapes. Despite everything that's been revealed in recent years about FBI abuses, the Bureau is highly regarded in this part of the country. Those efficient-looking men in dark suits and white shirts make credible witnesses in Texas. Jurors might be persuaded that the district attorney's office or the local police are involved in skulduggery. But not the FBI and the Texas Rangers. When Texans think of a Ranger, son, they visualize Gary Cooper. They remember the story of a Ranger who stepped off a train to quell a riot in a small town. The townspeople were upset when only one Ranger arrived to dampen the behavior of so many, but the Ranger said, "They's only one riot, ain't they?"

So, the Judge concluded, Racehorse Haynes would probably refrain from challenging the authenticity of the tapes, but rather would attack what is said on them.

"Entrapment?"

"Can't," the Judge said. "Entrapment is arguable only when the defendant pleads guilty, and that's not likely in Cullen's case. Haynes may focus on conspiracy, and claim that Cullen was framed by Priscilla, McCrory, and that Burleson fellow."

Then Haynes will face a major decision: whether or not Cullen should testify. If the tapes can be explained, the jury will expect Cullen to do the explaining.

The men approached the end of their walk.

"A moment ago," the Judge said, "you spoke of people being afraid. Look at *that!*" The Judge pointed down the street to the Davis place.

Work crews were erecting a tremendous fence around the grounds of the mansion where William Davis lived. Tall, spiked metal sections were being mounted on stone bases. A bulldozer was scooping a driveway for a new entrance to the house; it was two hundred yards further from the front door than the old entrance across the street from the tee on the fifteenth hole.

"The golfers are concerned," the Judge said. "They fear William will electrify that fence and they won't be able to retrieve golf balls hooked out of bounds onto his property."

The Judge did not smile.

"I've heard that fence was dismantled from some royal estate," the Judge continued, "and brought over here from Europe. What with that immense entrance gate and the statues of lions on each side of it, I'd estimate it must have cost William a hundred thousand dollars, or more. And now there are guards around this house all the time. William was frightened enough after the shootings in '76—they say he rounded up his family and took them up to the attic and sat there with a shotgun across his knees until police came to take them all to a judge's house. He must be thoroughly frightened now that he's reportedly on Cullen's alledged hit list.''

The two men sat on the stone bench in the tee house and watched the fence going up at the mansion.

"That's one hell of a fence," the journalist commented. "But I wonder if there is any meaningful difference between it and the barrier a poor man would erect to hide behind?''

"What's that, son?''

"Judge, when you and I discussed Cullen's case before the Amarillo trial you chided me about seeing it in sociological terms. Perhaps you were right; perhaps the only real difference between his plight and that of others standing accused of the same thing is his wealth. Maybe Cullen's is just another murder case written off to bad taste since he's rich. If he were poor, we'd blame it on a bad environment.''

"Just another murder case?'' The Judge drew back; he was astonished. "Do you really *mean* that? Do you really *think* that?''

The Judge was agitated. His lips began to tremble.

"But, Judge. . . .'' The journalist spoke carefully. "You said yourself that it looked like a simple case of murder to you.''

"*Goddamn* it!'' The Judge was almost shouting. "That was *Amarillo!* The case being tried was about a man who I think went on a rampage and slaughtered people because something snapped inside him. It could be argued that there was no premeditation in that carnage. But Cullen's Houston trial will determine something entirely different—ominously different. Don't you comprehend that someone has launched an assault against our system of criminal jurisprudence? That the *law* is threatened!''

The Judge stopped long enough to catch his breath. Then he spoke less stridently, but fervently.

"One of two things has happened," the Judge said, "depending on whether Cullen is guilty or innocent of this latest charge. If Cullen *is* guilty, it must mean that he was either testing or flouting the system because he is convinced he can use money and power to do whatever he wants. It would mean that one man has—with premeditation—taken us all on and challenged the law because he thinks he's above it. If this society"—the Judge flung his hand in the general direction of the golf course—"can produce a man who believes that and blatantly proceeds to prove it, we are in trouble."

Then the Judge shook an admonishing finger at the journalist.

"The *other* possibility is that Cullen is innocent. If he is guiltless do you realize what *that* means? It means the threat is even more ominous—because it follows that the *system* launched a calculated assault against a citizen. If Cullen is truly innocent, then we can only deduce that the district attorney's office, the FBI, the police, the Texas Rangers, all were engaged in a deliberate and monstrous conspiracy to put an innocent man behind bars. What got into them to do such a thing? Where does that leave our respect for the administration of justice? Its impartiality? Think a moment, son, of the implications of what happened here in Fort Worth if Cullen is *not* guilty."

The journalist pondered the impassioned argument as they returned to the Judge's home. At the gate the journalist bid him good-bye, explaining he had to pack for a flight to Houston.

·12·

CULLEN II—

THE HOUSTON TRIAL

The airline passenger was met at the Houston airport by a friend. "Welcome," went the greeting, "to the land of bilk and money."

Houston is America's fifth most populous city and the fastest growing area in the United States. It is located on 520 square miles of bleak landscape near the second largest port in America. Some residents call it the big swamp. The burgeoning city has modern skyscrapers, new and old oil wealth, and innumerable lawyers. Four of the nation's top ten law firms operate in the city.

On September 22, 1978, T. Cullen Davis celebrated his forty-fifth birthday—his third in custody—in two cities and on the highway between them. Judge Cave had ordered that the prisoner be transferred from Fort Worth to Houston "forthwith." Texas law requires that prosecutors bring a criminal defendant to trial within sixty days of arrest, or that they grant freedom under bond. Delays in criminal trials occur only when defense lawyers request an extension.

Two sheriff's deputies removed Cullen from the Tarrant County jail shortly before 8:00 A.M. for the 263-mile automobile trip from Fort Worth to Houston. There Cullen was confined in one of five cells reserved for inmates involved in sensational or well-publicized crimes. He changed from a light gray suit to jail attire: white pants, a white shirt with the identification "Harris County Jail," and plastic slippers to replace his wing-tipped shoes. Asked what he thought of his new quarters, Cullen replied, "Peachy," adding that in the Houston jail ice cream was sometimes available. But everything was not peaches and cream in Houston's Cross-Bar Hotel, where guests are awakened each morning at 3:30. In Amarillo, Cullen had been allowed to mingle with spectators and journalists during court recesses. In Houston, Judge Moore decreed that this nationally famous prisoner would not be permitted to meet and talk with media representatives. He would be granted unlimited access to his lawyers and lengthy conferences with his brother Ken and other executives of KenDavis Industries. Judge Moore allowed Cullen a thirty-minute visit each Saturday with Karen Master and permitted her to deliver a clean suit each day of the trial.

The Houston trial—Cullen II—was scheduled to begin on Monday, October 9. His confinement in the Harris County jail prevented Cullen from going to a Saturday night Fort Worth gala he had attended many times in the past. The annual Steeplechase Ball was a great success. Charles Tandy, the wealthy owner of Radio Shacks, gave the orchestra leader a handful of $100 bills for an extra hour's music. Tandy died the next afternoon of a heart attack while napping at his home. He was buried on Monday, the day Cullen's trial began, in the Tandy mausoleum in Greenwood Memorial Park near the even grander mausoleum where Cullen's father and mother already rested. Dozens of floral wreaths surrounded Tandy's bier; the card on one of them read, "From Cullen and Karen."

Karen followed Cullen to Houston and, except during brief trips back to Fort Worth, sat outside the courtroom (as a prospective witness she would be allowed inside only to testify) on a wooden bench. Cullen spoke of the future he anticipated with Karen, declaring for the first time his intention to marry her. "I just would like everyone to know," Cullen said, "that I would do anything for Karen, because I love her and her family. And the feeling is reciprocated. She is the best companion I have ever had."

Karen added her comment, saying that she and Cullen had first discussed marriage during a ski trip to Aspen. "Cullen knew I was not going to be the type of person who would live with somebody unmarried for the rest of my life." No actual arrangements had been made, Karen said, "because it's all so tenuous."

Judge Wallace C. Moore would preside over pretrial hearings and jury selection. Judge Moore announced emphatically that the entire process, including witnesses' testimony before the jury, would *not* be lengthy. "This case won't go on for two or three months," the judge declared. "I understand several people have made careers out of this case; I do not intend to be one of them."

One man who was on the verge of making a career of Cullen's case was skeptical. Glen Guzzo of the *Fort Worth Star-Telegram* had heard such optimistic estimates before. Judge Cave in Fort Worth had presided over nine months of legal wrangling before the mistrial there. Guzzo had been in Amarillo when Judge Dowlen's prediction of a two-month trial fell three months short of the mark. Not only was Guzzo cynical about Judge Moore's estimate of the trial's duration, he accused Moore in print of naiveté when the judge said he did not intend to sequester the Houston jury—he had never done so in previous cases. The judge seemed to be assuming that media representatives in Houston would confine their reporting to day-by-day court proceedings. Guzzo believed the daily newspapers and television accounts written by him and others would, on the contrary, recap lurid events of the past.

Perhaps, Guzzo supposed, Judge Moore did not realize how bright a spotlight would be cast on him and the trial in Houston. Glen Guzzo was to cover the proceedings for the morning *Star-Telegram* and his colleague, Jim Jones, the afternoon edition.* In

---

* The two men were an affable pair, quite different in appearance. Guzzo was slender and dark with a mod haircut over his ears. Jones was a huge man with flowing blond hair. He might have been a preacher; his usual beat was, in fact, religion.

addition there were reporters, photographers, and sketch artists from other Texas newspapers and commentators and cameramen for several television stations. Mike Cochran, who had covered the Amarillo trial for Associated Press, was in Houston, as was the UPI correspondent. Syndicated stories had been appearing throughout the country. On the day the trial began, the *New York Times* reappeared after a long strike and featured a story about Cullen II (a story in which reporter William K. Stevens described Cullen as a "conglomerateur").

Judge Moore probably suspected that his performance would be scrutinized, especially after the brouhaha which followed the Amarillo trial, and the speculation by some that Judge Dowlen had been unprofessionally permissive there. Had there been any doubt of this in Judge Moore's mind, it was resolved in pretrial hearings in Houston. During an informal meeting with attorneys involved in the case, the judge remarked—"off the cuff," he said later—on the question f whether or not Culen should be released under bond during the trial. "I don't care whether he gets out of jail or not. He's not going to run off and I doubt that while his trial is going on he's going to pose a threat to the community."

Judge Moore's assumption was hardly compatible with the prosecution's contention that Cullen was precisely such a threat to society. Almost everyone in Texas read what the judge had said in the next edition of their newspapers. Moore's phone buzzed with calls from journalists asking about his comment. "It's getting to the point," the judge said, "where I'm going to be afraid to say 'good morning.' " But Moore was not afraid to make his clarification unequivocal: "I have no intention of setting a bond. I inherited him in custody and he's going to stay in custody."

Judge Moore had received from Fort Worth Cullen's indictment: "The Grand Jurors of the State of Texas," it read, "duly elected, tried, empaneled, sworn, and charged to inquire of offenses committed in Tarrant County, in the State of Texas,

201

upon their oaths do present in and to the Criminal District No. 3 of said County that Thomas Cullen Davis hereinafter called Defendant, in the County of Tarrant and State aforesaid, on or about the 18th day of August, 1978, did

> then and there intentionally and knowingly with intent to induce David McCrory to engage in specific conduct that, under the circumstances surrounding the conduct of David McCrory as the defendant believed them to be, would constitute such capital murder and make the said David McCrory a party to the commission of such capital murder, and such specific conduct was as follows: to wit: the said defendant did request, command and attempt to induce the said David McCrory to employ another to cause the death of an individual, to wit: Joe H. Eidson, for remuneration and the promise of remuneration, to wit: money; . . .

The indictment continued with three other variations of indictment—alternatives for the jury to consider—in legal language, including conspiracy to commit capital murder.

The document which Judge Moore would use as his authority in trying Cullen was signed by the Fort Worth district attorney, just under the closing line: "AGAINST THE PEACE AND DIGNITY OF THE STATE."

When the pretrial hearings began on Monday, October 9, Haynes was ready to work in a familiar courtroom.

Racehorse Haynes's national renown was solid when Cullen's Houston trial began. He was profiled in the *Wall Street Journal*. "Haynes is one of the most successful and expensive defense attorneys in America. At fifty, his dashing courtroom style and impressive track record against long odds have already classed him with champion defense lawyers such as Percy Foreman, F. Lee Bailey, and Edward Bennett Williams. And in a branch of the profession that rests heavily on notoriety, Mr. Haynes has recently pulled ahead of his famous colleagues, and is believed by many to be America's premiere criminal defender."

Another Texas lawyer grudgingly conceded, "He's good,

he's very good. But on account of him, there are a couple of dozen people walking free in Texas who wouldn't blink before blowing someone's head off. He's a menace to society.''

Haynes had a retort: "I sleep fine at night. It isn't my job to be judge and jury, but to do the best I can on behalf of the citizen accused.'' Haynes seldom referred in the courtroom to those he defended as clients—usually they were "the citizen accused.''

Haynes described what Cullen would have called the behind-the-eight-ball positions of most of the citizens accused he defended: "My clients admit they pulled the trigger, plunged the knife, swung the club. I have to show why, because sometimes the pulling, plunging, or swinging is justified. When all else fails, I just ask the jury for mercy. They usually oblige me.''

Shortly before the Houston trial began Haynes revealed his courtroom strategy during a New York meeting of the American Bar Association. "Say you sue me because you say my dog bit you. Well, now this is my defense: My dog doesn't bite. And second . . . my dog was tied up that night. And third, I don't believe you really got bit, and fourth''—he grinned slyly—"I don't have a dog.''

If Haynes's flair for the dramatic was impressive in Amarillo, it was at Cullen II that Haynes was subjected to the scrutiny accorded one accustomed to the limelight.

Pete Axthelm of *Newsweek* traveled to Houston to write about Haynes. Axthelm usually covers the sports beat, and he saw Haynes in ring rather than turf terms: "In court, Haynes is less a racehorse than a master boxer—now a long-range jabber, now a relentless body puncher, always a ring general in command of his special arena . . . whatever the verdict [in Houston] it will follow a show of gutter-fighting investigation and high-minded skepticism by a master of both arts: the veteran at the defense table, the current champion of the big trial heavyweights.''

Physically, Richard Haynes—standing five feet eight inches in his anteater-skin boots—was a trim welterweight. He wore pinstripe suits on a sturdy, prizefighter's body. "The tailor gets a piece of material,'' Haynes once said, ''wraps it around a refrigerator, cuts it, and sends it to me.'' In fact, his clothes were stylishly cut and he was well-groomed; there was never an errant strand in his dark gray-at-the-temples hair. He used half-moon glasses to read with and as a stage prop to gesticulate with when addressing the jury. His heavy, gold wristwatch was matched by a massive gold band. He constantly clutched a huge meerschaum; once lighted, the pipe became a machine creating billows of smoke which hovered over the defense table.

Cullen was the only nonsmoker at the defense table. He must have felt reassured by the team of defense lawyers who added to the cloud of smoke with their filter-tipped cigarettes. They were talented and prosperous attorneys. They dressed immaculately; their hair was modishly styled and they exuded an air of confidence. Like Haynes, each wore a badge of office: a tremendous gold timepiece banded with heavy gold. They were the Amarillo team intact. There were three Dallas lawyers on the defense team: elegant Phil Burleson, who had defended Jack Ruby; Mike Gibson, who had assisted Dr. Denton Cooley in surgery before turning to law; and the athletically handsome Steve Sumner, who had given up baseball to head Haynes's investigation squad. Haynes and his defense lawyers looked like what they were—the best stable of criminal defenders money could buy in Texas.

Haynes kept a touch of humility tucked away from sight. A reminder written on a piece of paper in his wallet read, ''Remember the plowhorse has accomplished a lot more than the Racehorse.''

Yet the real plowhorse at Cullen II sat across the room at the prosecutors' table. Tolly Wilson and his assistant district attorneys provided a strong contrast to the slick defense team. Wilson was a rumpled man with white hair and the countenance of a grumpy Santa Claus's helper. His style in the courtroom was competent but without flair. When exasperated by Haynes's pyrotechnics, he would throw up his hands in the middle of an argument and abandon his attempt to communicate with the jury.

Wilson was assisted by three Fort Worth colleagues. Marvin Collins was a stolid, heavyset man. Assistant prosecutor Paul Gartner, at five feet four inches, was the smallest of a number of men of small stature in the courtroom. Despite the familiar kidding he was subjected to because of his size, the twenty-six-year-old Gartner was respected in Tarrant County as a research expert. On loan from the Harris County district attorney's office, Terry Wilson (no relation to Tolly) provided local expertise to the visiting prosecution team.

The only Fort Worth prosecutor in the same sartorial league with the spiffily dressed defense team was Jack Strickland. The thirty-five-year-old attorney wore vested suits in court. A last-minute replacement for Jerry Buckner, the Fort Worth lawyer who had once bested Haynes in court, Strickland had a reputation as a criminal lawyer who could build his case step by step. He had asked Fort Worth jurors to assess the death penalty in five murder cases, and they had returned the ultimate sentence in each. Strickland also differed from his colleagues in demeanor. His thin, ascetic face, under a mop of curly hair, had a constantly bemused expression suggesting a choirboy cunning.

Strickland, the most articulate member of the prosecution team, was a frequent source of quotes for the journalists in Houston. He spoke his mind and spoke it well. At the beginning of the trial he remarked, "If Cullen Davis gets off this time he can do anything he wants. He can shoot me between the eyes on national television and he won't even be arrested. That scares me. Not because I'm worried about getting shot, but because of what it means for a man to be above the law."

"I'm used to 'Pete,' " presiding Judge Wallace C. Moore said. "It's hard to grow up in a small town with a name like Wallace." Moore was born in Majestic, a hamlet in Alabama. He left the University of Florida to become a flyer in World War II. He stowed a lucky penny in his boot during thirty-five combat missions over Italy and again while flying a hundred missions in Korea. Glen Guzzo attempted in an interview to characterize the judge in a wartime role he refused to accept. "I've finally been elevated to the status of Snoopy and the Red Baron," Moore complained. "I know some real war heroes and they're laughing at me. I just want to be a judge," he added.

After sixteen years on the bench the fifty-five-year-old district judge was about to hear the most momentous case of his career. After the intense press reaction to his off-hand remark about Cullen's being free on bond he realized that his conduct on the bench would be closely observed—especially by those aware he was a friend of Racehorse Haynes. Moore already had a well-established reputation as a no-nonsense judge; now it was to be seen if he could or would keep Haynes bridled and expedite the trial as he had promised.

Judge Moore began his task with a Benson & Hedges menthol cigarette between his fingers. He was seldom to be without one as the trial progressed.*

The pretrial hearings—Priscilla, McCrory, and Pat Burleson were called as witnesses—extended through the second week of October 1978. Haynes exercised the defense option of requesting a delay of one week, to permit his technical experts to examine the FBI tapes of conversations between Cullen and McCrory. The most recent motion for bond for Cullen was still under consideration. At the end of the week the bond was denied, and Judge Moore granted Haynes's request for a second week's delay. He scheduled the first day of jury selection for the following Monday, October 30.

During the fortnight between pretrial hearings and jury selection, Cullen made skiing reservations at Aspen for the Christmas holidays—a gesture of characteristic optimism. For

---

* British members of a BBC crew filming a documentary on Cullen's trial were astonished to observe Judge Moore smoking and wearing a business suit on the bench (many Texas judges do wear judicial robes and prohibit smoking in their courts).

her part, Karen had rented an apartment in Houston and was busy acting as Cullen's secretary, answering the increasing volume of mail he received at the Harris County jail.

"Cullen, keep that sweet smile," wrote one female supporter. "Don't ever lose a positive thought and you will win. . . . Soon you will be a free man again. . . . My heart grieves each day for you. . . . Pray to God for help."

Karen replied to fifty letters a week. "A lot of the letters are about the same," she said, "all wishing Cullen good luck and saying they are behind him." One letter was from a woman in trouble. "I have been informed," the woman wrote, "a warrant has been issued for my arrest. They say I shot my stepdaughter once in the stomach. She was expecting a baby last Sunday. Since I'm on the run and in hiding, I cannot go into details." The fugitive asked Cullen to help her locate a lawyer. Many of the letters were pleas for money. Karen declined politely on white and blue stationery with the letterhead "Karen and Cullen" printed in blue.

In Fort Worth, Priscilla's fortunes vacillated. The slander suit filed against her during the Amarillo trial by a former nurse who was dismissed on the grounds of courtroom testimony privilege. Then Priscilla's two divorce lawyers estimated their legal fees would eventually total $2 million—but it was Cullen who was expected to pay the fees.

Then it was reported that Priscilla's beloved white mare Freedom either was stolen or strayed from the steel-beamed stable at the mansion. The horse was found, however, within a few days. Police recovered the animal in Fort Worth's Lake Como area. A young boy had swapped the horse for a bicycle.

Some in Fort Worth had expressed their disappointment that District Attorney Tim Curry had elected to remain in Fort Worth while delegating Tolly Wilson as chief prosecutor in Cullen's trial in Houston. Developments in Fort Worth supported Curry's assertion that there was much work to do in Tarrant County. In early November a major sting operation in the

Dallas-Fort Worth area resulted in multiple arrests and, later, Curry's office uncovered a large illegal betting ring. His colleagues across the state apparently thought highly of Curry, despite his absence from Houston. On November 16, an El Paso convention of members of the Texas District and County Attorneys Associaton elected Curry their new president.

Then two days before Cullen's trial was to resume Carl Freund, of the Fort Worth bureau of the *Dallas Morning News,* reported new details from Cullen's medical records which had become public in connection with Gus Gavrel's civil suit against Cullen. Released on bond after the August 1976 shootings, Cullen had entered a clinic which specialized in psychiatric treatment. According to the notes of the psychiatrist who saw him then, Cullen was calm and cooperative, but had appeared bored and restless with signs of depression. There was one terse entry on the clinic record. Some interpreted it as a reference to Cullen's obsession about his property on Mockingbird Lane. The psychiatrist's observation read: "House is passion."

The first panel of fifty prospective jurors was summoned to Judge Moore's court on Monday, October 30. Because Cullen had faced the spectre of a death sentence in Amarillo, potential jurors had been questioned individually on the issue of capital punishment and the process had consumed eight weeks. In Houston, where the trial would not be for capital murder, the selection would be easier and quicker, with prospective jurors questioned in groups. The prosecution and the defense were permitted to maintain ten peremptory challenges not to be revealed or utilized until the panel of fifty had been reduced to thirty-two; the twelve survivors would constitute the jury.

Each prospective juror filled out a personal history questionnaire. Most who eventually did not qualify were dismissed because they admitted they were already convinced of Cullen's guilt or because of physical or financial hardship which would ensue in the wake of a long trial. One woman was excused because of an allergy to smoke in the courtroom.

Each potential juror was asked if he or she knew any of scores of persons connected with the trial. All said they knew two men on the list provided to them—Racehorse Haynes and T. Cullen Davis.

During the jury selection process one juror was intrigued while watching Paul Gartner "taking his little notes." The juror asked Haynes how old Gartner was. "Thirteen or fourteen," Haynes replied with a grin.

Another woman provided a light moment during the otherwise tedious jury selection by commenting that her son had decided not to become a lawyer with the explanation: "Mother, I've talked to several lawyers; all of them are crooked, and I don't want to be one."

After the laughter in the courtroom died down Racehorse Haynes, his eyes twinkling, related the ancient description of a lawyer's epitaph: "Here lies a lawyer and an honest man." A bystander provided the punch line for Haynes: "Glory be, two persons in the same grave."

On Thursday the initial panel of fifty prospects had been exhausted and another group of twenty was summoned.

The final jury was seated on Friday. There were seven men and five women. There were no blacks. There were no Hispanics.*

The State presented its first witness, FBI Special Agent Ron Jannings, on Monday, November 6.

Jannings testified he had been the FBI man contacted by Charles David McCrory. That initial encounter came about because Jannings had taken karate lessons in one of Pat Burleson's studios in Fort Worth, and Burleson had directed McCrory to him. The witness described how he and other FBI men had wired McCrory for sound in preparation for his two meetings with Cullen—first on August 18 and then on August

---

* Houston has one and a half million inhabitants. The city's blacks and Hispanics total about forty-five percent of the population.

20, before Cullen was arrested and charged with soliciting the murder of Judge Joe Eidson. Jannings identified the Polaroid photograph taken after the judge had agreed to tuck himself into the trunk of his car wearing a stained and torn T-shirt. It was used by McCrory to prove to Cullen that he had had Eidson killed.

Even so, before the day was over Racehorse Haynes had scored more points from the prosecution witness than Tolly Wilson had. In his reexamination he introduced the name of one David Binion, who Haynes said had visited Priscilla in Fort Worth. He intimated that Binion was a professional assassin Priscilla wanted to hire to eliminate Cullen. Jannings refused to reply when asked if Binion had any connection with the FBI.

Using the prosecution's witness as his medium, Haynes stated that Cullen had been the victim of an extortion threat just before Christmas in 1977, after his acquittal in Amarillo. Jannings confirmed that Cullen had reported the threat to the FBI and agents had been assigned to the case. The episode involved a letter mailed to Cullen at Karen Master's home demanding $10,000 to quash an attempt on his life. FBI efforts to apprehend the extortionist had failed despite the fact that the FBI had installed a recording device on Karen's telephone.

FBI agent Jannings was again in the witness chair when the trial resumed on Tuesday. He stated that McCrory had told him about the shopping list of persons Cullen wanted killed. Priscilla topped the list. The witness said that his notes were unclear, and he could not be sure if the price for Cullen's wife was $200,000 or $500,000. Others on the list, at $80,000 each, were Judges Joe Eidson and Tom Cave. A tag of $25,000 each was placed on the lives of Beverly Bass, Gus Gavrel, Jr., Gavrel's father, and W. T. Rufner. No price had been mentioned, Jannings said, for the murder of Cullen's younger brother Bill. Additionally, the FBI man said that the list was to include Dee, Priscilla's eldest daughter, a Fort Worth businessman named A. J. Pascal, and an unidentified Mexican friend of Pascal. Pascal was identified as the subject of a civil suit filed by Cullen, who contended Pascal owed him a large sum of money.

Meanwhile, in the early days of the trial, David Binion read in the newspapers that Cullen's lawyers had left the jury with the impression he (Binion) had been contracted by Priscilla to murder Cullen. Binion sought out newsmen covering the trial and denied the allegation. He had once visited Priscilla in the mansion, he said, and departed in a quandary without knowing why she had asked him to come. But Priscilla had not, Binion insisted, asked him to murder anyone. Binion admitted that he had been a volunteer informant for the FBI on several occasions in Fort Worth and had pretended to be an underworld type in the city's night spots. But he really wasn't, he protested, and he accused Racehorse Haynes of using his name to throw up a smoke screen.

"There's not a damn thing smoke screen about it," Haynes retorted. "He admits, even in the newspapers, that he has a reputation as a hit man and that he's visited Priscilla Davis."

On Wednesday, November 15, a second Fort Worth FBI man took the stand to testify about the circumstances under which Charles David McCrory had been wired for sound before two encounters with Cullen. Special Agent Gerald Hubbell was one of the four FBI men who hid in the van on the parking lot at Coco's Famous Hamburgers on the Sunday morning when Cullen was arrested. He stated that Cullen had peered into the van suspiciously before meeting McCrory; he had been unable to see the FBI agents huddled inside because of special curtains which concealed them. Hubbell described the recording devices he had strapped to McCrory's body.

On Thursday, Fort Worth District Judge Joe Eidson was again a witness for the prosecution, as he had been in Amarillo. At one point Tolly Wilson asked the judge if, prior to the most recent postponement of the Davis divorce trial, Cullen had made any attempt to "remove" the judge from the case.

Haynes bounded out of his seat. He objected strongly to the

connotation of the word "remove" and moved that Judge Moore declare a mistrial. Moore denied the motion. It was the third time Moore had curtly scuttled a dismissal motion by Haynes. But the episodes were in the trial record should Haynes, in a later appeal, claim reversible error by his friend Judge Moore.

As in Amarillo, the prosecution used Judge Eidson as a witness to impress on the jury the theory that divorce complications triggered Cullen's murderous forays. Wilson asked the witness, "Did you ever hear [Cullen] express an opinion as to your service?"

"Yes."

"When was that?"

"I saw him on a television newscast in Amarillo the day after his acquittal of a murder charge."

"What did he say?" Tolly Wilson asked.

"He asked what he thought of the Amarillo judge and he said, 'I liked him,' or, 'He was fine. I didn't like the Fort Worth judges.' "

Phil Burleson interrogated Judge Eidson in an effort to counter the prosecution's claim that Cullen wanted Eidson dead because of his role in the divorce proceedings. He suggested that Eidson's ruling on temporary monthly payments to Priscilla had actually been favorable to Cullen, because Priscilla had asked for $7,500.

"I'd say it was a compromise," Judge Eidson said. "He was offering $3500 a month and she was asking $7500, and I concluded that $5000 would be proper."

Judge Eidson described the circumstances which led him to pose as a corpse for the FBI. When the request was made, Eidson said, "Frankly, I was pretty shaken up by the situation." In a downtown Fort Worth parking garage he climbed into the trunk of his automobile.

"I removed my coat. I removed my shirt and I removed my undershirt," Eidson said. "Then the undershirt was placed on my back and I got into the trunk of my car. I laid [sic] down and some photographs were taken."

"Was anything done to your undershirt?" Tolly Wilson asked.

"When I had it off, cigarette burns were made in it."

"Was anything put on it?"

"Yes, ketchup."

George Ridgley, the FBI photographer in the van which had Cullen under surveillance when he met with Charles David McCrory, was the final prosecution witness on Friday. He testified that he had surreptitiously photographed Cullen twenty-two times when he met McCrory on August 18, and snapped other pictures on August 20. One of the latter photographs showed Cullen wearing sunglasses, peering toward McCrory's automobile; another depicted the two men leaning over the open trunk of a car.

On Monday, November 13, while Judge Moore prepared to preside over the second week of testimony in Cullen II, a colleague began jury selection for a murder case in Fort Worth. Judge Tom Cave, who had moved Cullen I to Amarillo, was now returning the favor in Fort Worth. He was hearing, behind his boiler-plate bench, a case which had been transferred from Amarillo due to excessive publicity. It was another capital murder case. David Grijalva, twenty-six, was charged with a 1977 robbery of an Amarillo Pizza Hut during which he killed an employee. He had "somehow or other crushed the head of the night manager, a woman, in a fashion that could be described as gruesome." The woman had died from repeated blows to the head, apparently inflicted with a fifteen-pound rolling pin. Her throat had been slashed and Grijalva, to insure certain death, crushed her head in the restaurant's pizza dough mixer.

Meanwhile in Houston, Judge Moore excused the jury on Monday while a third FBI agent, Joe Gray, discussed the physical characteristics of the devices used to photograph and record the meetings between Cullen and McCrory. The groundwork was being laid for the introduction of the tapes and films and, ultimately, monitored telephone calls.

On Tuesday, Judge Moore instructed courtroom artists to put away their sketch pads during the testimony of the next witness. Charles David McCrory was a ward of U.S. marshals under the Federal Witness Protection Program. McCrory and his family had been living under assumed names and had been relocated after his testimony during Cullen's bond hearing in Fort Worth three months before. This was the most recent prohibition for the media; previously there had been the standard rule prohibiting cameras and tape recorders in the courtroom and then, at the request of defense attorneys, television and press cameras and recorders were banned entirely from the seventh floor of the courthouse.

Cullen Davis turned to stare impassively at McCrory as his chunky former friend entered the courtroom, was sworn, and took the witness seat. McCrory wore a dark blue suit with a vest. He spoke in a low voice; Tolly Wilson frequently asked him to speak up.

McCrory nervously related the circumstances which preceded the two clandestine meetings with Cullen in Fort Worth. He elaborated by adding lurid details of what he claimed were suggestions by Cullen on how the bunch of people on Cullen's hit list could be killed and their bodies disposed of.

During the first meeting on August 18, McCrory testified, Cullen spoke in low tones and in broken sentences. When they met a second time, Cullen began by saying "just paranoid" to explain his inspection of the FBI van. Then Cullen had explained his inarticulate speech during the previous encounter. "[Cullen] told me he knew there were people capable of standing a long way off and reading lips through a telescope . . . and that explained why he put his hand over his mouth when he talked. . . . He instructed me to use great caution."

McCrory repeated the account he had given at the bond hearing in Fort Worth.

"He told me he was going ahead and have Beverly killed, and 'you're going to help me hire someone to do it.' "

Tolly Wilson asked what else Cullen had said.

"He said . . . he would have me and my whole family killed . . . that he had the money and power to have it done."

On Wednesday, the August 18 tape was played for the jury. Although each juror listened through earphones, it was sometimes difficult to understand because McCrory's automobile air conditioner had been operating during the conversation. The prosecution had prepared a transcript, and requested that the jurors be provided with the written dialogue. Racehorse Haynes and Phil Burleson objected. They protested that allowing a jury to read a transcription would set a precedent for Texas courts and, Haynes hinted darkly, such a landmark decision on Judge Moore's part might constitute reversible error. Judge Moore compromised. He ruled that the jurors could use the transcript one time, during the initial hearing of the tapes. It was a pivotal decision in favor of the prosecution.

Then there was more taped evidence. Recordings of three telephone conversations between Cullen and McCrory were introduced and for them there was no need of a transcript—the exchange between the two men was clearly audible. The first call was from McCrory to Cullen on the afternoon of August 19, the Friday before the Saturday on which McCrory had promised Joe Eidson would be killed. McCrory had telephoned Cullen at Karen's home from the Pilgrim's Inn Motel in Fort Worth; FBI agents in the motel room with McCrory recorded the conversation.

"How come you didn't invite me to that fucking football game?" McCrory asked Cullen.

"You haven't got time for a ball game," Cullen responded.

McCrory promised Cullen he would let him know how things had gone either later Saturday night or early the next morning.

"Good deal," Cullen said. "You'll be uppermost in my mind."

Another recording was of a telephone call from McCrory to Cullen at 2:40 A.M., August 20—early Sunday after the Saturday night football game at Texas Stadium. McCrory reported on the weekend chore of the Murder Incorporated hit man he had dreamed up for Cullen's benefit.

> McCrory: Need to, uh, see you. Uh, he's finished with the job and he's wanting to get out of here so, uh, gotta do it now.
>
> Cullen: Oh, shit. I haven't—How—How do I know?
>
> McCrory: I got the proof. That's no sweat.
>
> Cullen: Uh, well—
>
> McCrory: Just believe me, uh, I'll show it to you. Don't worry about it.
>
> Cullen: All that information is down at the office.

Tolly Wilson and his prosecutors were to contend, through subsequent testimony, that the "information" Cullen was referring to was in fact the $25,000 in $100 bills which Cullen passed to McCrory the next morning.

> McCrory: Oh, shit, man. You gonna have to go get it. I'm not—You know. I can't—I don't want to talk, but I can't face, uh—you understand.
>
> Cullen: Well, what's the matter with in the morning?
>
> McCrory: He wants to get gone.
>
> Cullen: Well, you—you can understand, uh—It's not, uh—
>
> McCrory: Hold—Hold on just a second.
>
> Cullen: Yeah.

McCrory pretended to turn away from the telephone and to speak with another person at his end of the line: "He's got to go to his office and he can't get in there tonight. It's gonna have to be in the morning."

McCrory: [To Cullen again] How early? Nine o'clock be all right?

Cullen: Yeah.

McCrory: Cullen, for God's sake, don't leave me hung on this.

Cullen: No. That—that—that'll work out just fine, uh.

McCrory's testimony continued through Wednesday and Thursday, when the jury saw the audio and photographic evidence presented in a theatrical manner: a motion picture—complete with opening music, the same refrain from Mc-Crory's automobile radio that was heard on the tape. The jury was not allowed to consult transcripts this time, but Judge Moore permitted McCrory to read from the transcript during his questioning.

McCrory was asked about Cullen's relationship with his adopted daughter Dee because defense lawyers had scoffed at the inclusion of her name on Cullen's hit list. When asked if Cullen had ever expressed his opinion about Dee, McCrory said, "Yes, he said that he hated the bitch."

Racehorse Haynes again moved for a mistrial when Judge Moore advised McCrory that he did not need to include all the transcript obscenities while reading from it. The motion was denied, but Moore then instructed McCrory to include the expletives.

The synchronized presentation of sound and images on five television sets in the courtroom was impressive. The jury could hear the rustle of paper while McCrory was testifying that at that moment he was receiving $25,000 from Cullen.

McCrory: I got Judge Eidson dead for you.

Cullen: Good.

McCrory: I'll get the rest of them dead for you. You want a bunch of people dead. Right?

Cullen: All *right*.

217

It was devastating evidence.*

On Friday morning Haynes attacked McCrory's credibility as a witness and planted seeds of doubt that he hoped would bloom into the suspicion that Cullen, not Judge Eidson, was the victim of a conspiracy.

Haynes amused the jury and the spectators by coming up with another of his courtroom ploys: he lugged huge calendars, taller than he was, into the courtroom. From McCrory Haynes elicited—and noted dramatically on his several calendars—that the former had visited the grounds of the murder mansion on the morning after the shootings in 1976; that he had been in the company of Pat Burleson, the karate entrepreneur; that McCrory and his wife had been remiss in declaring and paying income taxes and that he had secret bank accounts.

McCrory was not amused by Haynes's calendars. At one point he asked, "Was that a question you were mumbling, Mr. Haynes? I can't hear you too well when you are over there. You need a bigger calendar."

McCrory refused to answer some questions and equivocated on others when they pertained to members of his family or their whereabouts. The judge tolerated the evasions on the grounds that McCrory's relatives might be endangered.

Late Friday there were several clashes between Racehorse Haynes and Judge Moore. One exchange was about McCrory's testimony when Haynes insistently returned to a detail which Moore did not consider important. Finally Moore barked at Haynes: "We've spent twenty minutes on this and I don't want you sticking it in his ear all morning."

The journalists who had been at Amarillo exchanged glances.

---

* Journalists covering the Davis trial would often relax with a few drinks after filing their stories. On one festive evening a young Houston reporter conjured up the scenario he predicted Haynes would use in Cullen's defense. Haynes would explain the "I got the judge dead for you" tape in the following manner: Cullen had hired McCrory to assist him in a program to provide for the undernourished of the world. A step forward in that noble nutritional endeavor, Haynes would tell the jury, was when McCrory reported, "I got the judge fed for you."

It was obvious that Judge Moore—despite his friendship with Haynes—was of tougher mettle than Judge Dowlen. At one point Moore sustained a prosecution objection before it was made.

The final day of the second week of testimony in Cullen II was a frustrating one for Racehorse Haynes. Moore sustained most of the objections posed by the prosecution. McCrory proved to be an elusive witness. And the synchronized tapes were obviously going to be difficult to explain. Haynes was braced by a crowd of reporters when the day was over. "If you want to know why I'm less than my jovial, good-natured self," Haynes said, "I watched a newscast last night on a tv station I used to respect . . ." And Haynes launched into an attack on media coverage of the trial.

Friday was not a happy anniversary for Cullen: precisely one year before he had been acquitted in Amarillo. At that happy time one of his attorneys had lifted a glass, saying, "I propose a toast that at this time next year we'll all have another party at Cullen's rightful abode."

There were no festivities that night in Cullen's cell.

The third week of testimony began on Monday, November 20, with Charles David McCrory still on the stand. Racehorse Haynes's inquisition of McCrory, and the lengths to which the defense attorney went to impugn his character, became so detailed and time-consuming that spectators and jurors dozed.

On Tuesday, McCrory admitted that he had retained $5000 from the bundle of $50,000 he said Cullen had given him to launder in Las Vegas. He considered it a fee for services and gave it to his son, "so in case Mr. Davis had me killed, my son would have at least $10,000 to go to college on."

"Just thinking ahead, were you?" Haynes asked.

McCrory claimed he already had given his son most of the other $5000 he had been paid by Cullen to investigate Beverly Bass.

219

At the end of the day Haynes posed the last of several thousand questions he had hammered home to McCrory during the trial's third week. Tolly Wilson had no further questions—that would have opened the door for further reexamination by Haynes.

During the five days McCrory was on the stand, Racehorse Haynes had managed to reduce the prosecution's main witness from an argumentative cocksure one to an indecisive, agitated one. In the final hours McCrory found himself answering ''I don't know'' and ''I don't remember'' to dozens of questions.

''No sane person in the world,'' Phil Burleson declared, ''would believe Charles David McCrory.''

''I wish he'd been able to remember better,'' said Jack Strickland, ''but he corroborated the tapes.'' And Strickland added that while McCrory's memory was faulty on details, the defense team still would have to grapple with the problem of the tapes, which could not be explained away.

Indeed the tapes were a vexing obstacle for the defense lawyers. They had been played for the jury six times, and would be played again. During McCrory's testimony, Haynes shied away from the substance of the tapes. Only twice did he question McCrory about the tapes, and both queries concerned his suspicion that McCrory had deliberately introduced the subject of sex into the conversations with Cullen. McCrory explained: ''He and I had been discussing [sic] several times a girl he had been going with that he didn't want Karen to know about.''

The headline CULLEN GRINNED was the big news of the day.

An FBI man testified on technical matters on Wednesday, November 22, and then Judge Moore granted the jurors a four-day Thanksgiving break. The defense team would need the time to mull over a major decision which loomed: Should Cullen take the stand, or should the tapes be left unchallenged?

All in all, Racehorse Haynes was pleased with the way things had gone in recent days, and he exuded confidence. ''The opera ain't over,'' he reminded music and football fans, ''until the fat lady sings.''

During the Thanksgiving holiday Cullen visited with his two sons. His Thanksgiving Vermont turkey was served on a metal tray with dessert. He sipped Hawaiian Punch.

The trial resumed on Monday, November 27, with FBI Special Agent Joe Gray testifying as an eyewitness to Cullen's rendezvous with McCrory on early Sunday morning, August 20. Gray had been inside the white FBI van which Cullen inspected before talking with McCrory. Although Cullen could not see into the van, Gray said that he recognized Cullen.

Judge Moore began to express concern that the trial might extend through Christmas. He polled jurors to determine if they wished to work nights or on Saturdays. They elected to arrive at the courthouse at 8:00 A.M., an hour early, and to cut another hour from their lunch and recess periods.

On Tuesday the prosecutors called two of Cullen's secretaries to the stand. The testimony Brenda Adcock and Mary Ann Carter offered was damaging to their employer. Ms. Adcock said that, following Cullen's instructions, she had stowed a thick envelope marked ''Cullen Davis—Personal and Confidential'' in the office safe at Mid-Continent Supply Company several days prior to August 20. She had then gone on an Acapulco vacation. Her colleague, Ms. Carter, was the only other office employee with the combination to Cullen's safe.

Mary Ann Carter then testified that she was awakened on Sunday morning, August 20, by an 8:00 A.M. call from Cullen. He was at the office and wanted the combination to the safe. She told him where he could find a piece of paper with the combination noted on it and asked that he call again if he had any problem. Cullen did not call again.

Brenda Adcock, on returning from Acapulco, was the next person to open the safe. Cullen's thick envelope had been removed. She further corroborated McCrory's testimony by saying that she recognized McCrory's voice when he had telephoned Cullen using the name Frank Johnson. As she left the courtroom Ms. Adcock lingered long enough to pat Cullen on the shoulder.

On Wednesday prosecutor Jack Strickland—who had frequently expressed his admiration of Racehorse Haynes's colorful courtroom technique—had a dramatic scene to present. He directed that the lights in the courtroom be turned off so that the jurors could take turns squinting through a night vision scope with a telephoto lens. It had been discovered in the trunk of Cullen's automobile after his arrest on August 20. Strickland referred sarcastically to the contents of the Cadillac's trunk. "It's the stuff you usually find in a trunk—a ski, a gun with a silencer, a night vision scope, a file folder, and two ominous cans, one with tennis balls and one with Schweppes tonic water."

A Fort Worth investigator revealed that the Ruger pistol with a silencer which McCrory placed in Cullen's car was inoperable because an FBI agent had shortened its firing pin. The federal agents feared Cullen might use it against arresting officers after its delivery—or to dispose of McCrory. The silencer was brought into the courtroom and placed in evidence. Ever the one to avoid describing anything connected with his client in pejorative terms, Haynes called the ominous-looking instrument "a barrel extender."

On Thursday a Texas Ranger, John Hogg, testified on the circumstances of Cullen's August 20 arrest. Hogg said that he had treated McCrory to a glass of milk in Coco's Famous Hamburgers after Cullen had driven away from the meeting. He said that McCrory had been frightened for his life when Cullen inspected the FBI van. "He was visibly shaken," Hogg said. "Both cheeks were wet with tears. He was driven up [emotional]."

Later in the day an investigator from the Fort Worth district attorney's office was on the stand when there was a disturbance in the courtroom. A woman spectator, apparently believing the witness to be Charles David McCrory, began shouting, "But he's lying!" She was escorted from the courtroom by the bailiff. Judge Moore later opined that she should have been detained to find out if she was "either intoxicated or not wrapped too tight [mentally unstable]."

The district attorney's investigator indirectly indicated that even the prosecution team did not think too highly of McCrory as a person. "It would be a heck of a note to wind up dead," he said, "being mistaken for McCrory."

On Friday, December 1, FBI man Larry Tongate described how he had looked down from an airplane on the morning of August 20 to see Cullen drive from his office and then take several evasive actions before meeting McCrory at Coco's Famous Hamburgers. The plane had circled while the two men talked, then had tracked Cullen again, alerting mobile surveillance teams that they could move in on Cullen for the arrest.

The prosecution had presented its case in four weeks of testimony when the state rested early Monday, December 4. Judge Moore overruled the routine defense request for an instructed verdict, based on the thesis that Tolly Wilson had not proved his case against Cullen Davis.

Racehorse Haynes was unequivocal in his opening statement to the jury: "There was no specific intent of Thomas Cullen Davis to offend the law in any way and that [sic] in fact Thomas Cullen Davis was a victim of a conspiracy by and between Charles David McCrory, Pat Burleson, and others."

Haynes did not challenge the authenticity of the tapes so vividly exploited by the prosecution. But he told the jury that they would find before the trial was over that "things are not what they seem to be."

In his cross-examination of FBI Special Agent Ron Jannings, Haynes had established that Cullen had received an extortion note in late 1977. Haynes told the jury that the threatening letter had been signed "D.M.R." When advising the FBI, Cullen had suggested that the most likely suspect was Charles David McCrory.

Haynes had told the jury that "others" were involved in the conspiracy to lure Cullen into meetings with McCrory. One of the "others" Haynes was to accuse was his first witness—Priscilla.

The prosecution could not call Priscilla to the stand in Houston, as Texas law stipulates that a witness cannot testify against a spouse, except in cases where the spouse or a minor child is the victim. Had Tolly Wilson been able to summon Priscilla he might well have waived the option, for that would have given Haynes the opportunity to attack Priscilla's credibility and, in a rerun of his successful assault on her in Amarillo, convince the jury that Priscilla was a Mrs. Hyde. Since Priscilla was in Houston as *his* witness, Haynes could not attempt to discredit her.

Priscilla made a grand entrance into the crowded hall outside the courtroom. She had made so many public appearances that now she had the aplomb of a film star. Her ice-blonde hair dipped over one eye. She was dressed in black: a black fox collar framing two strands of pearls and a gold and diamond cross on a chain. Reporters clustered about her. Priscilla's thin fingers fluttered about her face. She apologized, explaining that a skin irritation was the reason for the several layers of makeup on her attractive but drawn face.*

Priscilla spotted the other woman in Cullen's life. Karen Master was sitting on her customary bench reading a paperback. Priscilla raised her hand in a half-salutation. Karen kept reading.

Before being called into the courtroom Priscilla was asked if

---

* In August, Priscilla had been in Fort Worth's Harris Hospital to have "some skin cancer removed" and, the same month, in the All Saints' Hospital for treatment of an undetermined "severe pain."

she had any qualms about testifying. "I'm used to it now," Priscilla said. "I'll just sit here and let them stick pins in me."

As Priscilla strode down the courtroom aisle to enter the witness box, Cullen followed her passage with an impassive expression on his face.

Cullen's wife was on the stand the entire day. In the morning the courtroom was frigid when the heating system in the Harris County Criminal Court Building malfunctioned. Unable to attack Priscilla directly, Racehorse Haynes repeatedly attempted to convey a deprecating image of Priscilla's life-style and background to the jury. Judge Moore repeatedly sustained prosecution objections that Haynes was impeaching his own witness.

Some of the flavor of Priscilla's life-style did come through. Yes, the children's bills had been as high as $500 monthly during "a busy summer at the country club." The color of the carpeting in her Lincoln Continental Mark IV? "Lipstick red," Priscilla said.

Haynes introduced into the record and into the minds of the jurors insinuations concerning Priscilla's relationship with Charles David McCrory and Pat Burleson, the karate-studio franchiser. He focused on the period just before and on the day Cullen had been arrested in Fort Worth on the solicitation-for-murder charge against Judge Eidson. The facts created doubt and suspicion. Priscilla said she had not seen or talked with Pat Burleson during 1978 until August. Then she had gone to his karate studio in downtown Fort Worth on August 16, the same day McCrory talked to Burleson about approaching the FBI. Priscilla confirmed that Burleson had visited her at the mansion on Mockingbird Lane—just after Burleson had arranged for FBI man Ron Jannings to interview McCrory.

And—Haynes narrowed his eyes and looked at the jury box as the revelation surfaced—Burleson was again in the mansion on August 20, early that Sunday morning, at the very time Cullen was saying to McCrory that it was good that the judge had got dead!

Racehorse Haynes was immensely satisfied as he lighted up his huge pipe, puffing until a cloud of smoke hovered over the defense lawyers' table.

The meetings with Burleson, Priscilla insisted, were in regard to her need for additional guard service at the mansion. Cullen's wife said her debts had mounted and the cost of paying off-duty policemen to protect the huge house had become exorbitant. Burleson was helping her to locate and hire more inexpensive guards.

The spectators in the court were shivering by the time a recess was called. Judge Moore announced as he left the bench, "I'll see if I can get some fire built."

During the afternoon session most spectators and some of the lawyers shed their coats in a courtroom so efficiently heated that it was stifling.

Haynes resurrected his giant calendars to record exactly where Priscilla was, and how long her meetings with Pat Burleson lasted, during the crucial period before and after Cullen's arrest on August 20. The lawyer noted the times on the plastic-covered calendars with a grease pencil; the jurors watched the courtroom show attentively.

Then Haynes directed another dramatic interlude. He summoned an unidentified witness. A large, hulking man in a trench coat entered the courtroom and stood silently before the judge's bench. He looked like a former professional football player who had become an actor specializing in hit-man roles in gangster movies. Then the man, on Haynes's instruction, left the courtroom. He had not spoken, nor had any questions been asked of him.

Haynes turned to Priscilla. Did she recognize that man? Yes, she said, she had seen him on television. He was David Binion, the man Haynes referred to during the first day of testimony as an underworld character Priscilla had hired to arrange a contract on Cullen's life. Priscilla said that she had never met Binion.

During the remainder of Monday, Racehorse Haynes interrogated Priscilla assiduously, peppering her with spicy questions. Frequently, Judge Moore interrupted to admonish Haynes that he must refrain from attacking his own witness. Jack Strickland passed the time by constructing a paper airplane.

Cullen smiled once during the day. Haynes had been prodding Priscilla to find out why she had written a certain check for $500; she couldn't remember. She added: "I'm learning to mark my checks now." That produced a grin on Cullen's face.

Priscilla was scheduled to take the chair on Tuesday at 8:00 A.M., but jurors had to wait until she arrived at 8:30. She explained that she thought someone was kidding when they said court would convene at such an early hour.

The tapes of Cullen's two meetings were played again while Priscilla listened from the witness chair. Tolly Wilson stopped the tapes at critical points during cross-examination to ask Priscilla if she had been involved in a conspiracy to trap Cullen into saying what he did. Each time she denied the allegation. She also denied even mentioning the name Cullen Davis during her several meetings with Pat Burleson.

Priscilla was only twenty minutes late on Wednesday, the third day of her testimony. Allowed to step down later that day, she chatted with reporters before returning to Fort Worth. Priscilla was asked if she knew of any explanation for Cullen's apparent reluctance to have McCrory's alleged assassin aim at her rather than Judge Eidson. (Cullen had told McCrory he'd "have to think on that one.") Yes, Priscilla said, she had an explanation. "I think Cullen had firsthand information on how hard I am to kill."

Pat Burleson followed Priscilla on the witness stand. He denied any role in a conspiracy against Cullen. He said that when McCrory had first contacted him on August 16 at a 7-Eleven store in Fort Worth, he had refused to listen to his friend once the name of Cullen Davis was introduced. "He

227

related to me that he was in a lot of trouble, that the company he worked for was owned by Cullen Davis and his problem related to Cullen Davis." Burleson did, however, contact FBI agent Jannings and had counseled McCrory to tell his story to the federal agent.

Jack Strickland, in a series of adroit questions, established that McCrory had long considered Burleson a fatherly advisor. Burleson's calm and steady answers undid some of the harm Haynes had done to the state's case by dwelling on the suspicious circumstances of the meetings between Burleson and Priscilla.

On Thursday the courtroom audience waited expectantly for Racehorse Haynes's next witness: David Binion, the ominous-looking character with mysterious FBI ties. Haynes had intimated he had been contracted by Priscilla to murder Cullen.

Binion testified—in a heavy, raspy voice which suited his appearance—that while living in Fort Worth he pretended to be a hit man although he was actually working as a paid informant for the FBI and the Drug Enforcement Agency. Binion said that Priscilla had telephoned him, then had invited him to visit her at the mansion. This was a contradiction of Priscilla's statement under oath that the only time she had seen Binion was on television. And, Binion said, much to the defense's delight, his impression of Priscilla during his visit was that she was "messed up on drugs."

But when it got right down to the facts of the meeting in dispute, the testimony warmed cockles on the prosecution's side of the courtroom.

Haynes asked the heavyset witness: "Did Priscilla say to you that 'He will get his' ?"

"No," Binion replied, Priscilla hadn't put it that way.

"What did she say, exactly?"

"I can't say exactly," Binion said. "It was in a religious sense, a religious manner."

"She didn't call you up there because you were a preacher, did she?"

"No, sir."

"She didn't call you up there," Haynes continued, "to buy a used car?"

"No," the secondhand car salesman replied.

"Did she say that Cullen Davis would get killed?"

"No, I already told you that."

"Well, what did she say?" Haynes demanded.

"She said God would take care of these things and he [Cullen] will get what's coming to him."

Binion had something more to say to Racehorse Haynes: "You and I are taking the conversation in a different light."

On Friday, December 8, the defense shuttled eleven witnesses in and out of the witness chair. All were women; all worked for Cullen. Brenda Adcock, Cullen's secretary, was called back to the stand, this time by the defense. She testified that Cullen, prior to his most recent arrest, hired a private investigator to "sweep" his office to discover if the office was infested with electronic bugs. And, she said, Cullen had given instructions to the men who cleaned the windows in his office that they should "wash them very carefully."

Cullen's behavior was characterized, during questioning of Ms. Adcock by Phil Burleson, as "cautious." Jack Strickland had another word for it: paranoid.

Then a blonde bombshell detonated in the courtroom. The last of the secretaries from Cullen's companies was Dorothy Neeld, a flashily dressed woman with a flamboyant manner. Ms. Neeld said that she was thirty-seven years old and had five children ages seventeen through twenty-four. After a messy divorce she had obtained employment at Jet-Air, Cullen's company where Charles David McCrory had worked.

On the Tuesday before her Friday appearance in Houston, Ms. Neeld had contacted defense lawyer Steve Sumner because, she told him, she had "something on my mind that you might need to know about."

Racehorse Haynes believed the jury should know about it as well. On the stand Ms. Neeld testified that three weeks before the then scheduled August divorce hearing in Fort Worth she had seen Charles McCrory get into a car with a woman who looked just like Priscilla Davis. Both Priscilla and McCrory had previously testified that they had not been together.

"I thought it was strange," Ms. Neeld said, "that Mr. Mc-Crory would be with Ms. Davis when he was an employee of Mr. Davis."

There were two other men in the car, she said. The witness said she did not know the driver and the front-seat passenger. Sumner offered Ms. Neeld a stack of photographs, all of men wearing mustaches. Ms. Neeld selected one. "That's the man who was the front-seat passenger," she said. It was a photograph of Pat Burleson.

Ms. Neeld wasn't able to identify the driver of the car, but she did recall that it was a burgundy-colored Lincoln. Ronald Aultman, one of Priscilla's attorneys in the divorce case, was furious. He owned a burgundy 1977 Lincoln.

Jack Strickland raised his eyes heavenward. "A platinum Ulewayne Polk," he labeled the witness. (He referred to the nurseryman who had created such a stir in Amarillo with his last-minute testimony.)

When the court recessed on Friday, December 8, after five weeks of testimony, Haynes and his stable of defense lawyers were satisfied with the impression made by their surprise witness. And, they hinted, the best was yet to come.

On the same Friday, in Fort Worth, another judge made an announcement which meant that Cullen's trials would not end in Houston, regardless of the verdict in Judge Moore's court. District Judge Charles Murray was to hear the five civil suits filed against Cullen as the result of the shootings of August 1976 at the murder mansion.

The first suit to be heard, Judge Murray said, would be that of Gus Gavrel, Jr., who had increased his claim against Cullen from three to thirteen million dollars. Gavrel would be a sympathetic witness when he appeared on crutches before a jury. Racehorse Haynes had petitioned that all five suits be heard simultaneously, so the issues could be resolved once and for all. There was not only the case of Gavrel to contend with, but also two suits filed by Priscilla, one for her own wounding and the second for Andrea's death; a fourth suit was filed by Jack Wilborn, also because of his daughter Andrea's death; the fifth was filed by the relatives of the murdered basketball player, Stan Farr.

The decision that Gus Gavrel's complaint would be the first to be settled was crucial. It was the most likely to go against Cullen, setting a precedent for the subsequent suits. And a new Texas law would influence the outcome of Priscilla's civil suits. (Previously in Texas one spouse could not seek a financial settlement from the other spouse in cases of assault and battery; instead the complaining party had to choose between divorce or a criminal suit.) Now Priscilla could hope that Cullen would have to part with some of his millions in the civil as well as the divorce courts.

Further, in all five suits Cullen could be called to the stand as a witness, and Judge Murray was highly respected in Fort Worth as an able, no-nonsense judge. Most important was that in a Texas *civil* suit jurors do not have to reach a verdict beyond a "reasonable doubt," as was true for the criminal trials in Amarillo and Houston. The verdict could be reached in the civil suits based on the preponderance of the evidence or testimony. To put it in different terms, the jury in Amarillo would have had to decide—as did the jury now in Houston—that the odds were probably in the ninety-nine percent category that Cullen was culpable. In the civil suits, fifty-one percent credence based on the available facts would be sufficient to warrant a guilty verdict.

Cullen could not be sent to the Huntsville prison as the result of any of the five civil suits which would be pending after the verdict in Houston. But, regardless of the Houston verdict, Haynes would have his work cut out for him to keep Cullen from paying many millions of dollars in damages to Gus Gavrel, Jr., Priscilla, Jack Wilborn, and the relatives of Stan Farr.

The sixth week of testimony in Houston began on Monday, December 11 with the defense calling a Dallas woman to the stand. Mary Ramsey told the jury that she had seen Priscilla Davis in Las Vegas in June. Priscilla had testified previously that she had not been in Las Vegas during 1978. Mary Ramsey said she was sure that the person she had spotted in Las Vegas was Priscilla. Ms. Ramsey said that her husband worked for Mid-Continent Supply Company.

The extortion letter received by Cullen in December 1977, was read into the record: "I have a contract to see that you don,t [sic] live to see Xmas. If you don,t [sic] want this contract filled get 16,000 dollers [sic] in twenty doller [sic] bills together, run a [sic] ad in the *Star-Telegram* in the personal section reading D.M.R. call home and a phone no. Do this right, no cops and I will see that you live and also tell you who put out the contract on you."

FBI Special Agent James Acree said he and another agent had worked on the case for more than two months but the writer of the threatening letter was never located. The jury had understood from earlier assertions by the defense team that Cullen had advised the FBI, suggesting that D.M.R. was Charles David McCrory. The two FBI agents were not convinced—they recalled that Karen Master's ex-husband was suspected—and said that a latent fingerprint on the letter proved not to belong to McCrory.

One witness that day had sensational information to disclose.

Larry Gene Lucas, who described himself as an unemployed paint contractor and longtime buddy of McCrory, was colorfully dressed in an iridescent green suit and blue Hawaiian print shirt. One reporter described him as having a "pool hall demeanor."

Lucas said he had borrowed $10 from McCrory at the Sylvania Recreational Club in Fort Worth in the early summer of 1978. McCrory had asked him if he needed to make some money and Lucas said sure.

"What happened then?" Racehorse Haynes asked.

"He offered me $10,000 to kill Cullen Davis." Then Lucas said he told McCrory, "You're crazy—the man has more security than the president." Then McCrory said, according to the witness's account, "Well, you obviously need the money," and upped the offer to $20,000.

Lucas said he had declined the offer. Questioned further, he admitted cheerfully that he was a thief. He had served four years in Del Rio, Texas, for smuggling marijuana, and two years of a four-year sentence for a burglary conviction in Missouri. Lucas stepped down from the witness chair but the court would later hear more from the ex-convict.

One Tuesday morning a familiar figure added color and a splash of comedy to the trial: W. T. Rufner, who had gained fame throughout Texas as the man with an appendage on his appendage—the red and white Christmas stocking which served as a fig-leaf in a photograph with Priscilla. During the Amarillo trial Rufner had been asked how long he had waited on a certain occasion and, after reflecting, he had replied that the time involved was "about a six-pack."

Now, in Houston, W. T. Rufner was wearing a belt with a buckle which read "I bring joy to women," a red felt cowboy hat with a feathered yellow band, and, under an embroidered western shirt, another of his famous T-shirts. This one had a drawing of Rufner and a chimpanzee and the message, "Is This a Courtroom or a Circus?"

Rufner explained to the reporters who gathered around outside the courtroom that the chimpanzee represented Racehorse Haynes. "That's what Haynes is doing here," Rufner pronounced. "He's bringing in a bunch of monkeys." Rufner made it clear that he was referring to the parade of witnesses who had testified in Cullen's favor. And, referring to Cullen, Rufner added, "And he sure has got one [a monkey] in there that he's defending."

The elegant Phil Burleson passed near Rufner's impromptu press conference. "Fink," Rufner hissed. He had vivid comments about others on the defense team. He said that Cullen's lawyers had "suitcases full of money." But, he said, "It looks like they don't have this man [the judge] in their pocket."

Rufner told reporters why Cullen didn't like him. "He didn't like me staying over at his house and drinking his whiskey. But that's his problem. He should have stayed at home more."

Rufner, subpoenaed by the defense as a witness, was not permitted to enter the courtroom at any other time. Despite the injunction, he made two brief invasions; each time he was tossed out by the bailiff. Rufner left the building for lunch and purchased $16 worth of beer and egg rolls. When Rufner finally appeared on the witness stand there was an acrid aroma of brew in the courtroom. Judge Moore smelled something more ominous—the possibility that Rufner's bizarre behavior might give Haynes reason to demand a mistrial. The jury was excused.

Rufner and Haynes were soon bickering. Rufner said there had been several attempts on his life after the Amarillo trial. One involved an incident when two men threatened him with baseball bats. Haynes shot questions at the bearded witness until he lost his temper. "I could sit here for twenty minutes," Rufner said, "and tell you a bunch about people pulling me off the road and throwing a blast of shit at me, with more than baseball bats—"

"*Wait* a minute!" Judge Moore pointed his filter-tipped cigarette at Rufner. "Let me tell you something. This ain't Fort

Worth. This is *my* show. I trust you appreciate the fact that the jail is back here." Moore pointed to the door behind his bench which led to the Harris County jail. "Do it *my* way, or you're going out the *back* door. You're volunteering a lot of information and using some profanity and I'm not going to stand for it."

Judge Moore leveled his gaze on Rufner.

"I'm not going to let you blow seven weeks' work down the drain because you're teed off at *him.*" Moore's V-shaped eyebrows were vectored on Haynes, then returned to the witness. "You solve this some other time, some other place, not on *my* time. If you do something to blow me out of the tub, you're going to be safe for six months, anyway."

No one in the courtroom doubted that Judge Moore meant Rufner's refuge would be in the Harris County jail.

When Rufner left the courtroom Judge Moore turned to Racehorse Haynes. "I'm not sure," Moore sighed, "that Houston is big enough for both of you."

On Wednesday, W. T. Rufner testified in the presence of the jury.

"He was a perfect gentleman," Judge Moore said.

When the docile W. T. Rufner departed, he set up shop in a van on the street outside the courtroom to peddle T-shirts, one of which read, "What Price Justice?"

Three convicts followed Rufner as witnesses for the defense. John Thomas Florio, his nephew Salvatore, and Randall Craig told the court that the Fort Worth district attorney's office had tried in May to persuade them to participate in a scheme to frame Cullen. John Florio—wearing dark glasses and a short-sleeved shirt which revealed tattoos on both arms—pointed to Tolly Wilson and said *he* was one of them. They had been promised a reduced sentence and no prosecution for other offenses, the trio testified, if they would cooperate with the DA's office and deliver perjured testimony against Cullen.

John Florio was serving a sixty-year sentence for robbery at the time, and Salvatore twenty years for the same crime. Now, in the courtroom, Tolly Wilson asked John Florio when he had first been convicted. In a New York accent Florio sought clarification: "As a juvenile or as an adult?" Then Tolly Wilson recited a list of ten felony convictions on Florio's record during the past sixteen years. Florio put the statistics in perspective: "I've only been in prison four times."

On Thursday, Bob Brown, the husband of W. T. Rufner's former wife, testified that Rufner had confided to him before Cullen's arrest that "a man is coming into town to take care of Cullen." It wasn't going to be clean and fast, Rufner had added, because they wanted to see the son of a bitch suffer. The witness was identified as a mechanic who worked for Cullen at Cummins Sales and Service in Fort Worth.

Late on Thursday, Haynes called Charles David McCrory's cousin, Garry Lee McCrory, to the stand. Garry Lee was a machinist at Stratoflex, one of Cullen's corporations. Haynes was just beginning to get into the subject at hand when Garry diverged to discuss a pistol silencer he had fashioned on Stratoflex machinery a short time before.

Jack Strickland jumped to his feet. He waved a copy of the statutes of the state of Texas.

Judge Moore quickly excused the jury. Then he rose from the bench and began to stride out of the courtroom, advising the surprised witness as he went, "I'm going down the hall to find you a good lawyer."

Garry McCrory had not been aware, apparently, that manufacturing a silencer can bring two to twenty years in prison in Texas, and a fine of $10,000, or both.

In a few moments Judge Moore returned to the courtroom. In tow he led Rusty Stanley, an astonished Houston attorney Moore had recruited in the hall. Stanley was dressed in jeans and a sports shirt. "I want to apologize to your honor," Garry McCrory's instant lawyer said, "for my dress."

On his new attorney's advice Garry McCrory took the Fifth

Amendment when questioned further about silencers he might have manufactured.

Judge Moore cautioned Racehorse Haynes to warn his witnesses more carefully about giving testimony related to the commission of a felony, saying that such advice was a legal obligation.

"My primary obligation is to my client," Haynes said.

"This is not the first time," Judge Moore said, "we've had a difference of opinion."

The next morning, Friday, Garry Lee McCrory testified that three men had tried to kill him shortly after he contacted Steve Sumner of the defense team. Phil Burleson said, "We don't know whether the events are related or not, but it's sure an interesting coincidence."

Next, Karen Master, after weeks of waiting on a bench outside the courtroom, had a new seat in the witness box at the right of Judge Moore's bench. She wore a turquoise dress. Whenever she mentioned Cullen she referred to him as "Mr. Davis." Her testimony was accompanied by frequent smiles at the jury.

Karen said that after she and Cullen had returned from a trip to New York and Washington in mid-July 1978, Charles David McCrory had telephoned Cullen at her home on July 13. After the conversation Cullen had gone out, to return with a thick brown letter-sized envelope. The envelope contained money, Karen said; she had peeked inside. She did not count the money, but Cullen "took it to the office with him the next morning." Defense attorney Steve Sumner told reporters that the envelope was the same one that Cullen's secretary had previously testified Cullen had asked her to keep in the office safe. "Remember that Brenda Adcock testified she received a brown envelope on July 14," Sumner said. Sumner was not reluctant to imply that the $25,000 Cullen had given McCrory on August 20 was money that belonged to McCrory—*not* a payoff for Judge Eidson's murder.

Jack Strickland countered by saying that he found the idea that Cullen had simply been holding McCrory's money an unlikely one.

"Cullen didn't mind being called at three in the morning, didn't mind getting up at seven in the morning, going to the office, and meeting with McCrory on a parking lot on a Sunday, huh?" Strickland added, "I guess Cullen was in the money-delivering business. I guess that's why he needed a gun with a silencer on it."

Karen Master was still on the stand when the court recessed on Friday to end the sixth week of testimony.

It was apparent that the trial would not end before Christmas, but it was moving toward a climax. Would Cullen testify? Would the "fat lady" sing for Haynes? Certainly Haynes would have to explode a bombshell before resting his case.

On Monday, December 18, Karen testified again. Based on her testimony, and that of other defense witnesses who would appear before the Christmas break, the defense presented the following version of Cullen's life and times during the months immediately preceding his August 20 arrest.

In June, Karen testified, Charles David McCrory had telephoned her to warn her: "Karen, I have some information that I think you should know. I know that Priscilla Davis and Gus Gavrel, Sr., have a contract on Cullen's life. . . ." Gavrel, Sr., was the father of the young man wounded at the mansion and was on Cullen's alleged hit list.

In July, Cullen had picked up an envelope from McCrory and taken it to his office.

On August 10 a caller identifying himself as an FBI agent spoke with Cullen on the telephone. Karen's description of this event hung tantalizingly incomplete.

And, during the period just before his arrest, Cullen had been concerned about his safety. He had acquired a bulletproof vest. The man who supplied the vest corroborated Karen's testimony.

Karen listened to the tapes of the meetings between McCrory and Cullen, and told the jury yes, that was Cullen's voice. The admission signaled Haynes's intention to produce a star witness—his client.

Cullen's coming!

The alarm came from Jack Strickland. He had repeatedly predicted that Cullen would never take the stand, but now he reversed himself. "It's not what she *said,*" the prosecuting attorney remarked in reference to Karen's testimony. "It's what she *didn't* say."

Tolly Wilson agreed. He believed that after Karen's identification of Cullen's voice on the tapes, Cullen's appearance as a witness was inevitable. "Until she said that," Wilson said, "I thought they might not call him. Now I think they will have to."

On Thursday afternoon, December 21, Racehorse Haynes and his defense team confirmed that T. Cullen Davis would indeed testify in his own defense. He would explain the tapes.

Judge Moore wished the jury a Merry Christmas and dismissed them for the holiday.

Karen Master canceled skiing reservations in Aspen.

In Fort Worth the people who lived around Rivercrest exchanged gifts. Two popular presents were half-gallon jugs of Chivas Regal and popcorn from Neiman-Marcus in five-gallon oil cans. On Christmas Day in the Houston jail the richest prisoner in America received two gifts from the state of Texas: a pair of socks and a candy cane.

During the holidays those involved in Cullen's trial had the opportunity to mull over an unrelated but thought-provoking development that had occurred on December 20. On that day, in Austin, the Texas Court of Criminal Appeals overturned the conviction of Elmer Wayne Henley, Jr. Henley had been indicted in Houston in 1973 for his role in the mass slaying of twenty-seven teenagers involved in a bizarre homosexual sex-and-torture ring. The trial had been moved to San Antonio,

Texas, due to excessive publicity in Houston. The late-1978 split vote of the Criminal Appeals Court judges was based on the premise that in San Antonio, too, there had been excessive publicity. The San Antonio judge had committed reversible error when he had not entertained a change of venue motion.

Wayne Henley, Jr., had been sentenced to six ninety-nine-year sentences. Now, five years later, he would have a new trial.

In Fort Worth it was revealed that Cullen Davis needed cash to pay court costs and the monthly allowances which sustained Priscilla and Karen. He was about to sell a uranium lease in New Mexico. Cullen could anticipate $7 million from the sale. Of that, 93.5 percent would be Cullen's and 6.5 percent would go to one of Cullen's Fort Worth civil lawyers, Hershel Payne.

T. Cullen Davis had spent several months sitting in courtrooms since August 1976, but never under oath in a witness chair. He took the stand on December 27, 1978, when the trial resumed in Houston after a five-day Christmas break.

Cullen was surprisingly calm. He answered questions in a clear voice. From time to time he smiled fleetingly at the jurors. He wore a light blue suit, white shirt, and dark tie as he presented his version of his meetings with Charles David McCrory and his explanation of the incriminating statements recorded by FBI microphones.

It had all begun, Cullen said, early in 1978 when McCrory began hounding him for a job. McCrory had lost his karate studio franchise and was broke. In January, McCrory had gone uninvited to Cullen's office in Fort Worth; Cullen discouraged McCrory from expecting work with one of his companies. McCrory continued to telephone but Cullen avoided him.

Cullen reported that Steve Sumner had suggested in early summer that McCrory might be useful in connection with the divorce. Judge Eidson had ruled that "fault before separation" evidence would be admissible at the trial. Perhaps McCrory could provide information about sexual misconduct by Priscilla before Cullen had moved out of the mansion on Mockingbird Lane. McCrory telephoned him on May 1, and Cullen agreed to see him at the parking lot of Coco's Famous Hamburgers. They met later in the day and talked.

"What was the subject matter of that conversation?" Racehorse Haynes asked the citizen accused.

"Well, he said that he was broke and didn't have a job . . . he started crying and wanted to know if I could help him and said he wanted to know if he could be friends with me."

"Did you agree to give McCrory a job?" Haynes asked.

"The way I left it with him," Cullen said, "was that there was a possibility of an opening with a new company we had bought and that he would call me or I would call him in three weeks."

Cullen told the jury he had arranged for McCrory to fill a $20,000-a-year position as a salesman for Jet-Air. The purpose was not to cover McCrory's activities as an investigator or as middleman in a murder conspiracy. "I was motivated mainly," Cullen averred, "by the fact he was going to help me with my divorce, particularly matters related to Priscilla."

Then Cullen testified that a meeting between him and Mc-Crory had been recorded by McCrory one week *before* the August 18 encounter taped by the FBI. This was the first mention by anyone of such a meeting.

Cullen said he had received a telephone call on August 10 from a man he believed to be James Acree, one of the FBI agents who had worked unsuccessfully to apprehend the author of the extortion letter sent to Cullen in late 1977. According to Cullen, Acree told him: "We believe you are the victim of an extortion plot by McCrory. I want you to play along. Whatever he suggests, just go do it."

Cullen met McCrory the next day, August 11. He played along, as instructed by the FBI. He was (Cullen said) aware that his conversation was being recorded. McCrory told Cullen killers contracted by Priscilla were stalking him. He assured Cullen he could persuade the would-be killers to become informants and to provide information about Priscilla which Cullen could exploit in the divorce trial.

Cullen testified further that the $25,000 he had passed to McCrory on August 20, just before his arrest, was McCrory's own money, won at the gambling tables in Las Vegas. This could not be disputed by the prosecution; an effort to trace the bills had been fruitless. Cullen said he had been keeping it for McCrory since July and returned it that Sunday morning at McCrory's request.

Responding to questions from Haynes, Cullen flatly denied that he paid McCrory $5000 for investigative work, or that he had given McCrory $50,000 to be laundered in Las Vegas.

The prosecution had played the August 18 and 20 tapes repeatedly since the trial had begun. Now Haynes asked that they be reviewed again. At critical points he stopped the tapes so that Cullen could explain what he and McCrory had said. Cullen said he was aware on each occasion that McCrory was wired for sound.

"This conversation about killing people was some kind of insurance," Cullen said, "for his people." *His* people, Cullen explained, were the killers McCrory said he would be able to turn into sources of information for Cullen.

Cullen said that just before the August 20 meeting, McCrory had displayed the recording equipment strapped to his body. After that, Cullen added, "Whatever he wanted to talk about I talked about." But, Cullen made clear, he did not mention dollar figures in the dialogue with McCrory, "because I didn't want that turned against me. . . . I never told McCrory I was going to pay any amount of money to do anything."

Cullen was asked to explain his recorded statement that "I'm always covered." Cullen said he made it a habit to be around other people because "I might get caught alone and get killed myself. Or something might happen in Fort Worth I would get blamed for."

Cullen said that he became accustomed to taking extra precautions: wearing a bulletproof vest, hiring investigators to check on Priscilla's activities at the mansion, and taking evasive action in his Cadillac to thwart surveillance. He explained his circuitous approach to the August 20 meeting with McCrory. "I wanted to find out real fast if anybody was following me. I thought there was a good possibility that McCrory told somebody I was bringing him $25,000. There's no telling what could have happened en route."

The witness insisted that the conversation of August 20, just before the arrest, was a spiced-up remake of the August 11 meeting with McCrory. "McCrory said I wasn't coming through enough," Cullen said, explaining that McCrory's killers would want stronger stuff before switching their allegiance from Priscilla.

Later during the day Cullen dropped a pebble of information and a name which caused ripples in Fort Worth. He said that before his arrest he talked with one of his Fort Worth lawyers, Hershel Payne, about the $25,000 he had kept for McCrory from July 13 to August 20, and that he mentioned Judge Eidson and the FBI to him.

Hershel Payne was a respected attorney in Fort Worth.

Was Payne Racehorse Haynes's "fat lady"?

On Thursday, Cullen continued to deny that he intended to hire a killer to murder Judge Eidson. He said it was all McCrory's idea.

"I was just going along with him," Cullen said. "I was just following his cue. I was going along with the FBI, in accordance with what they wanted me to do. There was no plan to kill anybody. We were using those tapes he was making as a tool. I didn't think McCrory could have talked me into that if I hadn't gotten that call from the man I thought was with the FBI."

Racehorse Haynes asked Cullen to explain his taped instruction to McCrory to "go back to the original plan." McCrory had said the statement meant he should begin getting a bunch of people dead.

"That's the plan that he was supposed to bring those people around to me," Cullen said, referring to Priscilla's hired killers. "That's what I was trying to get him to do. I didn't want to cut any more tapes."

Richard Haynes asked Cullen about the now-famous exchange concerning Judge Eidson, when McCrory said, "I got Judge Eidson dead for you," and Cullen's reply was "Good."

"Did you believe he was dead?" Haynes asked.

"Of course not," Cullen replied.

"What was the reason for your saying 'Good'?"

"I was just going along with his conversation," Cullen answered in a steady voice. "I had no reason for wanting him dead."

Chief prosecutor Tolly Wilson confronted Cullen in cross-examination. "Did you believe Charles David McCrory wouldn't turn on you?"

"That's why I wouldn't use my money," Cullen said.

"You did, though, put your whole self in their hands by making those tapes?"

"I thought I'd be safe if I didn't consummate a deal or agree to kill anybody."

Wilson continued. "The thought didn't occur to you that they might take these tapes and blackmail you for the rest of your life?"

"Yes," Cullen admitted, "that's why I was being a little bit careful."

Cullen went on to say he really didn't *know* who it was on the telephone who said he was FBI agent James Acree. But he had *thought* it sounded like Acree, whom Cullen remembered from Acree's investigation of the 1977 extortion letter. But now, after hearing the FBI man testify in Houston about the letter, he was pretty sure it was *not* Acree's voice.

It was revealed that the telephone number Cullen said he had called to talk to someone pretending to be an FBI man belonged to a karate studio owned by Pat Burleson.

Before the court adjourned on Thursday, Haynes posed a question to Cullen.

"Are you guilty of conspiring with Charles David McCrory . . . to cause the death of District Judge Joseph Eidson?"

"As God is my witness," Cullen said, "I certainly am not."

On Friday morning Cullen answered more questions about his telephone consultation, while he was dealing with McCrory, with his Fort Worth civil lawyer Hershel Payne. He had asked Payne whether or not he might find himself in trouble if his recorded conversations with McCrory were later revealed. He told the lawyer about the FBI sponsorship of the intrigue and, "I told Hershel that David was wanting to talk about killing people." Cullen testified: "I said, 'Can David and I be prosecuted for it?'"

Cullen quoted Payne's reply: "If you don't intend to do it and you don't consummate the deal, no law is broken in this state. People talk about killing people all the time with no intention of doing it. There's no law against it." And Payne cautioned, "You better be careful you don't do something David will try to blackmail you with."

Payne also assured him, Cullen said, that possession of a silencer was legal if registered with Alcohol, Tobacco, and Firearms agents. If Payne said that, Tolly Wilson pointed out, he was wrong. Further, Wilson found it strange that Cullen should have telephoned Payne rather than consult with one of his several attorneys who were expert in criminal law. "Because Hershel doesn't charge me when I call him," Cullen explained.

A juror became ill and on December 29, Judge Moore excused the jury until after the new year. There was still work for the judge and the lawyers in court on that Friday, however. Cullen's attorneys had argued that a recent ruling of the Texas Court of Criminal Appeals dictated that Cullen be freed on bond—he had been jailed for more than four months—not later than the next day, Saturday.

Phil Burleson drafted a motion with the expectation Judge Moore would grant it.

Then the defense lawyers suddenly and inexplicably retracted the bond motion which, if granted, would have made Cullen a free man. Phil Burleson said that it had to do with an unspecified legal point, and neither he nor his colleagues would say more. Asked what Cullen's reaction had been, Burleson snapped, "He didn't cry about it; he didn't jump up and down. He accepted it." It was a mysterious development. (The mystery was cleared up after the trial: Judge Moore had told Burleson he would *not* grant Cullen bond.)

When court recessed on Friday, December 29, Cullen went back to his cell at the Harris County jail.

In Fort Worth another murder trial had finished. David Grijalva, accused of stuffing a woman's head into a pizza dough machine, was sentenced to death by lethal injection after a speedy trial.

The ongoing trials of T. Cullen Davis were headlined daily in Fort Worth. On Saturday, December 30, 1978, the *Star-Telegram* announced that its editors and readers, in separate polls, had voted for the third straight year that "the continuing problems of Cullen Davis" was the top local news story.

One of Cullen's continuing trials was the matter of his divorce from Priscilla. Judge John Barron, who had come out of retirement to replace Joe Eidson, said, "I don't shoot loaded dice," to emphasize that he would be fair in hearing the divorce petitions. His personal attitude would be crucial, as Cullen had changed his mind and waived a request for a jury in the case. Priscilla's lawyers voiced concern that Cullen was sloughing off financial assets to his brother Ken, with the intention of retrieving them after the divorce trial. The judge vowed that this would not occur. "I can take those assets," he proclaimed, "and I can starve them to death." He referred to Cullen and Ken. "I can absolutely starve them to death, by injunction, by receivership, and by lien, before they cheat her out of five cents. I can take Cullen Davis's stock. I can put it in escrow, and I can enjoin him from doing a frazzling thing with it." Then the judge moved the divorce trial from January 10 to February 20.

The divorce trial and the five civil suits pending against Cullen—not to mention three capital murder indictments never pursued—were discussed animatedly by a group of Fort Worth *cognoscenti:* the city's lawyers. Over the New Year's weekend the talk concentrated on Cullen's testimony in Houston. Most lawyers were surprised that Cullen had been such a good witness, poised and articulate on the stand. Some Fort Worth lawyers faulted Tolly Wilson. They had been stunned at the brevity of his low-key cross-examination of Cullen. In Amarillo and in Houston it had been assumed that harsh, tough interrogation would inevitably puncture Cullen's composure, provoking a display of his fiery temper on the stand. If young Strickland had handled the bulk of that cross-examination, some said, it would have been a different story.

Tolly Wilson defended his performance. "As far as trying to get him mad, that's not my cup of tea. If he wants to get mad, that's all right."

The consensus among Fort Worth attorneys about Cullen's future shifted abruptly. Before, it had been figured that Cullen's chances of acquittal were about fifty-fifty. Now the odds improved in Cullen's favor, and it appeared likely that Racehorse Haynes would pull another rabbit out of a courtroom hat. The difference lay in Cullen's surprise testimony that he had confided in and sought guidance from Hershel Payne. Payne was prominent in Fort Worth; he was the chairman of the local zoning commission and highly regarded by his colleagues. If Hershel Payne were to testify in Cullen's defense the odds would be different. But before the trial resumed in the new year the odds tumbled back to fifty-fifty.

Carl Freund, of the Fort Worth bureau of the *Dallas Morning News,* sought out Hershel Payne for a comment.

"Cullen never mentioned the FBI or Judge Eidson to me," Payne said.

Cullen was still on the witness stand when the trial resumed on Tuesday, January 2. On the previous Friday he had testified that he had told Hershel Payne about a discussion with McCrory which concerned Judge Eidson.

Now Cullen offered some clarification and a retraction. He had *not,* he now remembered, mentioned Judge Eidson to Payne.

"I don't think I said that," Cullen said. "If I did I didn't mean that." In the Friday testimony Cullen had also said he told Payne that he was in contact with an FBI agent named Acree. Now Cullen recanted. "Karen is the only one I told."

Phil Burleson said that Cullen wanted to clarify his testimony after "he reflected on it" over the New Year's weekend.

Jack Strickland snorted. He suggested that Cullen was changing his story because he had heard of Hershel Payne's printed denial in a Dallas newspaper.

Cullen stepped out of the witness chair after four and a half days of testimony and returned to his place at the defense table.

On Wednesday, Hershel Payne, subpoenaed as a witness by the defense, took the stand.

The Fort Worth lawyer was uncomfortable. He was Cullen's friend and was involved in profitable business ventures with him. He corroborated Cullen's story of asking him about possessing a silencer, of McCrory's talk about killing people, and that McCrory had given him money to safeguard.

But Payne said that Cullen had never mentioned a specific sum of money. Cullen had never, Payne continued, said anything about tape recordings, the FBI, an extortion attempt, or plots to kill Judge Eidson. Finally, Payne testified, he did not talk to Cullen at all during the period from August 10 to August 20—and when he did see Cullen the day after his arrest, Cullen mentioned neither the name Acree nor the FBI. But Payne, who wasn't representing Cullen in any civil or criminal actions against him, testified that he didn't consider himself to be giving any legal opinions.

"Couple that," Tolly Wilson said, "with Cullen's own testimony that he spent an hour or two in the federal building in downtown Fort Worth after his arrest and that he never sought out the FBI agent he says called him."

Jack Strickland confronted Payne.

"Did you feel that in some way you were being set up to provide an alibi for Cullen Davis?" Strickland asked.

"I don't think my friend of ten or twelve years, Cullen Davis, would set me up. No, sir."

"Have you not, in fact, said that you don't want to be number sixteen on his hit list?"

Haynes leaped out of his chair to object, but Strickland pressed on.

"You do not *think* your friend Thomas Cullen Davis would set you up or manipulate you to provide a cover; but, in fact, has that thought crossed your mind in the last five or six months?"

Payne was distraught but candid. "I guess it may have crossed my mind, when I've seen [sic] the sequence of events."

"Have you been able," Strickland asked, "to discern this pattern of asking you, not a criminal lawyer, about matters which might appear to be violations of criminal statutes?"

"That needs to be put in context," Payne replied. "I may be Cullen's closest personal friend. With that in mind, yes, sir."

Hershel Payne stepped down, saying he didn't know if he had helped his friend Cullen, or hurt him.

Wednesday continued to be a busy day in Judge Moore's court. James Stephens had testified previously that he had seen

McCrory, Priscilla, and Pat Burleson together in Fort Worth before Cullen's arrest. He claimed he had mentioned this to an investigator in the Fort Worth district attorney's office, and that the investigator had cautioned Stephens, after Haynes had called him as a witness, "not to get involved" in Cullen's case. He was asked to name the investigator. He refused.

Judge Moore pointed to the door leading to the jail again. Six months, he promised, if you don't name the man.

Stephens retreated. "I wish somebody hadn't gotten me involved," he sighed, and named the investigator.

Haynes summoned to the chair several private investigators from Fort Worth to establish that they had been hired by Joe Shannon to investigate the defense team first in Amarillo and then, most recently, in Houston. One of the men, Jay Hand, had previously denied that he had been involved in such surveillance. Joe Shannon had been one of Tim Curry's assistant prosecutors in Amarillo, along with Tolly Wilson, and was now in private practice. It was ominous, Haynes said. While Hand had denied participation, three other members of Shannon's squad had testified that they—and Hand—had indeed shadowed the defense lawyers, going to the extreme of rummaging through their trash. It was all very mysterious and interesting, Haynes reiterated.

Judge Moore did not dispute the interest of the development. But after sending the jury out of the courtroom he asked Haynes why an investigation that had begun seven weeks after Cullen's arrest was relevant.

"Who would hire these people?" Haynes asked. "Who would pay a substantial amount? Why would someone make a heavy investment of more than $50,000 for an investigation in this case? Who had the wherewithal to pay the money these people make?" His questions were fired at the judge in staccato bursts.

Judge Moore reflected, lighted another cigarette. "Who cares?" he asked.

"I care!" Haynes retorted.

"*I* don't care," Moore replied. "It's not relevant in any sense. It's a complete waste of time and a fishing expedition."

"Yes," Haynes said, "but there are fish to be caught."

"The whole system is being abused," Moore accused. "You are fishing in the wrong pond."

But Judge Moore did allow Haynes to proceed with limited questioning and, later, some testimony in the presence of the jury.

When the trial recessed on Wednesday it had become obvious that Haynes believed he knew who had sponsored the investigation of the defense team, and, he hinted broadly, had been the *éminence grise* and paymaster behind the conspiracy against Cullen Davis—his brother William.

On Thursday, Racehorse Haynes began to build his case against William Davis—in front of the jury when Moore would permit it, and without their presence when he would not. The defense team had been attempting to subpoena William Davis for weeks, but Cullen's elusive younger brother could not be found.

Haynes called six witnesses to the stand to embellish his scenario that William Davis was responsible for Cullen's tribulations. Two appeared before the jury, but Judge Moore ruled the evidence provided was not relevant. Five witnesses involved in the investigation of the defense team testified that they had uncovered nothing pertaining to Cullen's case.

Joe Shannon, summoned from Fort Worth, confirmed that the investigation had been fruitless. Shannon said that he did not know the identity of his financial sponsor. A Denver lawyer had hired him to recruit the investigators. "He told me he had a client, but did not tell me who it was," Shannon said. "He told me who he was *not.*" Shannon had asked if William Davis was the client, and the Denver lawyer had said no.

Haynes used broad strokes to paint William Davis into a picture of conspiracy. There were mysterious shadows to be explored, especially the murky manner in which Joe Shannon was paid through an unknown corporation by a Colorado lawyer known to William Davis.

On balance, however, Haynes failed to make a credible case against the missing William Davis. And Shannon said, "Our investigation developed nothing. It was a complete cipher." Back in Houston, Shannon had the opportunity to take a parting shot at his old adversary in Amarillo, Racehorse Haynes. "We were looking for illegal activities, if in fact they went on, as we suspected they went on in Amarillo."

One of Joe Shannon's investigators, Jay Hand, was a casualty of that day's testimony. His previous statement that he had not conducted surveillance of the defense team was shattered by Shannon's testimony. Hand hastily hired an attorney and took the Fifth Amendment. Hand also revealed that he had appeared in Judge Moore's court with recording equipment hidden under his clothing and had taped his testimony.

An employee of a building maintenance firm which cleaned William Davis's office in Fort Worth testified that he had seen Charles David McCrory's name in William's desk telephone directory. He had entered the office one night—not breaking the law, he claimed, because his firm was expected to work on the premises—and had photographed the telephone directory page which had McCrory's name on it. Haynes passed ten Polaroid pictures to the jury so they could inspect the evidence connecting McCrory and William.

Thursday wound down with Haynes continuing to conjure up dramatic if inconclusive visions of William Davis as the mastermind behind the plot against Cullen. Why was William avoiding subpoenas?

Some remembered that Haynes had once successfully conducted a cross-examination of an empty witness chair. Would he now end his case by interrogating a William-less chair?

The word was out. The defense would very probably rest the

next day. Who would Haynes's bombshell witness be? Who would be the fat lady who would sing before the curtain went down on the opera in the Harris County courtroom?

On Friday, January 5, the defense called its final witnesses in twenty days of testimony which they hoped would vindicate Cullen. The final testimony was exploited by Haynes to spin out his theory that William Davis was being elusive because he was afraid to talk about his role in a conspiracy to frame Cullen.

Gerald Brannon, the president of several William Davis enterprises in Fort Worth, testified that he had been in frequent telephone contact with William before and during the trial. But the calls were always in-coming, and he did not know where William was. Jack Strickland tried to let the jury know that one reason William was in hiding might be fear. He asked Brannon about security measures being taken at his home. Judge Moore sustained Haynes's objection, and so the message was not delivered.

As for the notation of McCrory's telephone number in William's directory, Brannon said, he had been responsible for that. He had instructed a secretary to type into a new directory for William the names and numbers from an old one, long out of date. And Brannon related an anecdote which revealed how deep the split between William and his brothers, Cullen and Ken, had become. Brannon had been an executive for KenDavis Industries for twenty-three years. Four months after Cullen and Ken had voted William out of the business in 1976, Brannon had attended a Christmas party at William's home across from the fifteenth tee on Rivercrest Road. Two days later Brannon was fired and, subsequently, went to work for William.

Racehorse Haynes called his final witness—after reserving the option of summoning William, if he could be located, before the case went to the jury. Haynes also obtained a promise from Judge Moore that perhaps a few additional witnesses might be called.

Spectators in the crowded courtroom were tense as they

turned to see Haynes's bombshell. The reporters in their reserved seats exchanged glances. *Now* the big story was imminent.

The witness who approached the clerk to take the oath was a large woman, with the immense bosom of an opera singer. Her hair was red, and she wore a russet sweater. She sat in the witness chair and the questioning began.

The reporters took down every word. The sketch artists bent over their pads.

The witness said her name was Sandra Merriman. But she added that this was not her real name. She and her husband had once been under the Federal Witness Protection Program, as Charles David McCrory now was, and it would be dangerous to reveal their true identities. She said she had met Charles David McCrory in Las Vegas when she had worked there in 1975 as a cocktail waitress at the Jockey Bar in the Stardust Hotel. She had chatted with McCrory and explained to him that the Federal Witness Protection Program was a program whereby the government would relocate a witness involved in a federal case, providing monthly financial payments and a new identity.

That was about all the fat lady had to sing about. She knew nothing about the case being tried.

The reporters in the courtroom were stunned. Was this Racehorse Haynes's bombshell?

Tolly Wilson was mystified. He asked a newsman: "Is the defense theory that this whole thing"—the alleged conspiracy against Cullen—"was done to get McCrory on the federal witness program?"

The defense rested.

At the end of the day Haynes was surrounded by television crews as he was about to enter the garage where his car was parked.

"You've been famous," one tv reporter said, "for your big bang endings. What happened to the big bang?"

"Watch for the nexus," Haynes said. "Keep watching for the nexus. It's not over yet."

The cameras focused on Tolly Wilson. "Their [the defense team's] case went down the tubes," the chief prosecutor said, "when Hershel Payne told the truth."

On Monday, January 8, Tolly Wilson began to call the state's rebuttal witnesses. Racehorse Haynes retained the option of summoning William Davis, if he could locate him, and two other witnesses.

On Monday night Larry Gene Lucas—who had testified that McCrory had wanted him to kill Cullen—was arrested by Harris County police. The charge was aggravated perjury. News of the detention of Haynes's witness was in the morning papers on Tuesday.

Haynes was furious. He moved for a mistrial; Judge Moore denied the motion. Haynes asked Tolly Wilson how word of Lucas's arrest had leaked. Wilson responded that he understood a reporter had received an anonymous tip.

"The *old* anonymous tip?" Haynes's voice was heavy with sarcasm.

"I'm sure you're quite familiar with that," Wilson replied.

"Do you think I placed the anonymous tip?" Haynes shot back. "Are you suggesting that I had it done?"

"Yes," Tolly Wilson said.

"Is that the result of some recent illness?" Haynes asked.

"Are you dethroned of your reason, Mr. Haynes?"

Judge Moore stopped the bickering. His irritation at the continuing delays—even now after both defense and state had rested their cases—was increasingly apparent. He warned lawyers on both sides that the time to send the case to the jury was near. "I'm going to land this monster," Moore said, with an allusion to his air force service, "if it blows all four tires."

Mary C. Weir appeared as a state rebuttal witness. She said

she had lived with Larry Gene Lucas off and on for several years. She produced a letter written by Lucas from prison which made it clear he hoped to profit by claiming that McCrory had offered to sponsor Cullen's demise. She said that from her personal knowledge she knew Lucas's testimony was false.

Haynes began his reexamination. He questioned the woman on Tuesday afternoon until court recessed, and began hammering away at her testimony and credibility when court resumed the next morning. Once, after saying he had just a couple of questions more, Haynes peppered the witness with thirty-three additional queries. She admitted that she was a prostitute, but the incessant questioning continued until the exhausted witness stepped down after five hours (during two days) in the chair.

Haynes used one of his remaining witness options to produce a seventy-year-old woman who vowed that Larry Gene Lucas, her son, was a fine boy.

David Childers, Priscilla's brother, took the stand to swear that Priscilla could not have been in Las Vegas at the time Mary Ramsey had said she had seen her there. Other witnesses provided testimony that made the claims of the Florio family—the convicts who had sworn the Fort Worth district attorney's office had subverted them—seem highly implausible.

Racehorse Haynes had not been able to locate and subpoena William Davis, but he came up with a bombshell witness, the kind everyone had expected: a last-minute appearance by a seemingly impartial observer who would cast serious doubt on Charles McCrory's already tattered credibility.

Harold Sexton was a former Fort Worth resident who had recently become a golf instructor in California. He was not an ex-convict, and he had not worked for Mid-Continent Supply Company.

Sexton testified that he had met Charles David McCrory in Fort Worth the previous summer, before Cullen's arrest. They had something to eat at Sambo's restaurant on East Lancaster Street. McCrory had mentioned that he understood things had not gone well with Sexton, and McCrory "asked me if I would like to make some money."

Sexton said he had asked McCrory what was involved.

"We need someone," Sexton said McCrory had answered, "to place a telephone call to Cullen and to present himself as a police officer."

Sexton said he had declined the offer. Then, a few days ago, he had read about Cullen's trial in the newspapers and he decided to contact Richard Haynes to volunteer his information.

Within hours after Sexton's testimony Tim Curry's office in Fort Worth marshaled a squad of witnesses to fly to Houston the next morning to tell the jury what they knew about the restaurant where Sexton had seen McCrory. The witnesses— including a fire chief—were prepared to testify that the Sambo's on East Lancaster had burned to the ground some time before the day Sexton said he met McCrory there.

On Friday morning Harold Sexton had second thoughts about his meeting with McCrory in Fort Worth. He told the jury he had made a mistake. The encounter was at *another* Sambo's on Division Street. The confusion resulted from the fact that both Sambo's were located on U.S. Route 80 and both Division and East Lancaster were a part of that road. "Hell, they all run together," Sexton said.

Tolly Wilson forced Sexton to admit that he knew the area well and to acknowledge that the two Sambo's were seven miles apart in business sections separated by vast undeveloped areas.

Cullen's current case had begun at Coco's and now had ended, indecisively, at Sambo's.

The tenth week of testimony was over on Friday, January 12.

On Monday, January 15, Judge Moore prepared his instruction to the jury while the lawyers readied their final arguments.

Racehorse Haynes requested that Judge Moore ban any mention of Cullen's financial standing during closing arguments. Tolly Wilson objected. The judge ruled that the jury could hear Cullen described as wealthy but not as immensely wealthy.

Judge Moore overruled a motion by Haynes that jurors seek a verdict on only one of the four options posed in his grand jury indictment. Moore said the jury could base their verdict on either of two charges: solicitation of capital murder (if a defendant "requests, commands, or attempts to induce another to engage in specific conduct that . . . would constitute capital murder or make the other a party to its commission"); or, a criminal conspiracy to commit capital murder (if the defendant "agrees with one or more persons that they or one or more of them engage in conduct that would constitute the offense, and he or more of them performs an overt act in pursuance of the agreement").

On Tuesday closing arguments began. Each side was limited to four hours to make its case.

Tolly Wilson began by characterizing Cullen as an arrogant, calculating, stone-faced man. After describing Cullen's final meeting with McCrory, Wilson asked the jury, "Doesn't it tell you something about the mental process of that man"—Wilson pointed at Cullen—"who sat [sic] there with the same cold stare on his face for the last twelve weeks?"

Wilson reminded the jury of McCrory's remark on the tape: "I got Judge Eidson dead for you."

"And from the cheering gallery," Wilson shouted emotionally, "came the reply, '*Good!*' "

The chief prosecutor cautioned the jurors that Racehorse Haynes's rhetoric could lead them into disagreement from which a hung jury would result. Haynes, Wilson said, had made "a deliberate attempt to extend the trial to see if something would happen . . . so we could not continue with this trial." Wilson said Haynes's objective was to confuse the issue of Cullen's guilt with piecemeal versions of various conspiracies from different witnesses. Haynes had attempted to create a situation where at least two jurors "would be so irritated with each other that no verdict would be possible." Wilson urged the jurors to remain united. "The very prospect of doing this again," he said, "makes me shudder."

Jack Strickland continued the argument. Referring to the tapes, he told the jury: "It's like you were in the back seat of that car, ladies and gentlemen. You can hear them and see them and you don't have to guess about what is being said. What a different lawsuit this would have been without that videotape. Do you think the defendant would have admitted saying all that if he didn't have to? But the defense was stuck with that. . . .

"You don't have to guess," Strickland went on, "if Cullen Davis paid Charles David McCrory his blood money, because you saw him do it. You don't have to guess if Cullen said 'good' when he was told this man right here"—Strickland identified Judge Eidson among the courtroom spectators—"had been killed. What in God's name can be a reasonable explanation of that?"

Strickland said the defense strategy had been to lay "rabbit trails. It was an ABC defense," he said, "Anybody But Cullen."

The assistant prosecutor categorized the defense witnesses who had supported Cullen's version of the tapes: people who work for Cullen, convicts and ex-convicts, and witnesses with relevant information "who didn't tell anybody, and then suddenly searched their consciences and came forward." Some of those witnesses, Strickland added, "have shown up and come slithering into this court."

He ridiculed Cullen's explanation of the tapes. "What else could he do? We found out that kill doesn't really mean kill and dead doesn't mean dead; bloody and bleeding don't mean bloody and bleeding; waste doesn't mean waste; shooter doesn't mean shooter; and alibi doesn't mean alibi."

Strickland gestured toward Racehorse Haynes.

"Mr. Haynes suggests money is what brought the crowds into the courtroom. That's probably true. Money is always what brought Mr. Davis to the courtroom. The abuse of money. . . . One thing, I submit to you, that Mr. Davis can't buy is the system."

259

When the prosecution finished closing arguments the tension in the courtroom was almost palpable. High drama was in the offing. All eyes focused on Racehorse Haynes.

As he began his argument Haynes's voice was raspy. He had developed a cold overnight in the chilling rain which had been falling on Houston. He stood, removed his half-moon spectacles, and addressed the jury.

First he disposed of Charles David McCrory's character—"the unctuous, sniveling McCrory."

It was McCrory, Haynes assured the jury, who orchestrated the conversations on the tapes. He steered Cullen, led him on, elicited incriminating statements about murder. McCrory was the villain who enticed Cullen by promising evidence for his divorce trial while he conned Cullen.

"He had the ability to con," Haynes said. "He knew he had something to sell. Is there any question in your mind that David McCrory is a *liar?*"

McCrory had been able to con the FBI and its agent Ron Jannings with his wicked scheme. "McCrory has sold the FBI and he sold Mr. Jannings. He sold Mr. Jannings into letting him call the shots. . . . Charles David McCrory, the man who sells all things, now wants to sell this jury."

Why? For what motive?

Priscilla.

Priscilla was the explanation, Haynes told the jury, for the conspiracy against the citizen accused. Priscilla had acted because she feared her upcoming divorce proceeding would mean the end of her life of luxury in the mansion. "Priscilla Davis would rather be contesting her share of the community estate with Cullen Davis convicted of a *crime*. Priscilla Davis would rather be contesting her share of the community estate as a *widow!*"

Haynes's voice dropped to a dramatic whisper.

"Was she the guiding genius behind it all?"

Perhaps there was another malevolent genius involved. Where was William Davis? Where was the man who had been Priscilla's ally, who had financed her transportation to and from the Amarillo trial? Where was the missing witness who had once paid for security guards at the mansion?

Haynes whirled to the empty witness chair to confront the invisible William Davis. "*Why* are you dodging our subpoena? *Why* are you getting daily reports on the trial from your employees? *Why* did your employees not want to know where you were located?"

Haynes defended the veracity of his witnesses, although he did make the wry admission that Larry Gene Lucas was "a man, perhaps, you can say, only a mother would love."

As he approached the peroration of his eloquent two-hour oration, Haynes stood at the edge of the jury box. Four of the five women in the jury sat in the front row.

"McCrory was an opportunist," Haynes confided to the jury. "McCrory took advantage of a person."

It was so still in the courtroom that despite his whispers Haynes could be heard identifying the man McCrory had taken advantage of. McCrory had taken advantage of Cullen.

"In my experience," Haynes said, "people who are born into great wealth have an inferior feeling, despite their wealth. And they wonder if others really like them and *why* someone likes them.

"You can see," Haynes continued, "what the money does. You can see the attention it brings. What it has done for Cullen Davis is to make him the mark, the mark of David McCrory. This is the same Charles David McCrory who would ask *you* to destroy a life by a verdict of guilty."

Racehorse Haynes closed with an emotional plea to the jurors. "Do no violence," he beseeched, "to your conscience." Haynes's eyes glistened with tears. "If you can do that, I have no quarrel with you, and God speed to you."

261

The sky was clear and the winds chilly in Houston when the second trial of Cullen Davis ended.

During the first trial in Amarillo the jury had been out just over four hours before returning a verdict of acquittal.

In Houston, at Cullen II, when the jury delivered its final report on Friday, January 22, the jurors had been sequestered since the previous Monday. During that period the jury's buzzer frequently sounded; the jurors wanted to ask guidance from Judge Moore, to review evidence that had been presented weeks before, or to be urged by Moore to arrive at a verdict. During forty-four hours of deliberation the jurors cast fourteen ballots, all with the same result—an eight-to-four deadlock. Which way no one knew, nor could Judge Moore ask.

The cavernous courtroom took on the appearance of a bus station filled with stranded passengers. The prohibition against the presence of witnesses in the courtroom had been lifted and several waited in the crowd. Judge Joe Eidson and W. T. Rufner were there. Karen played gin rummy with Cullen to pass the time. Cullen's brother Ken and two of his children were there.

Journalists, photographers, and television crews fidgeted as deadlines passed; Judge Moore had allowed those previously excluded to witness and film the trial's end. There was a media mob including two reporters from the *New York Times* and others from the *Washington Post, Los Angeles Times,* and *Newsweek* and *Time.* The AP and UPI correspondents who had been at Amarillo were still filing stories about Cullen. A third *Star-Telegram* reporter and two photographers had flown from Fort Worth to work with Glen Guzzo and Jim Jones. Three dozen reporters and cameramen from other Texas newspapers and radio and television stations waited for the jury to return for the final time. Soon the courtroom floor was littered with empty coffee cups; no one strayed far in fear of missing the climax of Cullen's trial.

The last signal from the buzzer came late in the afternoon. The jury began to file in to take their seats.

Cullen waited, stiff in his chair at the defense table. He was wearing the subtly patterned blue suit he had worn on the first day of his testimony. Racehorse Haynes was immaculate in his usual black pinstripe suit; his pipe smoldered in an ashtray. Tolly Wilson wore his brown suit. Judge Moore kept switching his cigarette from hand to ashtray, but never smoking it.

The jury forewoman said they were hopelessly deadlocked, the ballots remaining at eight to four.

Judge Moore addressed Cullen, requesting his consent to declare a mistrial; to do otherwise would have meant that Haynes could claim double jeopardy in any future trial.

"You have my permission, Your Honor," Cullen said. "And I want to thank this jury."

Judge Moore excused the jury as the courtroom clock struck 4:07 P.M.

There was no emotion.

Cullen turned to Haynes and thanked him. Then he whispered to Karen, and the two disappeared through an exit at the rear, but not before W. T. Rufner overtook Cullen to thrust a T-shirt into his hands; it read "What Price Justice?"

The media converged on Racehorse Haynes.

Phil Burleson took an envelope from his breast pocket, removed three hundred $100 bills and paid bond for Cullen.

Cullen and Karen emerged from the Harris County jail release area an hour later, accompanied by relatives and lawyers. Cullen said, "I'm glad I'm out."

Word leaked quickly: The jurors had voted eight to four for conviction. Three of the jury's five women were among the jurors who held out for acquittal.

There was a celebration party. Not as rambunctious as the one in Amarillo, but lively. Haynes proclaimed, "A classic example of the integrity of the American jury—they debated the

263

pros and cons every way and in the end they voted their consciences."

A journalist at the party asked Cullen if he had been uncomfortable in the witness chair.

"Well, I thought I was going to be nervous," Cullen replied. "But I wasn't. I guess I'm a cool cat."

Judge Moore, who was *not* at the party, was asked how he felt. He named no names when saying, "The entire system has been abused by this case. I'm talking about the way the case was tried. It was just more than a jury can remember."

Would Moore preside at a retrial?

"Hell, no," snapped Judge Moore.

After the celebration party Cullen, Karen, and Racehorse Haynes and his wife flew to Fort Worth in the Lear jet, first leg on a ski trip to Aspen.

In Fort Worth a *Star-Telegram* reporter interviewed thirteen pedestrians for a quick, informal poll. Nine citizens said they believed Cullen to be innocent or that the case against him was too weak to be convincing.

Priscilla, in the mansion, said that the fear was still there, and that she would continue to live with it. She noted that Andrea would have been fifteen that day.

Andrea's father, Jack Wilborn, predicted: "He'll have to look over his shoulder from now on. It may be when he dies a natural death, but I feel justice will be done."

District Attorney Tim Curry remained convinced that Cullen was guilty. "If Cullen Davis really received a call from a man he considered an FBI agent," Curry asked, "why didn't he tell other FBI agents about it when they questioned him after his arrest ten days later? I'll tell you why. They hadn't concocted his story yet. It was invented later."

Fort Worth is a small town. Tim Curry and Cullen Davis had known each other as they grew up in the western section of the city. Tim Curry, too, was a member of the Steeplechase Club.

Now Curry would have to decide whether to prosecute Cullen for the third time. Politically, it might not be wise. District attorneys in Tarrant County are elected, not appointed.

A Fort Worth woman began a drive to circulate petitions calling for an end to Tim Curry's prosecution of Cullen. Within four days she had 6000 signatures from Tarrant County taxpayers.

The *Star-Telegram* conducted a formal poll, as it had after the Amarillo trial. This time the question was simpler. Not was Cullen guilty, but should Cullen be tried again? Of the several thousand calls received by the *Star-Telegram,* fifty-five percent of the citizens said there should be no retrial. Despite this tally of popular opinion, the newspaper's editorials called for a retrial.

Curry was aware that people in his own office were saying that Cullen's trials were Curry's personal Vietnam. "He keeps sending men and money and nothing comes back."

"It boils down to whether a man with his money and his resources should get a free ride," Curry said. "From the point of time and expense, we have already reached the point of diminishing returns in our efforts to send this man to prison. But I don't see that as the issue. We've got to show the public that you can't put a dollar sign on justice in this state.

"We intend to re-try the case at the earliest possible time," Curry added. "That could be in six months. But that may not be realistic."

The decision was Tim Curry's. His was the signature on the grand jury indictment of Cullen—still valid—just under the line which read, "AGAINST THE PEACE AND DIGNITY OF THE STATE."

·13·

THE OLD JUDGE

Although a late afternoon sun lurked behind January clouds, only a shallow residue of bourbon remained in the old Judge's tumbler. He and the journalist had been discussing Cullen's trial and its inglorious climax.

"It's been an eventful period," the Judge said. "While you were in Houston, Gene Tunney and Margaret Mead died. Texas suffered the exquisite pain of inaugurating its first Republican governor in 150 years. And that *incredible* development down in Guyana."

"After Amarillo," the journalist said, "you were critical of Judge Dowlen's performance. What about Judge Moore?"

"I sincerely believe," the Judge opined, "he should have sequestered that jury. And the trial went on too long. *Five hours* of interrogation of that admitted prostitute after the defense rested. Too goddamned *long.* There's some new law to be written about the time a lawyer can spend on cross-examination and reexamination of a single witness. The truth is lost and obscured in all those questions." The Judge paused. "In any event, I'm writing a letter to the Texas State Commission of Judicial Conduct in Austin. Those people pay some attention to my opinion."

"But, Judge, I—"

"Don't misunderstand me," the Judge said, raising a hand. "Given the circumstances, Pete Moore did a superb job. He knew that Racehorse Haynes would exploit any opportunity, any ruling he made, to claim a mistrial or, on appeal, reversible error. No, son,''—the Judge drained the last of his bourbon —''I'm sending a letter of *commendation* to Austin.''

The journalist asked the Judge what he thought of the large number of Fort Worth residents who had signed petitions demanding that Cullen not be tried again.

''Legal opinion from the crowds?'' The Judge grimaced as he turned his thumbs up, then down. ''That's the way they voted in the Colosseum, son.''

The Judge rose from his chair and began to pace.

''If you had to sum up your reaction to the trial,'' the journalist asked, ''what would it be?''

''My reaction?'' The Judge turned. His face was drawn; he was disturbed. ''I'm sad. The whole thing saddens me. I've never had any children, you know. My only child has been the law. Now I feel as if my daughter has been raped.''

''There's something wrong with the system,'' the Judge continued. ''Perhaps it's the fault of our society, Texas society: a place where money still means something in terms of public attitudes, buying forgiveness, buying justice. Where money is still an acceptable substitute for respectability. A society where men are still expected to be men and women virtuous women—and ERA be damned. Where you assess blame and forgiveness according to that standard, and not by any damned fool laws. Where second- and third-generation oil heirs are spoiled rotten and showing it, and unable to adapt to not having their way—the H. L. Hunts and the Howard Hugheses and the Cullen Davises. Maybe that Rufner fellow spelled it out on his T-shirt: 'What Price Justice?' '' In many ways Texas is still a frontier—an oil and gas frontier—and the people here still have frontier attitudes: You're entitled to get away with anything as long as you're big enough to get away with it. And by and large folks go along with it, right or wrong.''

''I'm not sure I agree, Judge,'' the journalist said. ''During the past three months I've scrutinized the society that spawned

Cullen Davis. I'm not convinced the blame should be placed there. Most of the people who live around this golf course, despite their enormous wealth, are pretty much like other people. They live under a bubble of money which magnifies their faults, but not always their virtues."

"Maybe I don't adhere to that view," the Judge said, "because if it's valid then the blame has to be laid elsewhere. And that would mean the problem is with the goddamned *lawyers*. Now it appears that Cullen will be tried for murder for the *third* time. If he gets off again there's something radically wrong with the system—and maybe we'd better start correcting things with the lawyers. I don't care what any of us say. The purpose of the legal system is to produce justice. In plain language that means—to me, at least—that the guilty are punished and the innocent released or protected. And the god-damned *lawyers* can talk all they want to about a lawyer's duty to his client being to get him the best break he can possibly get under the system, including getting his client off scot-free if he is actually guilty. But I say his first duty is to *justice!*" The old man's voice was rising, his lips were trembling. "And if that conflicts with justice the lawyer's first duty is to justice—which ain't the product of skill or manipulation like shooting pool."

The Judge walked to the bookshelves and touched the volume of Disraeli. "Truth in action?" he asked himself.

The Judge turned to the journalist.

"Well, son, what about *your* verdict? Do you know whether or not Cullen was guilty of those crimes?"

"Yes," the journalist said. "I'm convinced I know the truth."

"And will you share that knowledge with your readers?"

"No, Judge." The journalist was apologetic. "That's not really my responsibility, my obligation. I've arranged my material for the book as objectively as the bizarre case of Cullen Davis demanded. But my job is to present the facts and let the reader decide for himself if Cullen is guilty."

The Judge smiled mischievously.

"Is it possible, son," the Judge asked, his eyes twinkling, "that the laws of libel in the state of Texas have something to do with your equivocal posture?"

The journalist sighed.

"I suppose," the Judge said, "I'll have to be tolerant of your less than noble compromise between duty and the practicable. But in return I'll ask you to do something for me before you go back East. I've never seen that big place on Mockingbird Lane. Will you take me over there?"

The trip by automobile from Rivercrest to the mansion where Priscilla dwelled was only ten minutes. During the drive the Judge and the journalist discussed the various myths and intriguing theories which would inevitably surround the mansion's past and present occupants.

One conspiratorial theory would never die. Many people in Fort Worth were convinced that Priscilla was clever enough, audacious enough, and had the motive—revenge for the murder of her daughter Andrea—to have become the sinister mastermind behind a plot to trap Cullen using Charles David McCrory as her instrument.

But most people in Fort Worth, the Judge and the journalist agreed, would be content to wait for the truth to emerge in yet another trial for Cullen. The question they wanted answered was a simple one: Was Cullen guilty or innocent of the crimes charged to him?

The journalist stopped his rented car at the gate at 4200 Mockingbird Lane. Beyond the gate the drive wound up the hill to the trapezoidal mansion, across the field where Priscilla had run to seek aid from her neighbors two and a half years before.

"No wonder Fort Worth never catches up with Dallas," the Judge said. "What an *indolent* town. Look at that sign! You would think that someone would take better care of the sign."

The sign at the entrance gate read, "Do no en er—pr va e pro erty."

The two men looked at the mansion for several minutes without speaking. Finally the Judge said, "You can take me home now, son. I think I'll break my rule and have another drink. At my age sleep is precious, and I just may have trouble sleeping tonight."

The journalist started to back away from the gate.

"Wait!" The Judge laid his hand on the journalist's arm. "Just a moment longer."

The rain clouds on the western horizon had opened momentarily, unveiling an orange disk of setting sun. The rays of sunlight slanted across the scrub-and-brush plains and painted the mansion with a twilight glow, the ineluctable between-day-and-night beauty that transforms bleak prairies into luminous landscapes. The TCU stadium on the bluff behind the mansion—TCU was the school where Stan Farr had played basketball—loomed over the Davis property. The mansion, splashed with gold, was eerily beautiful. Then the clouds closed, dropping a dark curtain over the scene. The mansion was ugly, ominous, a proper setting for a murder or two.

"I'm an old man," the Judge said, "and I'm a little drunk. But somehow I imagine I hear something. I hear the sound of a child's laughter—faintly, but I hear it—drifting down from that mansion."

The Judge turned.

"There's something that bothers me, son. It bothers me a great deal."

The Judge challenged the journalist with his gaze.

"If Cullen didn't kill that twelve-year-old girl," he asked, "who *did*?"

And then, after a long pause, "And *why*?"